O9-CFT-483

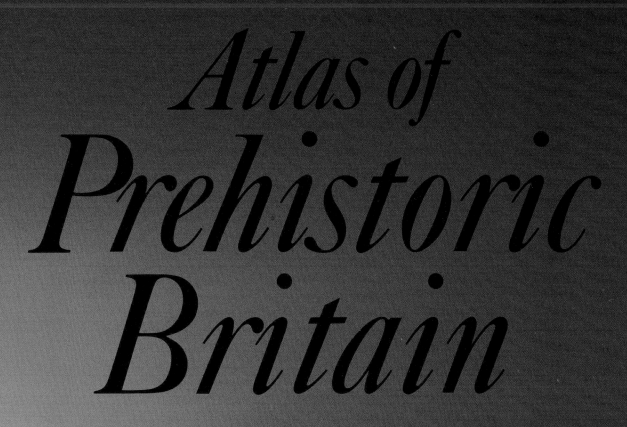

Atlas of Prehistoric Britain

John Manley

Photographs by David Lyons

New York
Oxford University Press
1989

Phaidon Press Limited, Musterlin House,
Jordan Hill Road, Oxford OX2 8DP

First published 1989
© 1989 Phaidon Press Limited
Photographs © David Lyons
Text © 1989 John Manley
Reconstruction drawings © 1989 Anthony Kwill

Published in the United States of America
by Oxford University Press, Inc.,
200 Madison Avenue, New York, NY 10016

Oxford is a registered trademark of
Oxford University Press

All rights reserved. No part of this publication may be reproduced,
stored in a retrieval system, or transmitted, in any form or by any
means, electronic, mechanical, photocopying, recording or
otherwise, without the prior permission of the publisher.

ISBN 0-19-520807-2

Printing (last digit): 9 8 7 6 5 4 3 2 1

Designed by Brian Lock
Printed in Great Britain

BOMC offers recordings and compact discs, cassettes
and records. For information and catalog write to
BOMR, Camp Hill, PA 17012.

Acknowledgements

The drawings for this book have usually combined data from a
variety of published and unpublished sources. Major sources are
indicated below. The numbers refer to the figures.

1, P Drewett; 2, P Mellars; 3, H Green; 4, M Todd; 5, P Woodman
& R Jacobi; 6, P Drewett; 7, P Woodman; 8, J Coles; 9, P
Woodman & R Jacobi; 10, R Mercer; 11, S O'Nuallain; 12, G
Childe; 13, T Darvill; 14, J Coles; 15, T Mckclough, T Darvill, I
Longworth & J Cherry; 16, T Mckclough; 17, T Darvill, A
Henshall & P Harbison; 18, M O'Kelly; 19, M O'Kelly; 20, G
Wainwright; 21, A Burl & A Harding; 22, RCAHM (England);
23, D Clarke, T Cowie & A Foxon; 24, Clwyd SMR; 25, P Ashbee,
RCAHM (Scotland) & P Harbison; 26, A Fleming; 27, D Spratt,
C Burgess & P Fowler; 28, P Harbison & L N W Flanagan; 29, G
Wainwright & K Smith; 30, RCAHM (England); 31, RCAHM
(England); CADW; 32, F Gardiner; 33, J Hamilton; 34, B
Cunliffe; 35, B Raftery, D Harding & Ordnance Survey; 36, G
Stout; 37, P Harbison, P Fowler, J Morrison; 38, R Whimster, R
Turner.

Date Chart I. Wymer

The following photographs are courtesy of the Trustees of the
British Museum: 7, 8, 9, 10, 11, 20, 27, 28, 49, 50, 51, 52, 53, 54,
55, 56, 87, 88, 89, 90, 91, 92, 93, 94, 99. Photographs 71 and 74 are
reproduced courtesy of the Clwyd-Powys Archaeological Trust.

The publishers would also like to thank the Irish Ministry of
Works for allowing David Lyons access to the Irish Monuments;
the Royal Botanical Gardens in Edinburgh for their help in
research; Joanne Freeman of the British Museum and Chris
Musson of The Clwyd-Powys Archaeological Trust.

Conversion Table

1 kilometre (km) = 0.62 mile
1 metre (m) = 1.09 yard
1 centimetre (cm) = 0.39 inch
1 hectare (ha) = 2.47 acre
1 tonne (t) = 0.98 ton

Frontispiece. Lough Gur, Co. Limerick, Ireland.

Pl 1 (*Title page*). Callanish, Isle of Lewis, Scotland.

Contents

Preface

The principal aim in writing this Atlas of Prehistoric Britain was to convey something of the fascination of the prehistoric period, and the distribution of its monuments, to as wide a readership as possible. To that end jargon has been avoided, dates have been kept to a minimum, and a simple, chronological approach has been adopted. Prehistoric sites possess an intrinsic appeal, just as later monuments, like medieval castles or stately homes, are attractive to so many. This appeal is a visual one, a combination of size, shape, material and landscape, and is admirably illustrated by the superb photographs of David Lyons. Most of the excellent artwork for this volume was compiled and drawn by Tim Morgan, while Anthony Knill produced the four graphic reconstruction drawings.

The core of any Atlas must be the maps. A word of caution is needed here. There are tens of thousands of prehistoric archaeological sites in Britain and Ireland; new ones are discovered every year; most cannot be dated securely without excavation. It was physically impossible to include all these sites in the maps in this book. Instead only a fraction, and a highly selective one at that, has been mapped. Essentially these maps depict the principal concentrations of major prehistoric monuments in Britain and Ireland. They are, therefore, no more than a rough guide. Likewise with the text. A very selective summary of nearly a half a million years of prehistory is all that is possible in a book of this length.

My debts are many and varied, and include a great number of people with whom I have corresponded during the writing of this book. My outstanding obligation is to thank all the thousands of archaeologists, both professional and amateur, whose dedicated work has provided the basic data for me to draw upon. I sincerely hope I have not misrepresented their findings overmuch. Some idea of my most frequented sources can be surmised from the bibliography and the map acknowledgements. A special vote of thanks is owing to Frances Kelly, and to Bernard Dod and Mark Fletcher of Phaidon who encouraged, cajoled and corrected where necessary. Although written in my leisure time, I am also grateful to my employer Clwyd County Council, for the opportunity to work in such an archaeologically interesting county. I am particularly appreciative of the efforts of Chris Musson, Frances Lynch, Gordon Barclay and Peter Drewett who read a preliminary draft of the text and to Karen Dunning Kirkby who did so much to help David Lyons with his photography. Needless to say even they could not correct all my archaeological errors nor do they necessarily agree with my interpretations. And to Marita, Michael and Barbara – many thanks for the tea and sympathy.

John Manley
Denbigh, Clwyd

St. David's Day, 1989.

Pl 2 (*opposite*). Stonehenge, Wiltshire, England.

Chapter 1

The Gathering Bands

c 500,000–5,000 BC

The Frozen North

For most of our time on this planet we have been hunters, gatherers and fishermen. It is only relatively recently that the majority of us have come to rely on farming, trading and manufacturing to supply our daily needs. Some, like the Aborigines, the Eskimos and the Bushmen, still cling tenaciously to their old ways. Others, caught up in the trappings of modern life, frequently break out. The fishing trip, the hunting expedition, and even the Sunday afternoon outing for blackberries are all echoes of a prehistoric past. They are, of course, a form of relaxation now, sociable occasions, to be enjoyed by close friends or families. But, unknowingly we re-create the closeness of our earliest communities – the gathering bands.

Bands who relied on hunting, gathering and fishing spread into southern Europe around two million years ago. These bands, probably comprising a small number of related families, must have crossed over from Africa by way of the straits of Gibraltar, from Tunisia, and across the Bosphorus via Asia Minor. Early camp sites are known from south-west Spain, Sicily and Romania. A million years later there is evidence, from several cave sites in southern France, of occupation by early man. In the northern half of France the gravels of the river Somme at Abbeville have produced rough hand-axes chipped with a stone hammer and dating to around a half a million years ago.

Some time after this the first human groups must have reached the British Isles. They did so not by some ancient feat of prehistoric navigation, but by walking across the dry bed of the now sunken plain of the North Sea from the European mainland. This singularly undramatic event took place during the Ice Ages, a period that lasted from about 700,000 years ago until about 11,000 BC. These hundreds of thousands of years were not ones of unchanging climate. On several occasions the temperature gradually fell and sheets of ice hundreds of metres thick slowly covered Scotland, parts of Ireland, Wales and northern England (Pl 3). Then after thousands of years the temperature steadily rose and the ice sheets melted and retreated, sometimes flooding parts of the

plain that joined the British Isles to the continent. The chronology and number of these oscillating cold and warm spells are difficult to estimate with any degree of certainty. More oscillations are known now than were previously anticipated and no definitive correlation between them and the early archaeological sites can be presented. The matter is further complicated by the fact that cold spells, or glaciations, could be punctuated by brief periods of warmth known as interstadials; conversely, warm spells, or interglacials, could be interrupted by additional cold phases known as stadials.

The dating of the traces of human occupation of such great antiquity, such as stone tools or bones, can be achieved through various methods based on the radioactive decay of unstable chemical elements known as isotopes. Decay of each isotope proceeds at a known rate. Approximate dates in years are obtained by measuring either the fraction of the original parent isotope remaining, or the percentage of new daughter isotopes produced. Three principal methods of dating are currently in use: radiocarbon, uranium and thermoluminescence. Radiocarbon dating is effective back to about 30,000 BC and therefore supplies most of the dates from the later prehistoric period. However, each date usually covers a broad range of one or two centuries, and then has to be 'calibrated' to produce a calendar date, by correcting for any irregularities in the rate of decay of the isotope Carbon 14. Despite the disagreements about the calibration process, it is calibrated or calendar dates that are quoted in this book. Uranium dating of cave stalagmites, or thermoluminescence dating by reheating a burnt stone or flint, can extend the dating range back to about 300,000 BC. So the archaeologist excavating a late prehistoric site dating from 5,000 or so years ago, will be looking for the remains of fires, or burnt grain or bone to supply samples for radiocarbon dating. The excavator of a hunting and gathering camp of greater age will search for burnt material in association with the stone tools, or stalagmite deposits if in a cave. Relative dating of hand-axes and other tools especially from excavations carried out some decades ago, can be approximated, either by comparing the type of tool represented with similar specimens from a

Pl 3. Alaska, USA. Ice-sheets of various glaciers, often hundreds of metres thick, periodically covered large parts of the British Isles during the Ice Ages. Groups of hunters may have deserted Britain during the maximum extent of the glaciers.

better dated collection, or by identifying whether the animal bones associated with the implements are of cold or warm-loving species and thus belong to an interglacial or to a phase of glaciation. This comparative or relative dating method, of course, can be used for archaeological finds of any age.

Whatever the absolute date it was probably during a warm spell that the first human groups walked to England. They, of course, would hàve had no perception of the sequence of geological events, just as we have little comprehension that we, too, could be living in a warm spell. During advances of the ice sheets the hunting bands would probably have left most of England unoccupied, only to venture across the great, marshy plain once more when temperatures rose. But what kind of landscape did those pioneer bands meet as they wandered westwards towards the forerunner of the Thames valley?

It was one shaped by slow but constant change. The cycle of rising and falling temperatures produced a cyclical response in the environment. As the great ice sheets melted and retreated to the north, the summers became steadily warmer,

Pl 4 (overleaf). Loch Garten, Highlands, Scotland. Forests of tall pine trees must have covered large areas of Britain during the climatic changes of the Ice Ages. Here some towering Scots Pine shade an undergrowth of heather and and bilberries.

the winters milder and the growing seasons longer. The vegetation changed in response to the changing climate. As the glaciers withdrew, vast quantities of water were released to scour and erode a bare, treeless landscape. Gradually grasses, ferns, lichens and hardy heathland shrubs like crowberry began to colonize the least eroded areas, and soon a kaleidoscopic pattern of sedges, grasses, lakes, and bogs filled out an otherwise bleak terrain. In summer the pools and lakes would perhaps attract herds of giant deer or wild horse, and flocks of migratory birds, but in winter the searing wind off the glaciers tugged and tore at the tough low grasses.

In time, as the winds lessened and the weather warmed, dwarf birch and then silver birch established themselves on the former heath, eventually clumping together into birchwoods. The slender white trunks reached a height of some 20 m and their crowns merged to form a protective canopy. Such a shaded and sheltered environment encouraged a more luxuriant undergrowth of mosses and shrubs, upon which fallen and lichen-encrusted tree trunks rotted. Animal populations had to adapt to darker and more closed habitats which favoured smaller species of deer such as roe deer. The valley sides of Caithness in Scotland give us some idea of these pioneer birchwoods.

The next significant change was the emergence of pine trees which mixed with the former birchwoods. The great advantage that the pines possessed was a higher canopy, reaching to some 35 to 40 m, so that the sun's rays were soaked up by a dense umbrella of blue-green needles, leaving the hapless birch to shrivel in the shade. These pines were much more varied than the regimented rows of sitka spruce that are such a blight on our present upland landscape. Some idea of the variety of forms and crowns can be obtained by visiting the ancient forests of Rothiemurchus in Perthshire, Ballochbuie in Aberdeen and Loch Garten in the Highlands (Pl 4). The early pinewoods also contained stands of very lofty hazel trees, much taller than their modern successors. An autumnal carpet of pine needles, cones and hazel nuts, therefore, began to cover the fallen birch foliage.

As temperatures reached a maximum during the warm period, the final phase of the environment's transformation occurred. Heathland that had given way to birchwoods, only to be colonized by pine and hazel, was now infiltrated by birds, small mammals, and wind and water that transported acorns and seeds of oak, elm and lime. Once these seeds had germinated the broad leaves of deciduous trees eventually broke through the pine canopy, mopping up the sun with their great, green crowns and starving the pine and hazel of life-giving light. The interior of the wildwood was dark; perpendicular trunks soared skywards, like the columns of some vast, prehistoric cathedral. The solemnity of the scene was only disturbed by the scurrying of shrews and woodmice, the scuffling of voles and hedgehogs, and the occasional loud squeal of a wild boar.

In the warm periods, as the ice sheets retreated farther to the north, many regions would have experienced the transformations outlined here. The opposite was true also, of course: as temperatures began to fall and the ice edged its way southwards, a similar sequence occurred in reverse.

These changes in turn produced differences in the variety of fauna; the large herbivores like wild ox or giant deer were more suited to grassland environments; others, such as roe deer or wild boar preferred woodland habitats; changes in the warmth of sea and lake water produced corresponding differences in the species of fish.

To return to those bands of hunters and gatherers and their journey into the Thames valley. At times it must have been hard going. We must imagine, in parts at least, a dense mixed woodland of daunting luxuriance stretching down to overhang the water's edge, harbouring in its silent shelter small deer, bear, and wild boar, feeding on the acorns and hazel nuts among the bluebells and wood anemones. The river itself would be replete with seasonally migrating salmon and eel, and with other familiar fish such as perch and pike. Further down-river, the waterway would divide and divide again, meandering slowly through a network of interconnecting channels, creating in its framework a patchwork of islands, floodplains, and marshes, covered with reeds, grasses and alder trees. This less wooded environment, and the attraction of easy access to drinking water, would have favoured giant deer, red deer, fallow deer, lion, bison, wolf, straight-tusked elephant, hippopotamus, rhinoceros and wild horse. The reed-beds at the swampy margins would have been settled by flights of crane, white stork, ducks, grebes, mergansers and lapwings. Away to the north, along windy salt-sprayed shores and treeless mudflats, millions of shellfish and crabs lay silently feeding; out in the coastal waters seals, rorquals and dolphins surfaced from time to time, while overhead guillemots, divers, and great auks would glide into the wind. And all around were countless roots and berries, nuts and herbs, fruits, flowers, and fungi (Pls 15–18).

Would these early bands of hunters and gatherers have considered the new environment of the Thames Valley pleasant to live in? It would seem that they did not need to hunt for hours, gather from afar, or fish when they did not want to. Their food was plentiful, easy to collect, and if it could and did decide to move, they could always follow. On the other hand the temptation to picture a prehistoric Garden of Eden inhabited by placid plant-eaters must be resisted. Hunting implements were primitive and comprised crude, hand-held stone tools. Hunting tactics must have involved communal stalking and the use of fire to drive big game into marshes, or over cliff edges, where wounded animals could be allowed to exhaust themselves before humans dared to approach. It is probable that a large number of hunting or fishing expeditions came back to camp empty-handed. A daily staple of uncooked or partially cooked plants, fruits, and berries cannot have been appetizing for long. Encounters with other human groups must have occurred from time to time. There is simply no evidence to suggest whether such meetings were friendly or hostile.

The Earliest Footsteps

The first human beings, then, walked from what is now the European mainland into southern England some time after

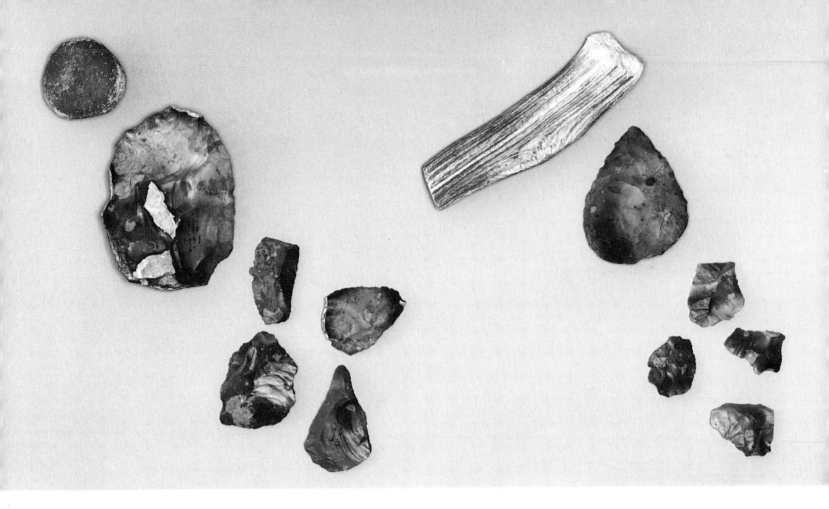

Pl 5. Making a Hand-Axe. Implements from Swanscombe in Kent demonstrate the process of tool manufacture. On the left a rough piece of flint is struck by the circular pebble-hammer, producing waste-flakes. The antler hammer is used for finer flaking to make the hand-axe on the right. (Length of hand-axe is 12.1 cm)

500,000 years ago. Their arrival may have coincided with a warm period known as the Cromerian interglacial, or with a shorter and warmer interstadial in the succeeding Anglian glaciation. Both glaciations and interglacials are conventionally named after sites or regions where they were first recognized. These early humans, or hominids, did not belong to the same species as ourselves, *Homo sapiens sapiens*, but to an early form of man called *Homo erectus*. We must dispel at once the stereotype of the stooping, grunting savage, however. These people were certainly slightly shorter than ourselves, with a more pronounced eye-brow line and a more solid jaw, but they did not stoop, were very athletic and probably possessed a basic language. They lived by hunting, gathering, and fishing, and fashioned implements from stone, bone and wood. Charcoal, ashes, and burnt tools from some sites show that they were capable of lighting fires. Although there are no traces of clothing from this early period, they must have made garments from animal skins, since survival would not have been possible without them. Camps would have been seasonally occupied in order to follow the migrating game or move to where there was good fishing, or the nuts were particularly abundant. The mouths of caves formed convenient shelters, but there must also have been many more temporary shelters constructed in open locations. Archaeology, however, will never reveal everything about the past, least of all that these people were probably capable of anger, love and laughter.

The archaeological remains of the early hunting camps are extremely meagre and confined mostly to southern and south-eastern England (Figs 1 & 2). All that survives of these temporary settlements are the flint and stone tools, sometimes associated with the bones of the animals that they were used to kill. The clothing, the plant and fish foods, the wooden shelters and usually the human bones have long since been destroyed or have disintegrated.

The first question to ask when looking at a map of past sites is: how accurate a picture of the distribution of actual settlements does it represent? The known sites of these early hunters conform quite closely to the area free of ice during the maximum extent of the ice-sheets. In the Hoxnian interglacial, which is named after a site in Hoxne, Suffolk, the ice had disappeared completely from the British Isles. England was still joined by a land bridge to the continent, and it is possible that Ireland was connected to the British mainland by one or more land bridges. In theory the first human groups could have travelled far to the north and west. In practice they probably did. The paucity of archaeological sites from these more distant areas is almost certainly caused by the destructive power of subsequent ice-sheets that could re-shape whole valleys and easily obliterate the remains of such camps.

The second problem concerns the nature of the sites themselves. Some of them are caves (Pls 6, 7 & 13) and some are open sites by lakes or rivers (Pl 14). It does seem likely, however, that the high proportion of cave sites represented in archaeological records does not reflect the actual distribution of settlement sites during the interglacials. This is partly a question of preservation and partly one of investigation. Seasonal use of caves was obviously made by early man.

13

Pl 6. Pontnewydd Cave, Clwyd, North Wales. The entrance to the
cave lies at the foot of the limestone cliff in the centre-right of the
photograph. The area in front of the cave was occupied by a band
of hunters and gatherers some 230,000 years ago.

Pl 7 (*opposite*). Creswell Crags, Derbyshire, England. Looking out
from Church Hole Cave across the gorge the cave system known as
The Arch is visible on the northern cliff-face. Occupation material
within The Arch indicates human activity around 12,000 BC.

Caves, however, are also the most likely and safest repositories in which these early archaeological remains would be preserved. A good example is Pontnewydd cave in north Wales, where implements and bone from a camp site at the mouth of the cave were carried by mud-flows into the cave interior, and therefore preserved from the destructive effects of subsequent glaciations. Knowledge that cave deposits could produce flint and stone objects acted as a positive attraction to generations of archaeologists, hence the probable bias in the type of site from which artefacts have been recovered. Open sites on river gravels, conversely, are much more likely to have been destroyed through later farming, gravel extraction or building. The image of the club-wielding cave man is a twentieth-century caricature that has little basis in fact. In reality, open sites must have been the norm rather than the exception.

The third difficulty with the evidence that has survived is that of trying to associate the stone tools found in certain deposits with the animal bones that are sometimes discovered with them. Individual caves may have been used for hundreds of thousands of years for a variety of purposes; indeed the Pontnewydd cave had a door fitted and was brought into service as a munitions dump during the Second World War. Animals, too, use caves either for hibernation or as dens and can die in them or bring other animals that they have killed into them. The layers filling caves can easily be disturbed by all this activity, and human and animal bones can quickly become incorporated into much earlier or later layers. It would be a very neat solution if the bones that the archaeologists found, together with the stone tools, displayed butchering marks that had been obviously caused by the very same artefacts, but frequently this is not the case.

Given that the variety of open sites is under-represented, the surviving settlements of our first hunters can thus be divided into cave locations, and camps in low-lying areas adjacent to water, such as river banks, shingle beaches or at lake sides. Two of the earliest cave sites, which probably pre-date the Hoxnian interglacial, are Westbury-sub-Mendip, Somerset and Kent's Cavern, Devon. The Hoxnian interglacial began around 400,000 years ago. Human occupation of Britain before this date would have been possible during an interstadial of the preceding Anglian glaciation, or in the Cromerian interglacial. Westbury-sub-Mendip is not really a proper cave, but rather a limestone fissure which has trapped and preserved some remains of a hunting camp. The material includes two flint choppers and bones of bear, sabre-toothed cat, wolf, horse, rhinoceros, and other mammals. Kent's Cavern lies in limestone on the western side of the Ilsham valley. The cave system is actually a large and complex series of cavities, produced by dissolution of the rock, and linked together by narrow fissures. In the lower levels of the Cavern crude hand-axes, chopping tools and flakes were recovered, possibly associated with the bones of bear, sabre-toothed cat, and two species of vole. It has been suggested that the material might be interpreted as evidence of specialized hunting involving the killing of hibernating bears. If this can be proved by a fuller study of the bones it would imply that the hunters had lamps or torches, and were able to penetrate the dark recesses of the cave in order to seek out the sleeping bears. An open camp, contemporary with these earliest cave sites, existed at High Lodge, near Mildenhall in Suffolk.

Coastal sites may have been used to take advantage of marine resources, as perhaps at Slindon and Boxgrove, in Sussex. A secondary attraction might have been the availability of fresh supplies of flint for tools from cliff falls. The site at Boxgrove, in West Sussex, is particularly interesting and appears to have been occupied around 450,000 years ago, towards the end of the Cromerian interglacial. Today it lies some 10 km inland, but at the time of the human occupation it lay close to an old cliff-line on the southern edge of the Sussex Downs, and not very far from the sea. The environment at the time seems to have been an open, grassy plain, subject to periodic flooding, with some deciduous and conifer tree cover in the vicinity. At Boxgrove exceptional conditions of preservation allow us to look at specific stone age incidents. Anyone who has been lucky enough to see a flint implement, such as a large hand-axe or a small arrowhead, made experimentally by chipping at a flint block with a variety of different hammers, will know that an enormous number of flint chips, or waste flakes, are produced in the process (Pl 5). Wherever the person making the object sits or stands, the numerous waste flakes are scattered in a rough area immediately in front of him. And just this sort of evidence has come to light at Boxgrove. In a small area of the excavation nearly 6,000 waste flakes clearly fall into two discrete scatters. Moreover, by painstakingly refitting some of these flakes together so that the original appearance of the flint block may be gauged, it is apparent that flakes from one scatter do not fit with any of those from its neighbour, strengthening the argument that here we have evidence of two separate flint-knappers, or one who moved from one area to the next, making two stone tools. The question then becomes what sort of tool? Two oval hand-axes have also come from the immediate area of the scatters, and it is very tempting to suggest that this tool type might have been the end product.

Not all hunting and gathering bands were using hand-axes. Some groups instead were manufacturing crude chopping tools which seem to have been used for butchering meat, hide-scraping, and wood-working. Like hand-axes, these chopping tools seem to have been multi-purpose artefacts. The explanation of these two different traditions of tool manufacture presents archaeologists with a typical problem. Are the differences, for instance, to be explained by chronology? There is some indication that chopping tools might be the earlier type. Or are the variations the result of different activities performed at separate sites? Or should we surmise distinct cultural groups with their own preferences for tool types, even at this early period? Whatever the solution, these chopping tools seem to have disappeared by the end of the Hoxnian interglacial. The best-known site where chopping tools have been found is in the gravels underlying the golf course at Clacton-on-Sea, Essex (Pl 8). At this temporary camp deer, bison, elephant, horse, and rhinoceros had been hunted or trapped. Similar tools came from a waterlogged deposit at Lion Point, Essex; these conditions preserved the

Pl 8. The Earliest Tools. The two principal types of flint implement used by the early hunters and gatherers are shown here. On the left is a chopping tool from Clacton-on-Sea, Essex, which is in contrast to the pear-shaped hand-axe on the right. (Length of hand-axe is 15.8 cm)

end of a wooden spear of yew, which had been fashioned with flint implements. Other comparable camps are those from Barnham St Gregory, Suffolk, Little Thurrock, Essex, and the lower levels at Swanscombe in Kent. All of these are waterside settlements and no cave sites are known.

Hand-axes, made from flint or other fine-grained stones, are common finds from some of the early sites, especially in the Thames valley, East Anglia, north Kent, and Hampshire. These axes are pear or oval shaped implements that, as the name suggests, were used as hand tools. They were fashioned by striking and shaping larger blocks of flint or stone with stone, wood and bone hammers. The hand-axes were multi-purpose artefacts used for a great variety of domestic and hunting chores, some of them quite minor as the small size of some examples suggests, a few being less than 8cm in length. Two deposits producing hand-axes were found at Hoxne in Suffolk and date either to the end of that interglacial or to an early stage of the glacial period known as the Wolstonian, which began around 350,000 years ago (Fig 2). In the earlier phase the camp lay beside a lake and finely shaped oval hand-axes of black flint were associated with the bones of horse, fallow deer, bison, wild cattle, macaque monkey and elephant. Fish bones of rudd, tench, and pike are consistent with the presence of a body of fresh water nearby.

It is uncertain whether the broken animal bones and teeth are the remains of meals consumed. Equally problematic, if these do represent food refuse, were the animals deliberately hunted, or were they merely the leftovers from carnivore kills that the humans preyed upon? Whatever the interpretation, butchery, plant processing and woodworking seem to have been the principal activities at the site. Another water-side camp occupied at this time is Swanscombe in Kent. Here wild cattle and horse were located together with hand-axes of pointed form. Of particular interest was the discovery of fossil animal footprints preserved in silt. These undoubtedly represent the trampling of animals as they came to water at the river. More dramatically, three fragments from the skull of one of the hunters indicate that the human, or hominid, to which they belonged was slightly more developed than *Homo erectus*, but not yet comparable with modern humans.

Both at Hoxne and another important site at Mark's Tey in Essex, there is some evidence to suggest a period of deforestation through burning of the trees, which may be contemporary with the human occcupation. The fires could have been started by purely natural processes, such as lightning strikes, but they might equally well have been started deliberately by the hunters, either as a device to stampede a herd, or perhaps to create a woodland clearing that would attract grazing animals.

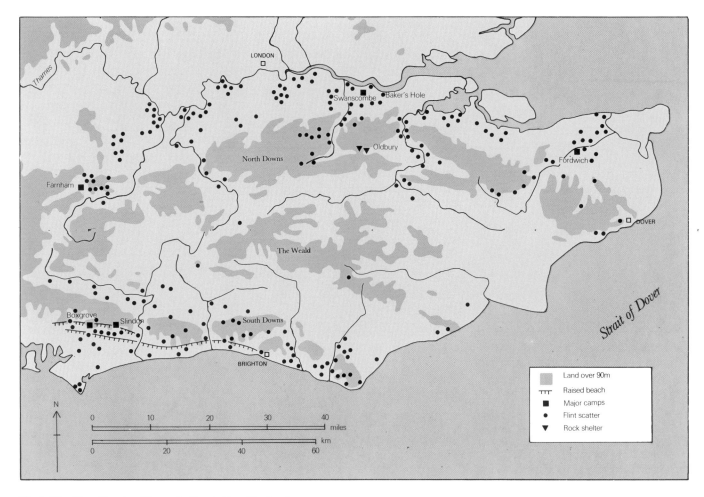

Fig 1. The First Hunting Camps in South-East England:
c 500,000–9,000 BC. Sites are concentrated close to the north coast
of Kent, along river-valleys, and on the South Downs adjacent to
raised beaches which indicate former shorelines.

The ice sheets of the Wolstonian glaciation re-covered
most of Britain and Ireland. The glaciation was interrupted
by two further warm phases, during the second of which the
already mentioned Pontnewydd cave was occupied (Fig 3 &
Pl 6). Here the area in front of the limestone cave seems to
have been occupied about 230,000 years ago. Today the site
overlooks a small valley along which flows the river Elwy. At
the time of these early humans the valley floor and river
would have been some 50 m higher than at present, bringing
it up to just below the cave mouth. Remains, in the form of
teeth and jaw bones, of at least three individuals have been
recovered, and these are thought to belong to an early form of
Neanderthal Man. This species of hominid takes its name
from the Neander Tal, which literally means the 'valley of
the Neander river' in West Germany, where a characteristic
skull and limb bones were found in the last century. These
Neanderthals were heavier and more muscular than modern
humans, but with a completely upright posture and a physi-
ology close to our own. Among the wild animals that may
have formed part of the food supply at Pontnewydd are bear,
rhinoceros, wolf, leopard, horse, roe deer and bison. Stone

hand-axes and sharp flakes for butchering prey have been
found along with stone tips of spears and scrapers for preparing skins. Burnt stones show that fires were lit, presumably
by striking stones together to produce a spark or by rubbing
wood against wood to achieve heat through friction.

Even at the height of this long, cold Wolstonian period,
however, parts of south-east England were still habitable, as
the open camp at Baker's Hole, Northfleet, Kent indicates.
The next interglacial, known as the Ipswichian, started
around 130,000 years ago and lasted for 60,000 years. During
this period the rising sea-levels flooded the North Sea basin
for the first time and Britain became an island. It is difficult
to say at present if the small hunting bands were confined to
mainland Europe, and Britain was therefore deserted. The
most recent glacial period is known as the Devensian and
lasted from 70,000 BC until about 11,000 BC. Once again
human groups were able to walk across the marshy North
Sea plain to reach Britain and many caves were occupied.

Fig 2 (*opposite*). The First Hunting Camps. The major difference in
these distributions is in the type of site, with caves predominating
in the north and west, and open sites concentrating in the east and
south, where naturally occurring caves are few in number. Early
Palaeolithic refers to *c* 500,000–45,000 BC, while Late Palaeolithic
equates with the period *c* 45,000–9,000 BC. (The sea is here
indicated by the orange area.)

18

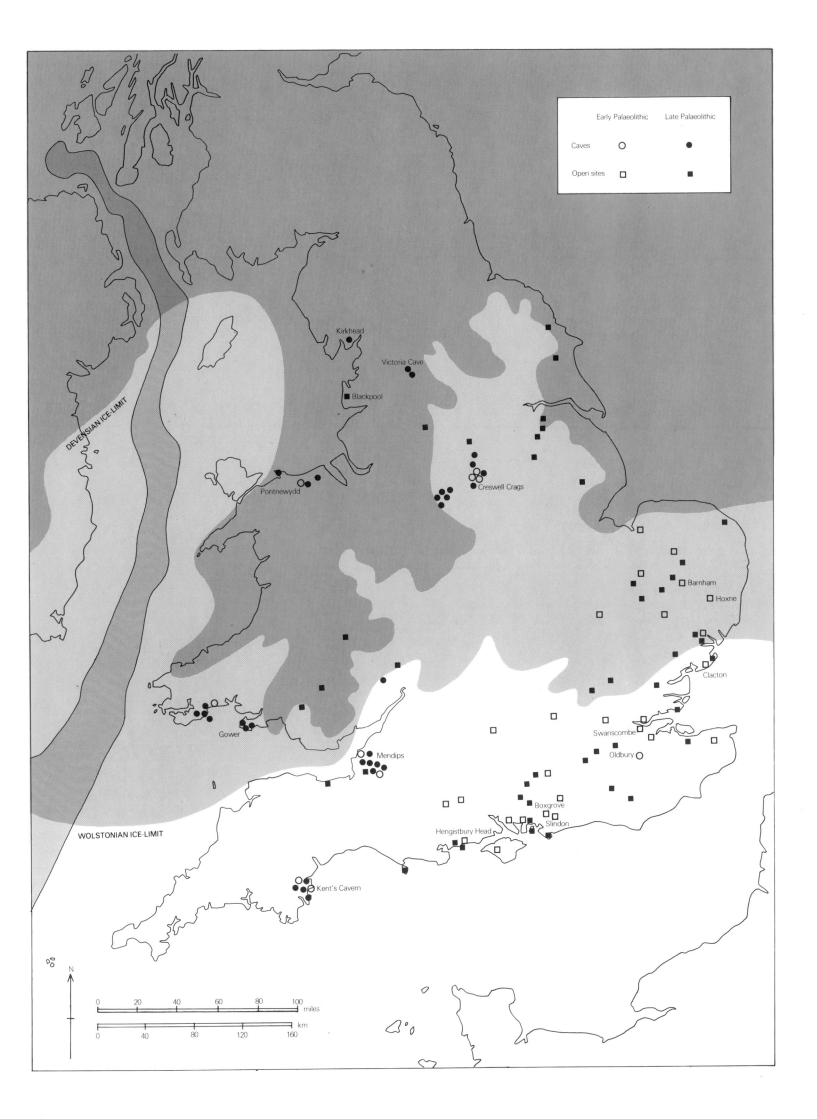

Early Palaeolithic   Late Palaeolithic

Caves   ○   ●

Open sites   □   ■

DEVENSIAN ICE-LIMIT

WOLSTONIAN ICE-LIMIT

Kirkhead

Victoria Cave

Blackpool

Pontnewydd

Creswell Crags

Barnham

Hoxne

Clacton

Gower

Swanscombe

Mendips

Oldbury

Boxgrove

Hengistbury Head   Slindon

Kent's Cavern

N

0   20   40   60   80   100
                                    miles

0   40   80   120   160
                              km

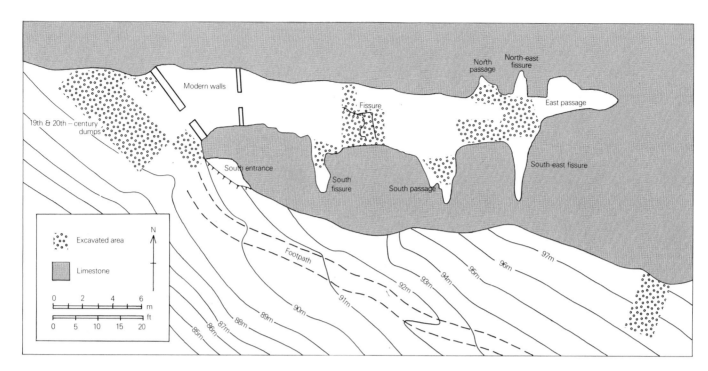

Fig 3. Pontnewydd Cave, Clwyd, North Wales. The area in front of the cave was occupied by hunters some 230,000 years ago. Many of the tools they discarded were swept into the cave by mud-flows.

A particular animal hunted at this time was the mammoth and in Ealing, north London, a pointed flake, presumably from the end of some kind of spear, was found lying amongst the bones from a complete skeleton, suggesting that a speared animal had successfully escaped its pursuers, only to die later from its wounds.

The First Modern People

It is to this last glacial period that we can trace our direct ancestry, for the human beings who camped in England and Wales belonged to fully modern man, *Homo sapiens sapiens*. The Neanderthals, who still inhabited Europe and the Middle East about 100,000 years ago, became increasingly inventive and resourceful as the glaciation developed, and may have gradually evolved into modern humans. There is no certainty on this point, however, and it is conceivable that our species can be traced back to earlier hominids, such as *homo erectus*. It may be no coincidence that during this period the technology of stone tool production was modified. The multi-purpose hand-axes which had been used for hundreds of thousands of years disappeared, to be replaced by more specialized tool-kits based on the use of long blades. Most characteristically, leaf-shaped points, some 10 to 15 cm in length, were made. These usually have very careful flaking on both sides of the implement and are thought to be spear tips. A much greater range of artefact types is now apparent with antler, bone and ivory being used to form a variety of awls, needles, points, harpoons, ornaments and musical

instruments including whistles. The maximum extent of the ice advance, covering most of Wales and running across from the west Midlands to the Humber, occurred some time after 25,000 BC and it is possible that Britain was again abandoned before being resettled as the climate again warmed up.

Cave sites were again used as camps during the Devensian glaciation (Fig 2). At Picken's Hole, Somerset, human teeth and animal remains have been recovered. The animal bones include arctic fox, cave hyena, cave lion, horse, woolly rhinoceros, reindeer and mammoth. A centre of hunting activity appears to have been the Mendip region of Somerset. The cave at Badger Hole, Wookey, has produced scrapers, awls, saws and leaf-points, together with bones of hyena, lion, otter, fox, brown bear, horse, giant Irish deer and reindeer. The caves in the limestone area of Derbyshire known as Creswell Crags were a frequent location for these hunters (Pl 7). The Crags form two sides of a gorge with caves in each cliff. In Pin Hole cave, scrapers, awls and a leaf-point have been found, along with bone and ivory tools, including a horse rib which was engraved with some crude decoration (Pl 9). From the neighbouring Robin Hood's cave came a piece of rib decorated with the engraved head of a horse.

The dramatic discovery of these first works of art from this remote period of our past has opened up exciting new avenues for research. They do not, of course, stand comparison with the cave paintings of south-western France or northern Spain, but they do provide an insight into the creative skills of these early modern men. The more usual finds from sites of this age – the stone tools, the settlement sites, the animal bones – inevitably compel archaeologists to study the economic aspects of daily life, through questions concerning the food supply, the uses of certain tools and the kind of habitation structures erected. But recognition of these small engravings allows us to consider the equally important ritual activities and artistic achievements of which we can only catch rare glimpses. The Derbyshire locations must have been close to the northern limit of human advance when occupied. Surrounded by an arid and treeless environment, and sheltering from the wind off the northern ice, it is testimony to human endeavour that some stone age hunter, perhaps huddled and with his back to the wind, engraved the head of the animal that he was in the process of hunting. In the south-east of England there were many more open sites, where perhaps similar works of art were fashioned; these still await discovery.

We have, therefore, with the appearance of modern humans evidence for the first art, the first music and, as we shall now see, the first formal burial suggestive of an interest in the after-life. At the Goat's Hole cave, Paviland, on the Gower peninsula of south Wales, early nineteenth-century exploration uncovered a remarkable find. In one part of the cave, under a shallow covering of soil, lay the headless, left side of a male skeleton, buried in an extended position. The body had been covered with red ochre at the time of its burial. Close to the thigh bone were found two small piles of shells that might have come from a decayed pocket. Between forty and fifty small, cylindrical rods of ivory lay on the chest of the person, together with fragments of ivory rings. This man constitutes the first known burial in Britain, and was laid to rest some time after 25,000 BC.

Around 15,000 BC the ice-sheets began slowly to melt for the last time and large herds of reindeer, elk, horse and red deer moved back into Britain across the North Sea plain, along with greater numbers of hunters. As the climate improved the large mammals of the ice-ages such as mammoth, woolly rhinoceros, bison and lion became extinct in Britain and Ireland, presumably because of increasingly successful hunting techniques and the changing environment. Forests gradually spread to cover the former treeless plains and the range of roots, berries, nuts and fungi must have increased considerably. These broad environmental changes must have been coincidental with a gradual shift by human groups towards a more diversified diet, exploiting a greater variety of smaller mammals and plant foods, with less reliance on successful kills of big game for meat. Caves continued to be occupied, however, and the same parts of the country were frequented, such as the Mendips in Somerset, Wales, the southern Pennines, with a limited extension into more northerly latitudes, as is demonstrated by the finds from the Victoria Cave, Yorkshire and Kirkhead Cave, Cumbria. On the Mendips Gough's Cave has provided exceptionally interesting implements. Two perforated bones have been found, which are thought to have been for straightening spear shafts, and a decorated piece of rib, upon which are incised groups of short lines that look suspiciously

Pl 9. The First Art. This piece of horse rib was found in Pin Hole Cave, Creswell Crags, Derbyshire. A crude engraving at the bottom of the rib appears to illustrate a person, perhaps wearing an animal mask, shooting a bow. (Length of rib is 20 cm)

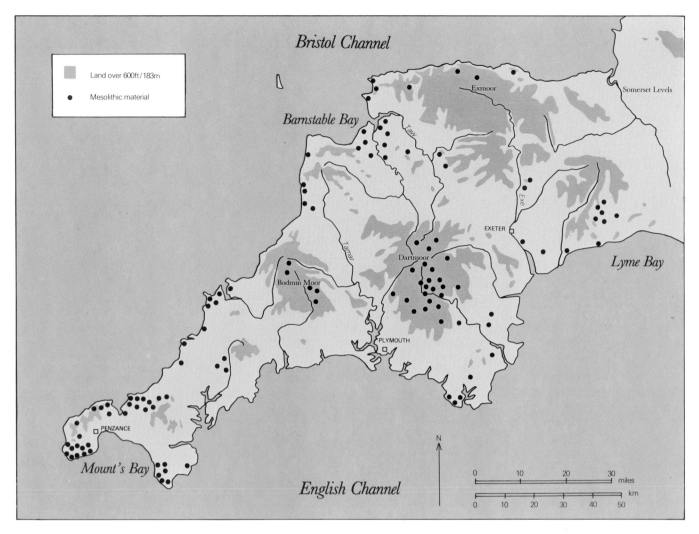

Fig 4. Post-Glacial Sites in South-West England: *c* 9,000–4,500 BC.
Camps are found both in the uplands on Dartmoor and Bodmin
Moor, and in low-lying coastal areas. The same band could
occupy both types of location, changing camp twice or more times
a year to gather, hunt or fish seasonal foods.

like tallies. Such are the problems of archaeological interpretation that this object has been variously described as a
gauge for spacing barbs on harpoons, a netting guide, a hunter's tally piece, a gaming object or a system for recording
genealogical information. An important open site of this
period is the promontory of Hengistbury Head in Dorset,
which now overlooks Christchurch harbour. In about 10,000
BC, however, it overlooked the confluence of major rivers,
with a broad flood plain beyond. At such a location a band of
hunters could have intercepted herds of reindeer on annual
migrations. The tools they dropped or left behind by their
camp fires might have been used in the preparation of deerskins. An unusual find was a highly worn ochre crayon
which, as experimental work has demonstrated, may have
played a role in both colouring and preserving the skins.

Only rarely does the completeness of the surviving archaeological evidence allow us to re-create a specific prehistoric
act in some detail. This is certainly the case with a complete

elk skeleton from High Furlong, near Blackpool in Lancashire. When the skeleton was located in muds and sediments of
a former lake, analysis of the bones showed indications of at
least seventeen lesions caused by the weapons of hunters who
had unsuccessfully pursued it around 10,000 BC. We can get
a fair idea of the animal's habits from contemporary comparisons. At present the elk, or moose as it is known in North
America, is to be found in North America, the USSR and
Scandinavia, mostly in regions where the vegetation is co-
niferous forest or birchwood. They are also frequent visitors
to lakes, rivers and pools, where they feed on aquatic vegetation, especially in the spring and summer. Standing up to
2 m at the withers and weighing over 350 kg, with antlers
over 1.5 m in spread, the long-legged elk must have been a
formidable prey for hunters equipped with only simple weapons of bone, stone and wood.

At High Furlong two encounters between the animal and

Fig 5 (*opposite*). Early Post-Glacial Sites: *c* 9,000–6,500 BC. People
reach northern Ireland for the first time. Britain is still joined to
the European mainland, and the occasional find of barbed points
under the North Sea may indicate the location of camps.

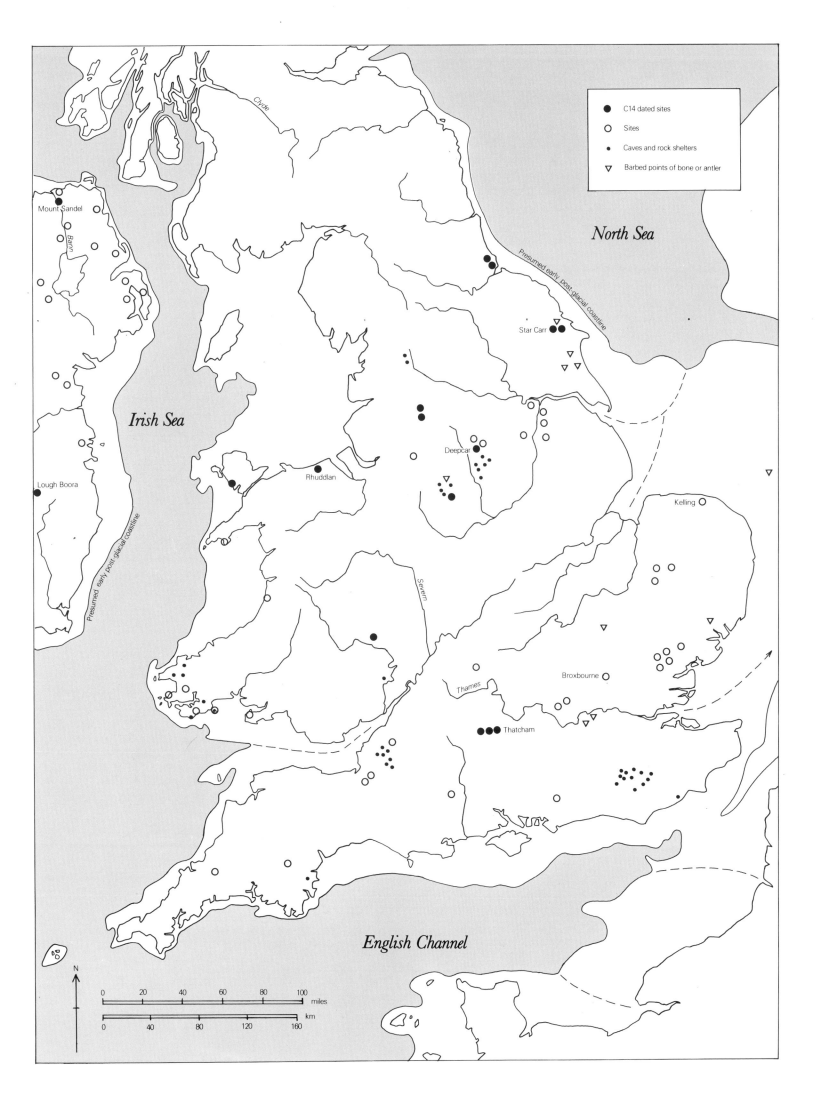

North Sea

Clyde

Presumed early post-glacial coastline

Mount Sandel

Bann

Irish Sea

Star Carr

Deepcar

Presumed early post-glacial coastline

Lough Boora

Rhuddlan

Severn

Kelling

Broxbourne

Thames

Thatcham

English Channel

● C14 dated sites
○ Sites
• Caves and rock shelters
▽ Barbed points of bone or antler

N

0   20   40   60   80   100
miles

0   40   80   120   160
km

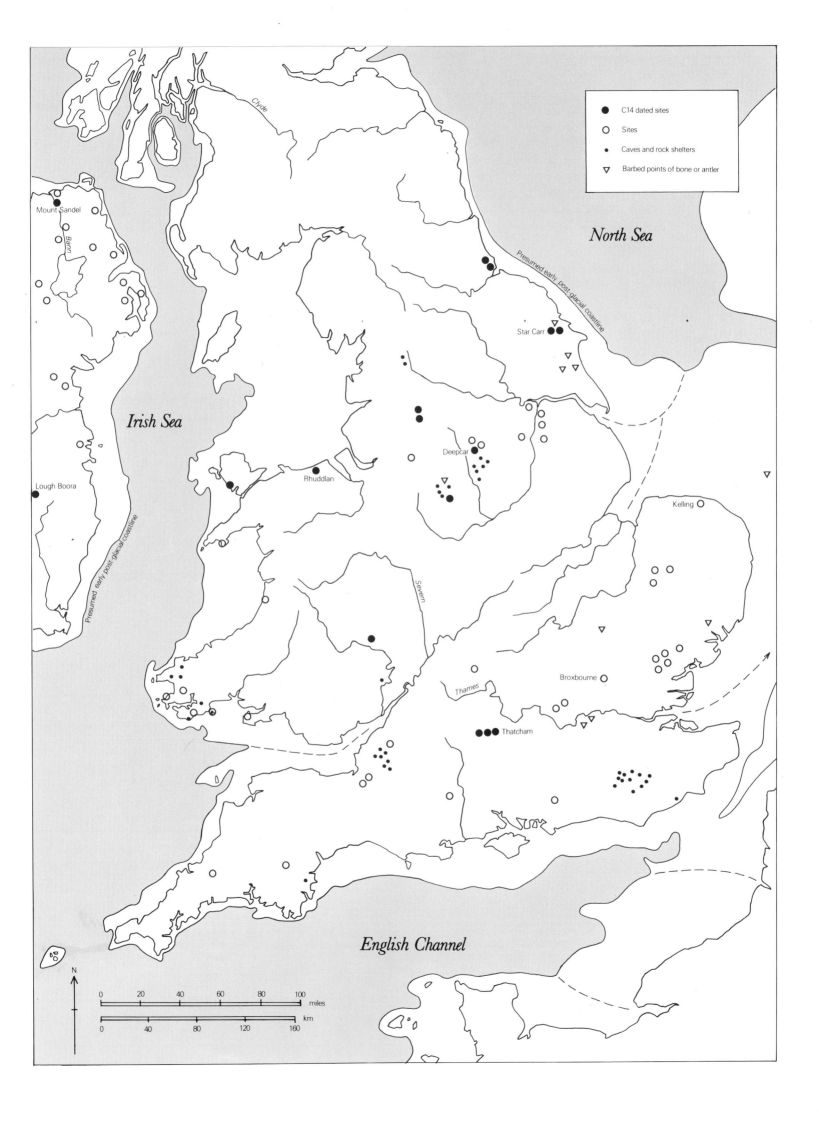

North Sea

Irish Sea

English Channel

Mount Sandel

Bann

Lough Boora

Clyde

Star Carr

Deepcar

Rhuddlan

Severn

Kelling

Broxbourne

Thames

Thatcham

Presumed early post-glacial coastline

Presumed early post-glacial coastline

● C14 dated sites
○ Sites
· Caves and rock shelters
▽ Barbed points of bone or antler

N

0   20   40   60   80   100   miles

0   40   80   120   160   km

the hunters are indicated by the pattern of cuts surviving on the bones. The first one occurred some two weeks before the death of the elk, when the hind legs of the beast were pierced by barbed points of bone shot from a bow. Bows and arrows had been used in Europe from around 20,000 BC, as a barbed and tanged arrowhead from the site of Parpallo in Spain demonstrates. We must imagine that the arrows did not travel over any great distance; the hunter or hunters had probably stalked the quarry and had approached to within perhaps 30 m of it before discharging their weapons. It is possible that the hind legs were a chosen target and that the intention at this stage in the hunt was to lame the animal.

Another, more intriguing possibility, is that the arrows were attached to cords for restraining the elk while the hunters attempted to take it into captivity. Contemporary evidence suggests that elks can be domesticated in order to provide milk and transport, including riding and drawing sledges. It is also, of course, much less hard work if such a large animal can be persuaded to walk back to your camp before it is butchered, rather than have to carry a heavy carcass. It is entirely possible that the close association of men and animals such as deer, would have led to herd management and perhaps a primitive form of domestication. Whatever the intentions of the hunters in this case, however, they went astray and the elk was allowed – at least temporarily – to escape to lick its wounds.

Archaeological evidence all too often comprises a collection of mute stones and bones; the job of the archaeologist is to make sense of the pattern and then interpret the design. Frequently and frustratingly the pattern is not complete. Often intelligent speculation must be used to assist interpretation. We can thus imagine that the elk escaped, but not for long. Days later some hunters closed in again on the weakened animal. This time the encounter was both close and bloody. The hunters unleashed a flight of flint-tipped arrows at their quarry; some of these penetrated the rib-cage of the unfortunate animal, and may have contributed to its death by collapsing its lungs. The pursuers were now able to approach the elk, and one of them used a flint axe to sever the ligaments and tendons on its left fore foot. The same foot was struck with a heavy, blunt instrument as the animal still refused to succumb to the inevitable. In a frenzy of desperation someone swung another flint axe wildly at its body, tearing through the bloody tissue and sinking the axe-head deep into one of the creature's ribs.

We do not know what happened next, only that the the final act in the drama did not go according to plan. The elk managed to get away on that cold, wintery day. Perhaps the hunters had used all their weapons; perhaps they had backed off to let the animal struggle its last few strides and tire itself to a fatal collapse; perhaps one of them had sustained an injury that needed attention; or perhaps they realised that this particular elk was not meant to be taken by men. Whatever the reason, the beast managed to stumble its blood-stained path without further attack towards a partially frozen lake. There it took a few faltering steps onto the thin ice, before crashing through the frozen surface into the depths below. Would the hunters have stood on the lake's edge and

cursed their wretched luck? Probably not. Luck does not seem to play much part in the lives of contemporary hunters and gatherers. By analogy, these prehistoric hunters may have believed that as soon as they set foot outside camp the animal-spirits of the herds had already chosen which animal was to be offered to them. This elk was not the one; they themselves had chosen wrongly.

People of the Forest

It is perhaps appropriate that our last picture of the 'big game hunters' of the Ice Ages is one of an unsuccessful pursuit of a solitary elk. If so then it was a sign that things were changing, and that human beings were going to have to adapt if they were to survive. For the period between 10,000 BC and 6,000 BC was one of rapid environmental transformation. The most obvious indicator was a steadily rising sea-level. As the ice-sheets melted and retreated northwards an enormous amount of water was released through streams and rivers flowing away from the ice. In 10,000 BC animals and their human predators could have walked from the coast of Yorkshire to Denmark, or stepped out on a tediously flat journey from the beach at Blackpool to the Isle of Man (Fig 5). Ireland may have been reached by one or more land bridges. Gradually, as the ice melted for the last time, these great coastal plains were submerged by the sea until, by about 6,000 BC, the coastline approximated to the present one. The occasional antler point dragged up in the nets of a North Sea trawler is a dramatic reminder of these former lands beneath the waves.

Temperatures, too, rose very rapidly at this time. From a yearly below-zero centigrade average in 10,000 BC the air temperature climbed during summers to a maximum of 18°C around 6,000 BC. Thus summer temperatures were higher than the present average of 15.7°C. This was coupled with an increased length for the autumn and spring seasons, less windy conditions and less precipitation. There was an inevitable effect on the flora and fauna. The heathlands which formed as the glaciers retreated north were gradually invaded by birch and pine forests which, in turn, gave way to deciduous woodlands of oak, elm and lime. The large mammals that had provided most of the meat and clothing requirements of the hunters and gatherers followed the retreating ice-sheets northwards, unable to adapt to the more closed environments of the dense woods. Elk, reindeer and wild cattle became more and more scarce. In their place species of deer more suited to forested environments thrived, such as red deer and roe deer, and also a range of much smaller creatures such as shrews, moles, hedgehogs, wild

Pl 10. The Hunters Kit. These implements from Star Carr in North Yorkshire show how tools had become much smaller by 9,000 BC. At the top are blades or knives, while the pointed pieces on either side may have been used to bore holes in skins. The serrated point is made from antler, and the microliths below it might have been used as barbs or arrowheads. (Length of antler point is 16.9 cm approx.)

boars, red squirrels, beavers, badgers, voles, brown hares and mice. Such was the transformation in the landscape that it is unlikely that our failed hunters at High Furlong in 10,000 BC would have recognized any of their surroundings 4,000 years later. And, undoubtedly more important, like the elk they would not have survived, since their skills and technology had become outdated.

So what were the human adaptations that had occurred? One possibility is that communities might have shrunk in size. Just as the larger mammals of the cold heathlands migrated and foraged in large herds, so the bands that followed them, or more likely intercepted them, were bigger. The number of people needed to organize the ambush of a migrating herd, to kill the animals once several of them had been trapped, to skin the carcasses and prepare the skins, and to share the meat was correspondingly bigger. In contrast the hunting of a wild boar in the forest could be undertaken quite effectively by only one or two people, and the skin and meat from the animal would clothe and feed far fewer individuals. This does not necessarily mean that the overall level of population began to fall as the tree cover increased. On the contrary, it seems highly likely that the population rose and, although average band size may have dropped, there would have been far more hunting groups in existence.

Another change that took place may well have been in the mobility of hunting communities. In previous periods groups might have been quite able to camp at a cave in north Wales during the summer and perhaps to retreat to the area of the English lowlands for the winter. During colder phases communities had come to England only during summer and walked back across the dry English Channel to winter on the continent. Now, as the large mammal percentage of the daily diet declined, other food sources, much nearer to hand, were increasingly used. There was a greater emphasis on gathering plant foods – nuts, especially hazel nuts, roots, leaves and fungi – and a tendency to trap waterfowl and collect shellfish. Long journeys may now have been uncommon and the seasonal shift from summer to winter camp may have been simply one of moving to the nearest substantial area of uplands at the start of summer to pursue grazing animals. A result of decreased mobility was a greater familiarity with the immediate locality and, of course, a greater awareness of the whereabouts of the most convenient sources of food: the best fungi, the most prolific mussel beds, the favourite spot for wild boar, the ideal place to position fishing nets in the river. As the self-sufficient band built up an intimate and detailed knowledge of its immediate surroundings there may have grown a tendency to frequent the favoured locations on a seasonal rota, so that the quest for food followed a well worn trail. It is easy to see how, with the realization that other bands existed in adjacent areas, this seasonal round might soon come to be appreciated by the band members as a sort of territory over which they had prior rights.

These small bands, therefore, by analogy with contemporary hunters, comprised perhaps four or five families each, and were economically self-sufficient. All their food and clothing requirements could be obtained relatively close to the base camp. Gathering or hunting the food, preparing and cooking, and repairing or making a range of goods from shelters to fish hooks, still left them with a few hours a day for gossiping or visiting neighbours. The bands were not socially or biologically self-sufficient, however. It must have been desirable for bands to get together from time to time, to exchange stories about people, or food sources, or outcrops of good stone for tools. It was necessary for there to be a good deal of inter-marriage between bands to ensure the survival of healthy communities, and to ease any tensions that might occur between different groups. We cannot rule out the possibility of fighting, and although there is some evidence for conflict among bands in Scandinavia in the post-glacial period, there is little indication of aggression in Britain and Ireland.

Finally there was a technological change in the production of stone tools. For this was the age of the microlith. Microliths are very small pieces of worked stone or flint, that were inserted in various wooden hafts for use as tools. The most obvious suggestion of their use has been as stone tips for wooden arrows. Instead of the earlier techniques of hunting animals using ambushes, or drives and stampedes over cliffs, where the beasts were eventually killed by repeated spear thrusts, bows and arrows were employed to hunt more solitary animals from a distance in wooded environments. Such are the uncertainties of archaeological interpretation, however, that frequently more than one explanation is capable of being supported by the facts. This is certainly the case with the humble microlith. Other suggestions for its function have been as barbs in harpoons or fish-spears, or as carefully positioned teeth in a wooden board to produce something that resembles a prehistoric cheese grater, used perhaps to shred plant foods. Indeed, the microlith was probably a multi-purpose tool, used for all these, and many more, functions. Easier to interpret are the stone axes and adzes that appear on sites in increasing numbers. These were presumably hafted in wooden handles and used for woodworking.

The distribution of the most important sites of this period, along with an approximation of the coastline, is illustrated here (Fig 5). Remains of seasonal camps have been found throughout southern England and as far north as Yorkshire. It is likely that coastal Wales was extensively occupied, with more intermittent settlements in the Welsh uplands. Human communities now reached Ireland for the first time. A particular concentration of sites lie in the Bann valley of northern Ireland, but this should not be taken as evidence that groups initially crossed using the shortest passage from the Galloway peninsula to Co.Antrim. In Scotland no sites of this age are yet known. Many thousands more sites are known than from the preceding periods, although most are still represented by only a collection of stone tools. In part, of course, this does not reflect population increase but simply that the locations of the camps have not suffered the scouring and destructive effects of further glaciations, and therefore many more have survived. The majority of the sites are open and from a few of the excavated examples comes the first evidence of constructed shelters and huts.

Star Carr in Yorkshire is one of the finest examples of a site of this period. In about 9,000 BC a platform of birch branches

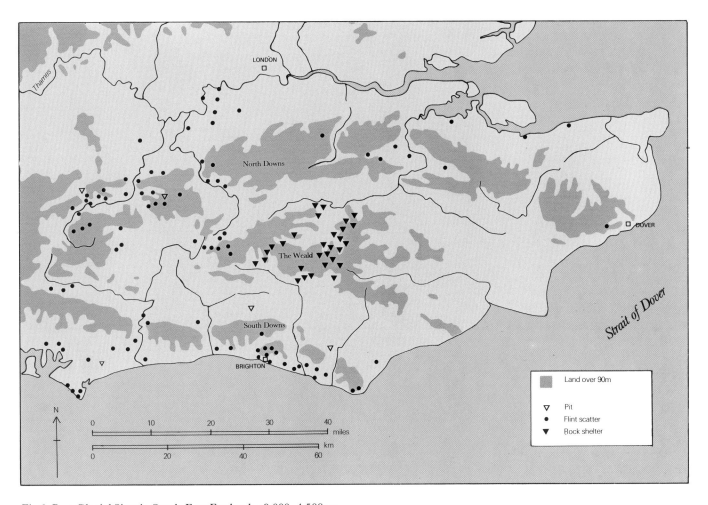

Fig 6. Post-Glacial Sites in South-East England: c 9,000–4,500 BC.
After the retreat of the ice-sheets bands of hunters and gatherers
penetrate The Weald and occupy a number of rock-shelters.
Concentrations of flint in fields indicate camps.

and trunks was laid down at the western edge of a small lake
in the Vale of Pickering. Flint axes and adzes were used to fell
trees of birch, pine and willow in the immediate vicinity.
Shelters or huts were presumably built adjacent to this platform and housed probably three or four families during the
winter months. They were remarkably industrious during
those cold and short winter days, manufacturing at least 191
barbed points, 187 of them from deer antler, which were discovered on the platform (Pl 10). The points were almost
certainly intended as spearheads, fastened using birch-bark
resin, to wooden shafts. It is not surprising, therefore, to
learn that among the animals consumed on site, red deer and
roe deer far outnumbered elk, wild cattle and boar. The close
association between this small group of people and the deer
herds is symbolized by the unique discovery of antler headgear made out of the animals' skulls (Pl 11). Perforations in
these front skull bones show that these were probably worn.
This strange headgear may have been used as a clever
camouflage to approach quarry, but it is more likely that it
was worn during rituals and dances at the camp, which were
performed to ensure the well-being and fertility of the herds.
There are three other fascinating discoveries at Star Carr: a
wooden paddle, the remains of a domesticated dog and a

quantity of deer bones. The paddle suggests that the occupants must have had some sort of dug-out or skin boat
moored alongside the platform for use on the lake. The discovery of the dog's bones implies that these animals could
have been used in tracking and collecting small game in the
same way as they are today. The dog from Star Carr is the
first tame animal from Britain, and one of the earliest from
Europe, and implies that the skill of breaking in an animal
from the wild had a long prehistory. Lastly, analysis of the
deer bones suggests that these hunters were being deliberately selective with their prey, and usually killed stags rather
than hinds or the young, implying that elementary practices
of deer-herd management had been appreciated and im-
plemented (Pl 12). During the summer months it is quite
likely that this highly skilled group followed the herds onto
the uplands of the North Yorkshire Moors.

There are a number of approximately contemporary sites
in the Kennet Valley west of Reading. At Thatcham, in
Berkshire, a very similar location to Star Carr was occupied
by a group during the winter and spring months. Here
concentrations of domestic rubbish and remains of hearths
formed an area of about 6m diameter, which might indicate
the position of a shelter of branches or skins. Hazel nuts, apparently something of a staple item in the diet at this time,
were found in the hearths. The finds included the expected
items such as a large number of microliths and animal bones

Pl 11. Hunting Rituals. Some of the hunters at Star Carr wore headgear made from stag frontlets with part of the antlers still attached. The interiors of the skulls had been hollowed, as if to lighten the bone, and the skulls were perforated. These deer-hunters may have worn them during hunting rituals.

of red and roe deer, elk, wild cattle and boar. All of the evidence suggests a tiny band of hunters, gatherers and fishermen existing at one particular location in its seasonal round, going about daily activities and also engaging in hide preparation and a little bone working. It is, however, difficult to ascertain during which season or seasons any camp was occupied. Often the food remains provide some clue. Hazel nuts, for instance, can be gathered in autumn, but, if stored, might last a group through the winter. Similarly, animals and fish have seasonal patterns of movement and the discovery of deer or salmon, for example, can lead to suggestions about the time of habitation.

The Cornish peninsula and the coasts of Wales also seem to have been frequently inhabited (Fig 4). An especially popular site lies at Rhuddlan on the Clwyd estuary in north Wales. Here communities camped out on top of a sandy bluff overlooking much low-lying land that stretched as far as the Isle of Man. Since the site was a long way from the flint bearing chalkland of southern and eastern England, microliths had to be fashioned out of a local substitute – a blackish stone called chert that was quarried out of the nearby limestone. Hazel nuts again seem to have been eaten in vast quantities. The profusion of wild plants, nuts, animals, fish and waterfowl that must have been available in this spot suggests that the group could have camped all-year round if they had wanted. They were artistic too. Four pebbles incised with patterns are a rather meagre reminder that such camps must have had a wide range of colourful decorated containers and clothing that have long since decayed.

The archaeologist specializing in this period has to be mathematically adroit and also possess a generous imagination with which to reconstruct the lives of people from the stones and bones that survive them. And there are rather an abundance of them – stones and bones, that is. At Deepcar, in Yorkshire, a total of almost 37,000 flint waste flakes were

balanced by only 144 surviving implements. In the southern Pennines alone there are over 1,000 sites of this type which have been discovered, and it almost seems that wherever an archaeologist digs a hole and looks for microliths then microliths will be found. But how many of these sites are contemporary, and how many were the result of a single band's wanderings? It has been suggested that, since red deer tend to congregate in the lowlands during winter and disperse over the uplands in summer, then human groups which depended on them may have done likewise. Whatever the population size we can be sure that it was growing and that people were deliberately trying to affect their environment. They created clearings by felling trees, either by axe or fire. Such open spaces improved grazing and influenced the movement of animals and the growth of particularly useful plants or trees, such as hazel. Ivy may also have been encouraged to use as fodder for deer herds. We have seen how familiarity with certain wild animals had resulted in the taming and the use of the dog, and the selective culling of stags. It is also quite likely that the advantage of storing food, such as hazel nuts or dried fish, was common knowledge. A significant shift had occurred in the balance between nature and humanity. Human groups were no longer at the mercy of, or even in harmony with, their natural surroundings; they were now capable of intentionally changing them.

Ireland was reached by various bands who may have walked across the possible narrow land bridges that linked the two countries, or sailed in dug-outs to the island. The key site is undoubtedly Mount Sandel, situated on a terrace on the east bank of the river Bann in north-east Ireland (Pl 14). Occupation was confined to the winter and may have been intermittent over hundreds of years before and after 8,000 BC. The local tree cover at the time was a mixed one of hazel and birch. Excavation revealed a series of egg-shaped huts constructed out of stakes that leant inwards and were presum-

28

ably tied at the top (Fig 7). The huts enclosed pits and hearths, and outside the shelters were further hearths, pits and a flint-working area. Only one hut seems to have been standing at any one time, and perhaps a group of less than ten people were seasonally returning to this camp and rebuilding their single shelter in approximately the same hollow. The food remains were particularly interesting. Bones of fish and young wild boar had been boiled, perhaps to make broth, before being thrown on the camp fire. Birds from a range of different habitats – woodland, riverside, estuary mouth and inshore waters – were consumed, along with the ubiquitous hazel nuts. Both fish and hazel nuts may have been stored for later consumption. An exotic element in the diet was the fruitlets of the edible white water-lily (Pl 17). The absence of red deer bones from the site is thought to be an indicator that their bones were not boiled for broth, and therefore were discarded elsewhere. It is likely that the hunters of Mount Sandel were just as partial to a piece of venison as their kinsmen across the water.

The seasons when Mount Sandel was occupied can only be determined by estimating the seasonality of the food resources. Salmon from the site indicate a summer period of occupation, while eel and hazel nuts suggest autumnal use.

Fig 7. Mount Sandel, Co. Londonderry, Northern Ireland. One of the huts erected around 8,000 BC. The stake-holes angled inwards towards the centre of the hut, and the archaeologist therefore suggested boughs bent and tied together at the top to form a dome-shaped structure.

Young pigs were also located at Mount Sandel, and this would imply a late winter activity. It can be argued, therefore, that the site was occupied either continuously from summer through to late winter, or in two separate seasons, one during the summer-autumn transition, the other towards the end of the winter.

Roughly contemporary with Mount Sandel are the remains of a temporary camp at Lough Boora, Co. Offaly. The lack of structures here argues for a camp of short duration. Around the hearths triangular blades and microliths were found, together with a number of stone axes. The importance of this site is that it demonstrates that settlements at this time had spread out into the Irish midlands, and were not confined to the north-east.

After the Flood

At some time after 6,000 BC the rising waters eventually lapped along the coastline that is familiar to us today: the shape of the British Isles was formed; the last land bridge to the continent had been submerged; Ireland became an island (Fig 9). What effect did this have on our now insular hunters and gatherers? Of course the rise in sea-level was not a sudden phenomenon; the process had been going on ever since the glaciers began to melt away to the north. And for much of this period the communities would have hardly per-

ceived any change in their immediate environment. There was one phase of sea-level change, however, that was much more rapid. Within 200 years, some time after 6,000 BC, the waters rose over a height of 7.7 m. Calculated on an annual basis this makes a rise of approximately 3.8 cm every year. This may not seem so catastrophic; yet it may have meant the loss of a valued coastal campsite within a matter of five or ten years. All of which demonstrates that the changes now underway had indeed reached catastrophic proportions, and that the groups then living must have been aware of the loss of vast quantities of low-lying land to the sea. Extensive territories, previously accessible for hunting or fishing now became sea-beds under the North Sea, or between the Lancashire coast and the Isle of Man. On them the camps, tools and hearths of hunters past were buried slowly under the accumulating silts, while hunters present retreated with the shore lines, telling tales around new camp fires of lands lost to the sea. Archaeological evidence for the stories does not survive, but a remarkable line of footprints preserved in the intertidal zone of the Severn estuary near Newport in Gwent seems particularly appropriate in this context.

The density of population in the British Isles must have increased as absolute numbers of hunters and gatherers grew and the land available to them diminished. It is not surprising, therefore, that at this time we have evidence for communities all over the remaining land surface, from the south of England to the north of Scotland. It is feasible that certain

favoured areas, such as the mouths of estuaries, became especially crowded and we cannot rule out the possibility of all-year round occupation at such locations. Average temperatures remained about 2°C higher than those of today, and increased the length of the spring and autumn seasons. However, severance from the continent coincided with the advent of a wetter and windier climate. Although the prevalent woodland was of the closed type containing deciduous trees such as oak, elm and lime, there are increasing indications that bands were able to open up clearings in the forest for the purpose of encouraging more useful plants and trees. This practice may have become so widespread that certain woodlands were completely prevented from regenerating. The increased precipitation slowly waterlogged some of these clearings, especially at higher altitudes, resulting in the onset of peat formation.

Among the most important camps in the south-east are those at Farnham and Abinger in Surrey and Selmeston in Sussex (Fig 6). At these excavated sites a number of hollows were discovered which were interpreted as pit-dwellings. The Abinger example was particularly interesting and was roughly oval in shape, measuring 4.27 m long by 3.2 m wide, with a maximum depth of about a metre. A sloping ledge running along its eastern side may have been a sleeping-place. Forked posts at either end of the pit may have supported a horizontal ridge-piece, against which would be lent a framework of branches, saplings, bracken and deerskins, forming a waterproof covering for a comfortable shelter.

Stone tool technology at this time was gradually becoming more sophisticated. The microliths became even smaller in size and more regularly shaped, with some evidence of their multiple use as barbs in wooden arrows or spears. New types of artefact appear such as the hour-glass perforated pebble, or so-called mace head. In reality these were probably hafted, but may have been used as weights on digging sticks rather than for ceremonial function. Partially hollowed or cupped pebbles are found which were probably held between thumb and forefinger as all-purpose hammer stones. More difficult to interpret are the limpet scoops – elongated beach pebbles – found on coastal camps in Wales. No doubt that the communities were feeding off quantities of shellfish, but whether the limpet scoops played any useful part in the extracting or eating of limpets is quite another question. Particular stone sources became prized and well known. The chert from Portland in Dorset, for instance has been found from sites as far apart as the Bristol Channel and Land's End.

Another type of hut or shelter of this period was excavated at Broomhill, Braishfield in Hampshire. Here fourteen posts were set out in an approximate oval around a shallow hollow. A number of smaller stakes helped to support the superstruc-

Fig 8. Morton on Tay, Fife, Eastern Scotland. This rocky promontory was occupied by a band around 6,000 BC. A pattern of stake-holes, an area of stained sand, a scatter of flints and a burnt area suggest that this was a roughly rectangular shelter.

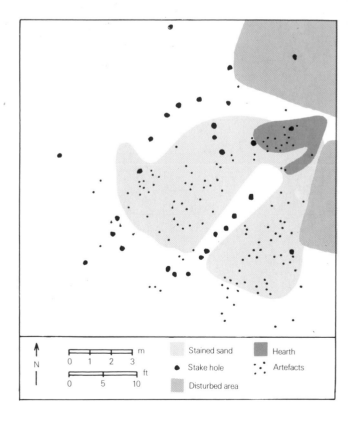

Stained sand	Hearth
• Stake hole	∴ Artefacts
Disturbed area	

Fig 9 (*opposite*). Late Post-Glacial Sites: *c* 6,500–4,500 BC. The coastline of Britain and Ireland takes on its present shapes as rising sea-levels separate Britain from Europe, and make an island of the Isle of Man. Hunters and gatherers now occupy the length and breadth of Britain and Ireland.

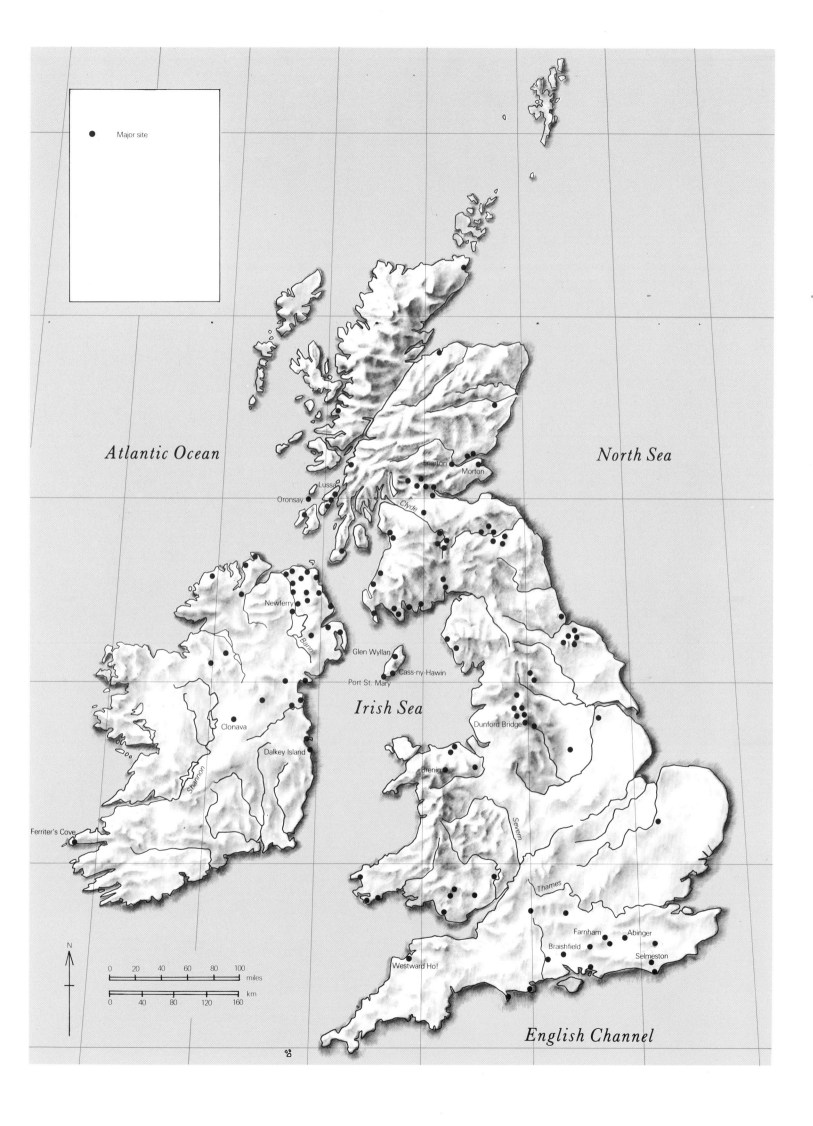

Major site

Atlantic Ocean

North Sea

Briarton
Morton
Lussa
Oronsay
Clyde

Newferry
Bann

Glen Wyllan
Cass-ny-Hawin
Port St. Mary

Irish Sea

Clonava

Dalkey Island

Dunford Bridge

Brenig

Shannon

Severn

Ferriter's Cove

Thames

Farnham
Abinger
Braishfield
Selmeston

Westward Ho!

N

0   20   40   60   80   100
                                    miles

0   40   80   120   160
                                    km

English Channel

ture. In the interior of the hut was a circular hearth that produced some charred hazel nuts, while on its south-eastern side lay an entrance flanked by inclined poles. The house had maximum dimensions of 4.5 by 5 m and seems to have been a rather substantial winter dwelling. Sea food now formed a greater part of the diet at settlements close to the sea. At Westward Ho!, Devon, a midden contained oyster, limpet and mussel shells, along with the more usual remains of deer, boar and even hedgehog. In Wales the bulk of the sites appear to be coastal, although there are indications that the uplands were also settled by small bands during the summer months. One such camp is that at the head of the Brenig valley in Clwyd, very much a windswept moorland location today, but still virtually in sight of the north coast of Wales.

There are a great number of contemporary sites in the uplands of northern England. At Dunford Bridge in West Yorkshire, an oval patch of flat stones may have provided a crude paving around a hearth and suggests a very small shelter of only 2.6 m in diameter. Just enough, one might say, for a man and his dog! In fact the preponderance of microliths at these camps may suggest no more than that, single families, or possibly men without women, engaged in summer hunting and pitching camp in a different place every night to rest, feed and re-barb their spears or arrows for the following day. Red deer, boar and birds were probably the prey. Small bands now foraged everywhere in Britain, including the Isle of Man, as is shown by the camps at Glen Wyllan and Port St Mary, and Cass-ny-Hawin, occupied around 6,500 BC.

Evidence from Ireland, too, is much more widespread. At Newferry, right out in the middle of the Bann valley, a small band seems to have relied for its food on the catching of eels and salmon. This would suggest that the site was occupied between June and December when the eels made their runs from Lough Neagh to the sea. A completely new type of tool appears at Newferry – the polished stone axe. Over forty were found on the site and the suggestion is that these implements were used in the construction and maintenance of a system of weirs and fish-traps. Much use was made of the good flint obtainable from the chalk outcrops of the Antrim plateau. There are many small camps in this area which contain quantities of flint-knapping debris, indicating perhaps, that groups made particular journeys to the chalk outcrops to secure fresh supplies of flint for their tools. From the evidence of the large middens that mark some of these sites, it appears that when they were not knapping they were spending at least some of their time eating oysters, periwinkles and limpets.

In Ireland the greatest concentration of camps away from the north-eastern coast lies in the Bann valley and its tributaries. There are some sites in the centre of the country, however. At the north-western end of Lough Derravaragh, Co.Westmeath, lies a low knoll at Clonava that was repeatedly occupied. Charred hazel nuts and the seeds of yellow water lily were two of the ingredients of the diet. Elsewhere on the coast the characteristic large flake tools of Ireland can be found associated with shell heaps or middens. Excavations at Ferriter's Cove in Co. Kerry have uncovered large flakes associated with a midden area of shells, burnt bones and fish

bones, while similar tools are being increasingly found in the Galway area. Why some of these tools are larger than their counterparts in England and Wales is not known; perhaps the reason may lie in a different production technique, or some variation in function. One shell midden at Dalkey Island, Co.Dublin was accumulating in about 4,200 BC.

In Scotland the distribution of camps is again principally a coastal one. Whether this is a reflection of the actual settlements at this time, suggesting that the rugged interior was largely deserted, or simply indicates the lack of archaeological research inland cannot yet be determined. What we can say with some assurance is that there is a particular concentration of camps around Oban on the west coast. Some of these were in caves, others were open sites, but as we would expect from their nearness to the sea, their occupants seem to have relied for the most part on shellfish, fish and sea birds for food. Most camps, too, are characterized by a large number of implements made from antler and bone, such as barbed points, the so-called limpet scoops, mattocks, pins and awls. Another remarkable cluster of camps, all marked by shell heaps, is to be found on the small island of Oronsay. These island sites were probably only seasonally occupied and the post-holes found during excavation suggest very flimsy shelters, or possibly racks for drying or smoking fish. Certainly fish, and in particular the saithe, contributed much to the food supplies, along with a range of local shellfish such as limpet, periwinkle, whelk, oyster, cockle, scallop and razor. There was enough time for more artistic pursuits, however. The large number of cowrie shells found, each with twin perforations, were probably strung as a necklace – a little hint of ornamentation. At Lussa on the island of Jura we have our first Scottish evidence of definite structures. Here three scoops were made in the gravels, and three contiguous rings of stone were laid out in the hollows, each being about 1 m in diameter. These seem to have been cooking pits, and from them came minute bone fragments, charred hazel nuts, limpet shells and some red ochre. This very early kitchen appliance was installed some time after 7,000 BC. Did the three fires burn simultaneoulsy, with separate foods being cooked on each, in order to serve a composite dish?

On the other side of Scotland a camp site at Morton, Fife (Fig 8), was repeatedly occupied. The location consisted of a rocky promontory that was turned into an island every high tide, but otherwise remained connected to the mainland by a sandspit. Two areas were excavated, separated only by about 40 m. One was clearly a midden at which butchering of animals and some preliminary preparation of food had been carried out. At the other, slightly higher up, lay the main occupation zone in which was located the remains of a roughly rectangular shelter with an external hearth. Some of the stake-holes suggested that the branches or timbers may have leant inwards to be tied at the top, as already suggested for the shelter at Mount Sandel. The covering could have been a mixture of skins, branches and reeds. A very extensive range of food resources was discovered: red deer, roe deer, wild cattle and boar supplied most of the meat; bird bones included guillemot, gannet, razorbill and cormorant; cod, haddock, sea trout and salmon were fished; a variety of shell

Pl 12. Deer. A variety of species of deer were hunted by early man. Familiarity with the behavioural patterns of the animal may have led post-glacial hunters into practising elementary forms of herd management.

Food for Free

fish was collected together with crabs. Many plant remains were found, including fat hen (today this is regarded as a weed but in the past was cooked as a green vegetable), which surprisingly contains more iron and protein than either cabbage or spinach. The presence of large specimens of cod indicates that some sort of boat was available to the Morton band. Just such a vessel was found in the river Tay at Friarton, Perth. Made from Scots fir, it resembled a dug-out canoe and measured overall some 4.5 m long by 1 m wide. The information from Morton indicates camps of about a dozen people, seasonally resident on the promontory, with the site remaining popular for hundreds of years.

What was it like to be a member of a hunting, gathering and fishing band in this long and distant period of prehistory in Britain and Ireland? It is very difficult to imagine, not simply because of the enormous time difference, but also because of the very different lifestyle compared with our own. Archaeologists are always faced with a dilemma when trying to flesh out the past from the evidence that is available to them. This is particularly true of early prehistory when a few hearths, post-holes, bones and stone tools are all that survive. Yet the attempt must be made. It is, after all, as Sir Mortimer Wheeler once remarked, the people that are interesting, rather than the bric-a-brac that they left behind. We can draw some comparisons between contemporary hunters and gatherers who survive today and those of the past. Such comparisons, allied to intelligent speculation, can throw some

Pl 14. Mount Sandel, Co. Londonderry, Northern Ireland. An early post-glacial hunting camp, occupied around 8,000 BC, was situated on the eastern bank of the river Bann. The hunters camped close to the site of the medieval Mount Sandel fort, the green mound in the photograph.

Pl 13 (*opposite*). Cefn Caves, Clwyd, North Wales. Just south of Pontnewydd Cave lie Cefn Caves, a labyrinthine cave system which meanders behind a limestone cliff. Cefn caves were briefly used by hunters and gatherers some 14,000 years ago.

light on this remote time.

It would seem that all the essential things needed for a comfortable life for the average band member were there for the taking, quite literally. Food swam in the rivers, hung from the branches, and wandered in the woods, the timbers and branches for shelters grew ready to be cut and trimmed, while quality clothing needed only a measured cut, a good scrape and careful curing to ensure a pleasant fit. These essentials were available to everyone. They did not cost anything and, miraculously, the shelves were always replenished by the unseen spirits of the forest. Faced with such a

profusion of desirables so near to hand it is very difficult to imagine a prehistoric equivalent of our expression work for a living. It seems quite likely that work would not have been recognized as a concept by our band members. Nor for that matter would wealth as we understand it, in terms of quantities of money or material objects. There was no point in hoarding what was available to everyone; nor was there any point in acquiring lots of objects when people moved from camp to camp and objects were heavy. And they moved around, perhaps, not because they had to, but probably because they wanted to. A mode of living which involves frequent changes of scene may be both more stimulating and relaxing than our accustomed residence in one permanent abode.

We can also speculate about the less rosy aspects of life at this time. Child mortality must have been high, and there would have been an ever present danger to adult hunters through contact with wild animals. Whether fighting took place within, or between, bands is difficult to assess, in the absence of evidence either way.

Amongst those hunters and gatherers who survive it is

particularly interesting to note that there is usually a clear division of activities such that, in general, the men hunt and the women gather. Often, hunting is more valued than gathering in terms of the prestige that a successful hunter can acquire, while paradoxically it is often the gathering that produces most of the daily calorie intake. While women in contemporary bands, therefore, undertake the more tedious tasks of providing the staple diet, men are often engaged in the uncertain, but highly exciting process of the hunt. There would seem to be no reason why this sexual division of labour should not have applied to the past, though in the nature of archaeological evidence, positive indicators are unlikely to have survived – certainly they have not been detected yet.

Using such inferences we can build up a contrasting picture of our bands by comparing the situation, say, at 200,000 BC and at 5,500 BC. In the former period large bands of some twenty or thirty members were accustomed to range over huge tracts of ground between one camp and another. There was probably no concept of the ownership of a territory. Gathering and fishing were important, and animals were hunted by relatively crude techniques (which still required careful planning, however), such as stampeding herds over cliffs. The time spent in obtaining food was perhaps slight, and maybe many hours of the day were passed in socializing and gossiping. There was some ability to store foods for a future date, but there was great emphasis on sharing among band members. Life expectancy cannot be estimated, but it cannot have been high. Clothing and fire were in everyday use, and so was language. Speech had evolved to the extent that knowledge of the immediate environment could be expressed in fine detail. The apparently less developed vocal chords of the early hominids, however, suggests a more limited range of sounds than we are capable of today.

By 5,500 BC the situation in Britain and Ireland had changed considerably, not least through the impact of modern man – *Homo sapiens sapiens* – and his increased mental abilities. Population had risen dramatically; there were more bands, but on average bands were smaller, comprising fifteen or twenty members. Tools, weapons and shelters were much more sophisticated, and so was hunting. A variety of techniques had been evolved, such as trapping, snaring, the use of bows and arrows and decoys, or intercepting herds in ambushes, to improve selective hunting. A much wider range of smaller game and other foods was sought than in previous periods. Distances between camps were much smaller and the concepts of a seasonal round and some idea of a band's accustomed territory were almost certainly appreciated. Life expectancy had probably improved although child deaths were still common. At certain times friction between bands may have produced altercations. There was more emphasis on storage and more insight into the future.

Undoubtedly the greatest change, however, was the effect of these bands on their own natural environment. Axes were available to fell trees, to make boats or to create forest clearings. After 5,500 BC the climate became wetter and certain cleared areas became permanently waterlogged. The desire to open up small areas of the forest may have been to improve

Pls 15–18. Food for Free. Limpets and edible seaweed were abundant on rocky coastlines (*opposite, above*); wild fungi, like the chanterelle, grew in profusion (*below*); wild strawberries were there for those who knew where to look (*opposite, below*). Fresh water lakes also supported numerous white water-lilies (*above*); remains of these were found at Mount Sandel, and the seeds of the lily might have made a type of gruel, or been fried to resemble something akin to popcorn.

grazing for animals to congregate or to improve the growth of desirable plants and trees. Selective hunting of deer allowed the stags to be culled while maintaining the reproductive potential of the herd. Familiarity with young animals, perhaps kept as pets, had led to the taming of dogs and possibly to experiment with other mammals such as pigs or cattle. Extensive knowledge of how plants propagated may have led to the deliberate cultivation of certain valued plants. Certainly the amount of time and effort invested in creating a woodland clearing was far more than usually expended on hunting and gathering. Such a realization might have induced a proprietorial attitude towards it on the part of the band that had created each clearing. Things were about to change irrevocably, however. Although those bands around 5,000 BC had no real conception of any different world, their own was about to alter fundamentally and, in some ways, for the worse. Food was never going to be as free again.

Chapter 2
Tribes and Tombs
c 5,000–2,500 BC

Pioneer Farmers

Some time after 5,000 BC the first evidence for farming begins to appear in Britain and Ireland. The evidence takes many forms, although these did not appear at the same time, and includes new types of settlements, large burial mounds, and industrial sites, like flint mines and stone axe factories. Together with these novel phenomena, different implements appear such as large numbers of stone axes, leaf-shaped arrowheads (Pl 20), antler combs, and, for the first time, pottery. Whereas the gathering bands tended to move around to take advantage of seasonal resources, the pioneer farmers, having invested time and effort in clearing woodland for pasture and cereals, stayed in one place, at least until the fertility of the soil had been exhausted.

One of the most characteristic tools of this early farming period is the stone axe (metals were still unknown) (Pl 28). While some of the axes could have been weapons and some may have had ritual functions or been used to cut leafy branches for fodder, their principal function was in woodworking or in felling trees from the wild woods. Deliberately made clearings for planting with wheat, and for grazing animals, and occupied for at least a few years until the soil became impoverished, were a new element in the landscape. The animals were of the kind that we associate with farming today, such as cattle, sheep, goats and pigs. They would have looked slightly different, however. The sheep would have been more slender and agile, with coats of various shades of beige and brown, and wool that moulted and which could, therefore, be plucked rather than shorn. The snub-nosed, pink-skinned pigs familiar to us had prehistoric ancestors with longer legs and snouts, and bristly coats, much closer in appearance to wild boar. The principal crops were wheat and barley, although like the animals, these early varieties were much closer genetically to wild grasses, and more naturally resistant to attacks from disease.

But where did these pioneer farmers originate? It is clear that the animals and plants for this early agricultural economy must have come from the European mainland since neither the wild progenitors of sheep, goats nor wheat and barley were native to Britain and Ireland. We are thus left with a simple choice. Did the existing hunters and gatherers in Britain and Ireland sail across the North Sea to bring back these strange but productive means of subsistence? Or was there a slow migration of farming families from Europe into our islands? The evidence, such as it is, favours the latter hypothesis. At some date after 5,000 BC, families who were already farmers decided that the grass was indeed greener on the other side. Their skin boats, no bigger than the canvas-covered currachs still used along the west coast of Ireland, were loaded with seed corn; domesticated cattle and pigs, which were found wild in Europe, and sheep or goats were tied and secured in the bottom of the boat, while the family squeezed in as best it could. Perhaps this happened after the crops were harvested, sometime between August and November. Breeding and milking livestock would be transported, along with seed-corn from the recent crop.

The change from a livelihood based on hunting, gathering and fishing to one drawn from farming seems to have been a slow process. It started in the Middle East around 10,000 BC and then spread slowly north-westwards across Europe until it reached northern France and the Low Countries in about 5,000 BC. We do not know, of course, whether it was the idea of farming that moved or the farmers themselves, or a mixture of the two. Neither can we be absolutely certain concerning the reaction of the hunters; whether these bands gradually adopted the new technology or whether they were confined to ever smaller tracts of territory, and cultural extinction. Studies of contemporary peoples tell us, however, that farming was probably much more laborious work than hunting and gathering. It is unlikely, therefore, that hunting bands would have willingly taken up agriculture if there had been no economic imperative to do so. The advantage of

Pl 19. Men-an-Tol, Cornwall, England. One of the most famous sites in Cornwall and one of the most enigmatic. Two standing stones are either side of a large circular stone with a central hole. Was the perforated stone originally the entrance to a chambered tomb?

Pl 20. Lozenge-Shaped Arrowheads. These flint arrowheads come from Seamer Moor in North Yorkshire. They would have been glued, perhaps with birch-bark resin, to wooden shafts. Shot from a bow, these projectiles would have been used in hunting or in hostile encounters with other groups.

farming was that more people could obtain a livelihood from the same area of ground than by pursuing a hunting and gathering way of life. It seems likely, therefore, that increasing density of population among the hunters produced conditions favourable for the introduction of agriculture, or unfavourable for a continuing reliance on a relatively finite supply of food from hunting and gathering.

Such theoretical considerations would not have been uppermost in the minds of our boatload of immigrants. They landed in south-east England, and probably elsewhere on the coast of Britain and Ireland, with seed-corn and animals to begin a long cycle of cutting and clearing the forest, preparing the ground for their plants, animals and houses. It was a typical contact situation, familiar to us today in more recent examples such as the discovery of the Americas or the landing at Botany Bay. Perhaps there had been a certain amount of trade or exchange between hunters and farmers across the Channel before the new settlers arrived. The resident bands may have been on friendly terms with the newcomers, possibly supplying them with meat or wild foods. On the other hand it is equally possible that hostilities broke out from time to time. The two methods of subsistence were to prove incompatible. The farmers themselves must have relied heavily on hunting and gathering while their crops and animals adapted to the different environment. One specific result of the increasing number of clearances may have been a growth in the local bee population, bringing more widespread use of honey as a sweetener and as an alcoholic base.

These first clearances, however, were to be the first of many and signalled the beginning of the end for the hunting bands. It would not be possible for the two different types of

economy to function together. As in the more recent contact situations new diseases may have been introduced by the settlers. Whereas hunting and gathering depended on maintaining much of the forest cover to preserve animals and plant foods, farming required the felling of those forests for fields. Likewise, just as the bands preferred to be mobile to exploit various scattered resources, so the farmers had to be resident in one place to ensure that they could harvest the crops they had sown months earlier. It is probable that the farming population grew much more quickly than that of the hunters. Whereas the latter would probably have favoured a considerable interval between childbirths, since children would be a heavy burden to carry between camps, farmers would have desired lots of offspring to help out with the tedious chores of the agricultural round. As sons and daughters took over from fathers and mothers, so land would be handed down through the generations, and with increasing frequency new settlements and clearings would spring from the old. By such means the covering of trees gradually shrank and divided, revealing a small but growing patchwork of fields, which was gradually to stretch into the farthest corners of Britain and Ireland.

Camps, Forts and Farms

It must have taken generations, perhaps hundreds of years, before farming settlements became a dominating feature of the landscape in Britain and Ireland (Fig 13). The climate was favourable, being slightly warmer than that of today, and there are indications of a widespread disappearance of elm trees, which probably owed something to the activities of the early farmers. Eventually, the population became so dense that regional groups began to emerge – the first tribes – formed by the common identity of numerous distantly related families with a certain area. In order to act as a marker and focus for these regional identities the first communal monuments were built, monuments that we can still see in the landscape.

The earliest of the communal monuments can be described, using archaeological shorthand, as causewayed camps (Pl 22). These are large circular or oval enclosures defined by one or more concentric rings of earthen banks and ditches. Their most distinctive surviving feature is that the ditches have been dug in short segments, leaving frequent causeways between the segments and corresponding gaps in the associated banks. There are far too many of these causeways on each site to consider them all entrances. The distribution of the camps is mainly confined to southern and eastern England, although there is one example known from northern Ireland. Similar causewayed enclosures are known from France and Scandinavia.

Excavations in these camps demonstrate that not all of them had the same function; many seem to have been the equivalent of medieval fairs, where large numbers of people would congregate regularly, perhaps in the autumn after the harvest. There would naturally be much eating and drinking at such festive times, with many exchanges of home-produced goods for items that could not be obtained locally. Similarly we may imagine that during such occasions future marriages were arranged between distant farms. Other camps seem to have been used for ceremonies connected with the dead. A particular funerary practice common at this time was the exposure of corpses prior to burial, so that the flesh decayed in the open air before the bones were formally buried. Supporting evidence for this practice comes from disarticulated human bones in some of the camps and in contemporary tombs. There are indications that funerary preparations of this kind might have been the principal function of certain camps. Conversely, a few camps may have been permanent settlements; examples such as Whitehawk and the Trundle in Sussex fall into this category.

One of the earliest camps is that at Hembury, Devon, which was constructed some time before 4,000 BC. In the interior, post-holes defined a wooden hut of approximately rectangular shape. It must be remembered that on large sites, such as Hembury, only a fraction of the site has usually been investigated by excavation. Conclusions are drawn, therefore, about the nature of the whole from a very small sample. It is quite probable that at Hembury additional wooden huts lie in the unexcavated areas. The camp at Windmill Hill, in Wiltshire, has produced a large number of finds from its ditches, including animal bones, flint tools and pottery sherds and the grave of an adult man from underneath its outer bank. Among the numerous animal bones many show evidence of being split to obtain marrow. Elsewhere on the site complete animals were thrown into the ditches which might be interpreted as sacrificial offerings. Often the deposits of bones at Windmill Hill occurred in layers more than 30 cm thick, which then seem to have been immediately covered by blocks of chalk rubble thrown down from the adjacent banks. While this could be evidence of some strange ritual, it might alternatively be no more than an understandable urge to bury the remains of rotting animals. It has usually been assumed that the occupation at Windmill Hill was of a seasonal nature, the site serving the local community as the prehistoric equivalent of a medieval fair. The refuse deposits in the ditches are interpreted, therefore, as the product of meals consumed by many people during a short space of time. Exotic axes, which were quarried from stone sources in Cornwall and the Lake District, hint at the kind of valued exchanges that were taking place at Windmill Hill, and also, perhaps, at other such camps.

At Etton, near Peterborough, the waterlogged ditches of a causewayed camp produced vast quantities of wood chippings and wooden rods fashioned for some unknown purpose, many neatly trimmed from wood obtained from a coppiced (i.e. managed) woodland. In one part of the ditch there was also a large piece of birch-bark, apparently folded over and left to soak in the ditch-bottom prior to being worked, perhaps into some sort of container. Remains of meals were present in the form of little piles of sheep bones, along with a number of pork spare ribs and a pile of hazel nuts. The interior of the enclosure was neatly bisected by a ditch which seemed to separate seasonal settlement from funerary activity. Limited excavation at a site in northern

Ireland, called Donegore Hill (Co. Antrim), has produced thousands of sherds of pottery and flint tools, including oval or leaf-shaped arrowheads, and many porcellanite stone axes which were quarried at Tievebulliagh, some distance away. Within sight of Donegore Hill, and only 5 km away, is the contemporary site of Lyles Hill which has produced a large quantity of round-based bowls; unlike the causewayed enclosures Lyles Hill was defended by a continuous earthwork.

In many traditional or primitive societies burial rites include the practice of corpse exposure. The dead person can be placed on a wooden rack, as happens among some North American Indian tribes, and animals and the elements will consume the flesh; or the corpse can be buried in temporary graves where there is a steady decompostion through bacterial decay. Something of this sort seems to have been the principal activity in the camp at Hambledon Hill, Dorset (Fig 10). The excavator found the anticipated deposits of animal bones, pottery and axes but also large quantities of disarticulated human remains, including several skulls carefully positioned on the floors of some of the ditches. It is suggested that over 350 individuals might have been exposed at Hambledon, probably during a century or more, with about

Fig 10. Hambledon Hill, Dorset, Southern England. The causewayed camp at Hambledon lies on the central part of the hill and was used principally for corpse exposure. The contemporary settlement and fort seems to have been the Stepleton enclosure on the southern spur of the hill. A much later hillfort was constructed in the first millennium BC on the northern spur.

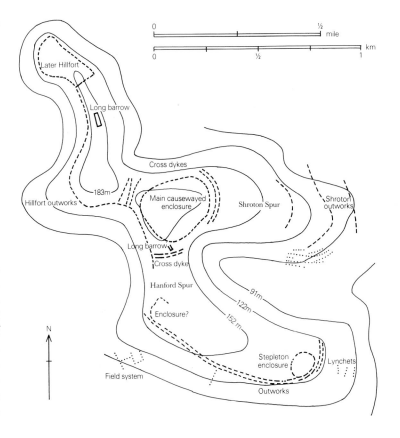

Pl 21. Skara Brae, Orkney, Scotland. Looking down into one of the houses, the rectangular central hearth can be seen, and beyond it a stone cupboard. On either side of the hearth are stone surrounds for beds, while cupboard-like recesses are apparent in the walls.

sixty per cent of the dead being children. The last figure reminds us of the high mortality rate among the young. In about 3,500 BC Hambledon would almost certainly have been a sacred place given over to the disposal, by decomposition, of the deceased and their consequent passage into the next world. In the words of the excavator Hambledon was a vast, reeking open cemetery, its silence broken only by the din of crows and ravens. A similar function has been suggested for the enclosure at Offham in Sussex. We cannot hope to explain all activities at these sites. Often in traditional or primitive societies there is a mixture of domestic and ritual acts, of the sacred and the secular, that seems quite incomprehensible to our compartmentalized cultures. Four engravings found cut into the chalk surfaces of the ditch of the camp at Flagstones, near Dorchester in Dorset fall into this category. Are these rough circles and hachures early efforts at graphic design ? Are they magical signs? Or are they the idle scratchings of some listless ditch digger?

Perhaps the most significant thing about these camps is not the activities that took place within them, but the fact that their outlines were defined by interrupted ditches. Some of these ditch segments were dug very irregularly and it would be more correct to describe them as elongated pits, rather than sections of a uniform ditch. Bearing in mind that people from widely-scattered farms probably converged on some of these camps for communal festivities and ceremonies, it does not seem too fanciful to wonder if each family excavated its own section of ditch. Following this reasoning we might then speculate that the filling of each segment – the remains of feasts, the pottery, flint and stone tools, even the human bones – might have been deposited by the self-same family in its own particular section. The circular pattern formed by the various segments would neatly symbolize the connection between the families and their common membership of the tribe, while at the same time preserving their individuality.

Pl 22. Knap Hill, Wiltshire, England. The remains of the causewayed camp are on the highest hill overlooking the Vale of Pewsey. The camp is 164 m in diameter and encloses an area of 1.6 ha. A single ditch, crossed by five causeways, forms the perimeter.

42

Many of the camps, therefore, were used for communal ceremonies of one sort or another, held under conditions of peace. Others have produced evidence which suggests that they may have been permanent settlements. There is also a growing body of information that suggests the presence of fortifications at this time, of warfare, or at least raiding, and of death in battle. The hill of Carn Brea is situated about 1 km to the south-west of Redruth in west Cornwall. At around 4,000 BC the eastern summit of the hill, comprising an area of approximately 1 ha, was enclosed at all points where sufficiently impressive natural rock obstacles did not already exist. The enclosing wall was built of massive stones, many weighing in excess of 2-3 t, and the original height of the defences was probably more than 2 m. The fact that the defences were constructed in stone may well be related more to the easy availablity of stone on the rocky outcrop than to any inherent advantage over the use of earth and timber. Evidence from radiocarbon dating suggests that occupation within the fort probably lasted for some 300 years or so, in rectangular houses and lean-to structures built against the inside face of the defensive wall. The average population at Carn Brea was probably over 100, assuming buildings similar in density to those within the excavated area. An extraordinary element amongst the finds was the very high number of leaf-shaped flint arrowheads. Many of these showed evidence of being burnt, as did many of the wooden structures in the interior. Furthermore, the concentration of arrowheads close to the presumed entrance into the fort suggests that the inhabitants may have been overwhelmed by an attack in which archery played a key role. We cannot reconstruct the conflict from archaeological evidence alone; we can only imagine the opening moments when the hiss of unleashed bow strings sent fire-arrows looping over that defensive wall, and the closing scenes when the settlement was put to the torch. Where did the attacking force come from? We will never know the answer; the nearest contemporary site is situated at Helman Tor, some 35 km away.

Something similar may have happened at the Stepleton fort, which lies on the southern spur of the hill crowned by the causewayed camp at Hambledon Hill. Indeed the two are almost certainly related, the Stepleton site being the defensive settlement, and the camp, some 1,000 m to the north, devoted to the burial rites of the inhabitants. The ditch of the fort, one of the earliest hillforts, was much deeper than that of the camp, with relatively fewer causeways. In addition, the fort seems to have been defended by one continuous bank on the inside edge of the ditch, apart from a single entrance on the eastern side. As at Carn Brea, there were many indications of the site being attacked with fire, so that some of the burnt wooden palisades which fronted the earthen defences fell into the surrounding ditch. In addition, in the butt end of a ditch close to the presumed gateway the excavators located the intact skeleton of a robust young man of about nineteen years. A leaf-shaped arrowhead, lodged among the bones of his rib cage, may well have been the cause of his death. The fact that he was given no formal burial may suggest that the successful defenders had no time for a dead attacker, simply covering up with chalk rubble an enemy who had died during the struggle. At some point during the life of the fort its defences were refurbished and additional earth and timber banks were constructed to link the fort with the camp, turning most of the hill-top into one vast defended area.

Indications of yet another such battle have come from excavations at Crickley Hill, 7 km south of Cheltenham in Gloucestershire. Here, on an eminently defensible promontory that faces west towards the Severn estuary, there originally stood a traditional causewayed camp. After a period of use there was a radical change and a new and larger ditch was dug outside the original enclosure, with a continuous bank erected on top of the filled-in remains of the earlier causewayed ditches. This new camp was obviously built with defence in mind since the new bank was protected by stockades on top and behind it, and was pierced by only two narrow entrances, both secured by timber gates. In the interior a cobbled road, flanked by fences, ran away from the entrance past at least two houses. The emergence of defences on this site, however, was ultimately to no avail since the defences, entrances, houses and fences were all destroyed by fire. That the fire was not the result of some domestic conflagration, but rather one produced during the heat of battle was demonstrated by the presence of nearly 400 leaf-shaped flint arrowheads, crowding around both entrances, against the face of the wooden palisade on top of the defensive bank, and scattered on the cobbled roads towards the interior of the settlement. The pattern of those mute points of flint reveal the course of the conflict, as the defences were overrun and the attackers pursued the retreating defenders through the fort. Such were the results of the battle, but as to the cause, we can only speculate.

Most people probably did not live in forts but in small farms that lay dispersed and rather isolated, in a countryside that was still quite heavily wooded. The number of such farms cannot be even guessed at; the evidence for them usually comprises scatters of flint or pottery in ploughed fields and few have been excavated. The available information, such as it is, suggests that single family groups of perhaps six to twelve individuals occupied these prehistoric farmhouses. A possible house came to light at Fengate, on the edge of the flat fen country near Peterborough. It was built of timber, with large posts and planked walls set in a foundation trench; its overall dimensions were 7.5 by 6 m. At Haldon in Devon, another rectangular house has been discovered. Composite walls of timber and stone supported a ridged roof, with an entrance at one corner of the building, and a hearth in another. The best evidence for these isolated farmhouses in England, however, comes from Buxton in Derbyshire. Here, on a flattish ridge between two branches of the river Wye, three rectangular timber buildings have been discovered. Two of them, measuring 7.5 by 5 m each, lie end-to-end and it is possible that one is later than the other, or indeed that the second is an enlargement of the original structure. Each has a central hearth and an internal cross partition. Fragments of pottery, a flake from a polished stone axe, pieces of worked flint and chert (including four leaf-shaped arrowheads), isolated pits, and grains and chaff of

Fig 11. An Early Farmhouse at Ballyglass, Co. Mayo, Ireland. The rectangular house is made of a timber framework, with a wattle-work infill, supporting a thatched roof. Internal divisions in the house presumably separated different areas of activity. The evidence for reconstructions such as these are the post-holes found by the archaeologist.

emmer wheat and barley are the only indications of their former inhabitants. A third and similar-sized building lies some 60 m to the east and also has indications of an internal partition. A pair of extra post-holes at the centre of its eastern end appears to represent an entrance.

In Wales, at least four sites have demonstrated the presence of rectangular houses. At Llandegai, on the coastal plain of north Wales, an arrangement of post-holes defined quite a large structure, measuring about 15 by 8 m. By contrast in the south-west, on the hill-top of Clegyr Boia near St David's, two much smaller rectangular buildings were found in association with a refuse dump containing fifty or more broken pots, flint tools and animal bones. Another rectangular timber structure was found beneath a megalithic tomb at Gwernvale in southern Powys. On the highest point of a terrace, post-holes and bedding trenches suggest a roofed building, the foundations of which were subsequently covered by the later stone tomb. Whether the building was an isolated farmstead, or had some ritual use connected with the tomb is difficult to judge. In Clwyd, excavations within the later hill-fort at Moel y Gaer, Rhosesmor, revealed a scatter of flints around a slot and post-holes that may suggest the presence of a rectangular building.

In Ireland the pattern of timber-built rectangular farm-houses is repeated. In about 4,000 BC a substantial settlement was constructed on a low hill of sand and gravel at Ballynagilly, Co. Tyrone. The house was almost square, being some 6.5 by 6 m in size; the walls were fashioned from thin planks of radially split oakwood. A total of nine leaf-shaped arrowheads came from the site, three being found within the structure. A much more impressive building has come to light at Ballyglass, in Co. Mayo (Fig 11). The foundations of a larger rectangular timber house were found, with dimensions of 13 by 6 m. There were clear indications of hearths and internal partitions in this house, with the possibility of a porch at one end. Particularly fascinating is the fact that the building seems to have been demolished to make way for a tomb that was constructed on top of it. We can only speculate on the relationship between the occupants of the house and the tomb-builders. Were the tomb-builders perhaps converting a house for the living into a house for the dead? Similar in size to the Ballyglass structure is the larger of the two houses uncovered at Tankardstown, Co. Limerick, where excavations took place in advance of a pipeline. Another example of a rectangular house stood beside Lough Gur, Co. Limerick. Round-houses also occur at Lough Gur, constructed with posts and wattle-and-daub, and no doubt, roofed with thatch. This suggests that both rectangular and circular building traditions may already have been established at this early date. Ireland has also produced remarkable evidence for the fields that were farmed from these pioneering settlements. In Behy and Glenulra on the north coast of Co. Mayo, a geometric system of field walls has been

Pl 23 (*above*). Whitepark Bay, Co. Antrim, Northern Ireland. In the chalk cliffs of Whitepark Bay can be seen horizontal lines of good-quality flint which was utilized by early farmers for tools.

Pl 24. Whitepark Bay, Co. Antrim, Northern Ireland. The Bay may have been an attractive landfall for immigrant farmers. Certainly the local flint, and food sources such as oyster, mussel, limpet, periwinkle and cockle were gathered by the early settlers. Three chambered tombs overlook the bay, and the small mound in the centre of the photograph was also used for prehistoric burials.

located beneath later blanket bog. The pattern of fields covers an area in excess of 1 sq km; a series of parallel walls 150 to 200 m apart run from the edge of the sheer cliffs inland for a considerable distance; the long strips formed by these walls are divided by offset cross-walls into rectangular fields up to 7 ha in area. The complete pattern has the appearance of being planned and built as part of a communal and co-ordinated effort. The large size of the individual fields suggests that they were designed for animal management rather than tillage. A large number of pre-bog field walls have also been located in Connemara.

In Scotland the rectangular building-tradition is represented by a massive structure at Balbridie, on the banks of the river Dee, west of Aberdeen. This fine timber building must have been more like a hall than a house since it was over

Pl 25. Knap of Howar, Papa Westray, Orkney, Scotland. This small farm was in operation before 4,000 BC. The smaller of the two adjacent buildings was a workshop and barn. It was fitted out with cupboards and shelves to store the farm's equipment and produce. The roof was probably timber-framed and thatched.

26 m in length and some 13 m wide, making it at least double the size of all the houses discussed so far. As you would expect in a structure of those dimensions, there were internal partitions, and various modifications were carried out on the hall during its lifetime. The most spectacular evidence for houses and farms, however, comes from the stone monuments of the Northern Isles. The four key sites are Skara Brae on mainland Orkney (Fig 12), Links of Noltland on Westray, Knap of Howar on Papa Westray and, least well preserved, Rinyo on Rousay. On these exposed islands tree cover must have been minimal and there quickly developed a stone architecture based on the available flagstones. Stone buildings, and the fact that some of the houses gradually became enveloped in encroaching sand dunes, meant that these structures have survived remarkably well, with walls standing to over 1 m in height. At Knap of Howar there are two rectilinear houses with rounded ends, built side by side and connected by a low passage through their conjoining walls (Pl 25). Both houses are divided internally by upright slabs, an architectural feature also seen in contemporary tombs in the same area. The larger structure may have been the residence, with separate areas for cooking, sleeping and working,

while the smaller building, with its stone wall-cupboards at one end, may have functioned more as a working and storage unit. Doors were probably wooden or wood-framed with a skin covering, while roofs may have been timber-framed and thatched. It is clear from the finds that the inhabitants lived by rearing cattle and sheep, and by gathering shellfish and fishing. Self-sufficiency was obviously the key to survival. Pottery, stone and bone tools were all manufactured on site from locally available materials, like fine-grained stone for the polished axes and whalebone for spatulae and mallet-heads.

At Skara Brae six houses of similar stone construction are grouped together in a village and linked by a covered passage running through the whole complex. An additional house is separated and entered from a passage running at right angles to the principal thoroughfare. The individual houses are all square with rounded corners (Pl 21). Stone furniture has survived to leave us with a vivid impression of domestic life five thousand years ago. In the centre of each house was a stone-lined hearth; on the wall opposite the entrance a stone dresser, with stone box beds on both side walls. Stone tanks and cupboards complete the interior design. Roofs may have been corbelled with stone, or more likely made of turf or thatch laid on rafters of whalebone.

Pl 26. Pike of Stickle, Cumbria, England. At the head of Langdale valley, the Pike of Stickle is the prominent rounded summit of volcanic tuff in the centre of the photograph. The debris from axe manufacture stretches from the summit at 600 m to the foot of the screes.

The First Industrial Revolution

As farming spread across Britain and Ireland the gradual rise in the population increased the need for agricultural and subsistence equipment. Axes of flint and stone were in great demand, not only to fell trees to create new fields, but also for the numerous tasks involving woodworking, such as the building of houses, fencing and manufacture of wooden handles for flint or stone tools. Stone axes were used by 6,000 BC, of course, when communities still lived primarily by hunting and gathering. Now, however, a vast number were required. It was no longer sufficient to search the beaches, the river beds or the high moors for isolated stones that could be fashioned into two or three implements. Extensive sources had to be located and this led to the development of quarrying and mining (Fig 15). It was much the same with pottery. Clay vessels are not known from the period when small bands obtained their food by trapping wild animals or gathering nuts. However, it is quite likely that the knowledge that clay, when heated by fire, turned into a much harder substance, had long been appreciated. There must have been countless times in the camps of the hunters when old fires were raked out, exposing baked and cracked clay surfaces beneath. Pot-

tery is not easily carried from place to place, however, and it really only became useful when permanent settlements of farmers developed a growing need for it. It is still more than likely, therefore, that the technique of pottery production was imported with the other elements of agriculture. Pottery vessels were useful in a number of agricultural tasks such as milking, and storage of food and liquid.

Some of the earliest evidence for this industrial activity comes from the flint mines in the chalk regions of southern and eastern England. At Cissbury in Sussex some of the pits and shafts can still be seen, and mining in this area seems to have been under way before 4,000 BC. The basic technique was fairly simple. A shaft was excavated through the chalk to a depth of as much as 15 m. Flint occurs in the chalk in horizontal bands and it is clear that the miners were excavating for the best quality stone, since often the higher and poorer bands were ignored in preference for the deeper, and better quality, floorstone. Once the floorstone was reached, galleries were driven horizontally out from the shaft to exploit as much of the layer as possible.

Who were these early miners? We can speculate that they were not full-time specialists but rather members of farming communities who would travel to the mines for a few days or weeks each year, during slack periods in the agricultural seasons. They would camp out at the site, dig out quantities of fresh flint and, as the excavation evidence shows, trim and flake the rough blocks into rough-outs something like the

49

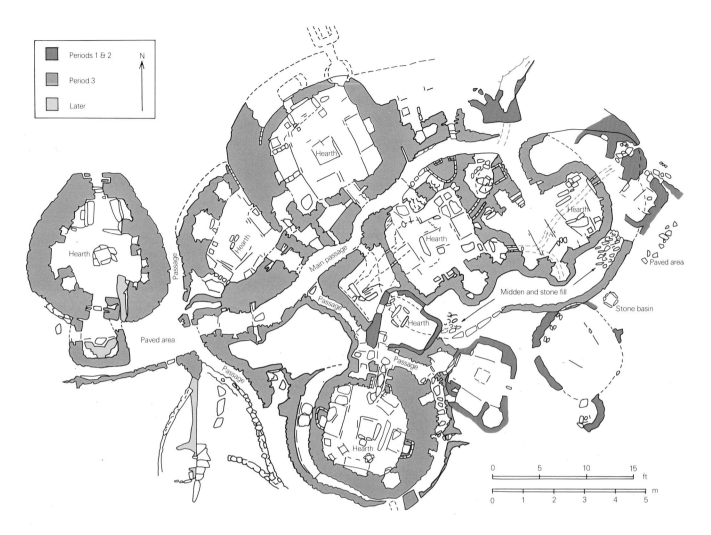

Fig 12. Skara Brae, Mainland Orkney, Scotland. This remarkable settlement was occupied around 3,000 BC. The plan shows the cellular construction of the houses, each with its own central hearth. A covered passage-way links most of the houses. The village may have had several resident families, perhaps thirty to forty people.

required finished shapes before returning home. Their tools to excavate the shafts must have been rudimentary. Wooden poles or ladders would be used to get in and out of the shafts, while antler picks, wooden spades and fire, to crack the chalk, would have been the principal means of mining. The galleries had to be lit, to allow them to be worked. Soot marks have been found on the ceilings in some cases, probably from burning torches, while small chalk cups discovered in various mines almost certainly held animal fat and served as lamps.

There was a religious side to this industrial activity. Mining is a hazardous occupation and miners are prone to superstition. Yet there is some evidence to suggest that the process of extracting suitable flint from a mine was regarded as comparable to the process of giving birth to good sons and daughters. A remarkable chalk figurine of an obese and pregnant woman, and alongside it a chalk phallus, were found at a much later flint mine, at Grimes Graves in Norfolk which dates from around 2,500 BC. Similar objects to the phallus

have come from a number of causewayed camps. One interpretation is simply that these chalk figurines were good luck tokens. Another, more speculative explanation is that these flint miners would not have looked upon the earth and their mines as impersonal entities, but rather as places imbued with spirits who had to be pleased, courted, worshipped and placated if they, in turn, would bless their admirers by the present of quality flint. Each shaft dug, perhaps over a number of visits, must have been a semi-spiritual undertaking, with frequent attempts to ensure the continued favour of the spirits if the prize was to be delivered. The birth of a healthy son or daughter must have been a similarly lengthy and magical experience. Whether good quality flint or robust offspring was the desired result, expectations were conditioned by ritual practices and their outcome, rather than any more rational appreciation of how the pregnancy was developing

Fig 13. Early Forts and Farms (*opposite*). The enclosures in the south and east of England are mostly causewayed camps, although some forts occur as at Crickley Hill and Carn Brea. Wooden rectangular buildings are popular, as at Buxton and Tankardstown, while the unique domestic architecture of the Orkneys owes much to the easily split local stone.

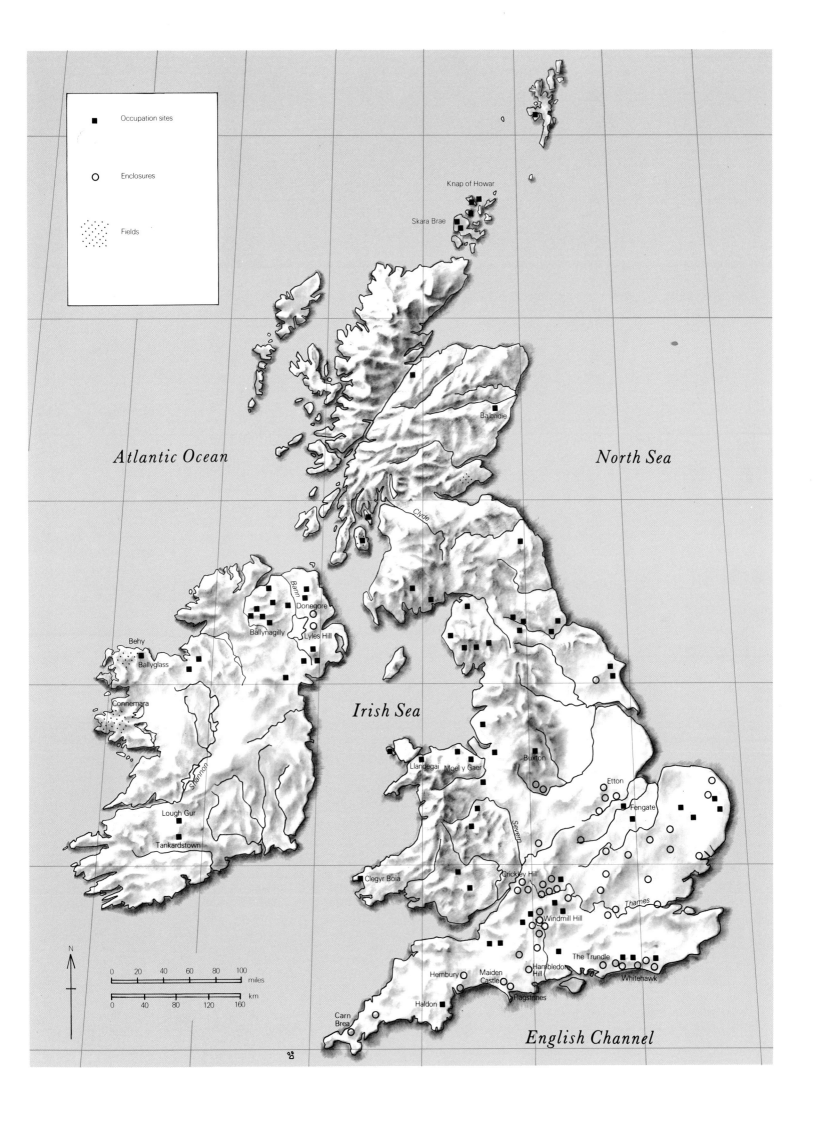

Occupation sites

Enclosures

Fields

Atlantic Ocean

North Sea

Knap of Howar

Skara Brae

Balbridie

Clyde

Bann

Donegore

Ballynagilly

Lyles Hill

Behy

Ballyglass

Connemara

Irish Sea

Shannon

Lough Gur

Tankardstown

Buxton

Llandegai

Moel y Gaer

Etton

Fengate

Severn

Clegyr Boia

Crickley Hill

Thames

Windmill Hill

Hembury

Maiden
Castle

Hambledon
Hill

The Trundle

Whitehawk

Flagstones

Carn
Brea

Haldon

English Channel

N

0   20   40   60   80   100
                              miles

0   40   80   120   160
                              km

or what the geological signs were from the mine shaft. Human beings alone did not decide their destinies and miners were not sole masters of their mines.

There is also evidence of extensive exploitation of deposits of flint at Dun of Boddam near Peterhead in north-east Scotland, where dozens of pits dug into the sides of a valley can still be seen. However, flint does not occur in quantity in the north and west of Britain, and in these areas a range of metamorphic and igneous rocks, which fracture in much the same way as flint when struck, were quarried from surface outcrops to make a variety of tools, including axes. A number of heavily-used outcrops have been identified, ranging from the Shetlands to the Cornish peninsula and the north of Ireland. Much the same sequence of activities must be imagined at these quarries. Small groups would journey to a particular source and detach a suitable block by using hard hammerstones, fire and water. This would then be split into smaller lumps and these would be flaked and trimmed until a rough shape of an axe was obtained. The axes would be finished at the settlements where the laborious processes of pecking, grinding and polishing and the tricky business of hafting could be carried out in more congenial surroundings. One of the major stone sources in northern England was the fine-grained tuff around the Langdale Pikes in the Lake District (Pl 26). Here hundreds of small sites have been identified. They can be divided into three categories: quarry sites where there are hollows, suggestive of open-cast working; scree sites, far below the parent outcrop, where boulders loosed by frost have come to rest and been utilized for axe manufacture; and finally glacial erratics, boulders left by the retreating glaciers which bear no relationship to the local stone but which were occasionally used. In Wales the most famous site occurs on Penmaenmawr mountain, called Graig Lwyd (Fig 16), while a similarly placed coastal site utilized the metamorphic rock of Mynydd Rhiw on the Lleyn peninsula. The proximity to the sea of most of the Welsh quarries may suggest that groups were arriving and departing by sea with their collection of axe rough-outs; alternatively, it may be that the most suitable rock happens to outcrop in the coastal locations.

That such voyages were undertaken is underlined by the fact that an Irish origin has been proved for over sixty axes found in Scotland, predominantly in Aberdeenshire and the Clyde estuary. Local production has been identified in Perthshire, Orkney and Shetland, although it is only in Perthshire and Shetland that quarry sites have so far been found. At Killin in Perthshire, a fine-grained grey-green stone was selected for axes, while in Shetland a blue-grey felsite was chosen not only for axes, but also for oval knives. The north-east tip of Ireland was especially favoured with mineral resources. Flint was regularly taken from coastal exposures in the chalk cliffs of Antrim (Pls 23 & 24). Outcrops of porcellanite were quarried at Tievebulliagh, 300 m up the side of a mountain overlooking Cushendall in north-east Antrim, and from a geologically identical source at Brockley on Rathlin Island. No polished axe-heads have been found at the quarry sites, but at Newferry, Co. Antrim, six axe-heads had been left close to a polishing stone hollowed out of sand-stone, indicating that the finishing was done in the farming settlements.

Since clay was probably available to most settlements at no great distance, many pottery vessels may have been modelled and fired in simple bonfire kilns, close to the farms. Potting and firing is, or becomes, a skilled activity and it eventually produced skilled potters in communities who passed on their techniques to future generations. In this way regional styles of pottery emerged. In southern France and Italy, for instance, early farming groups who utilized the resources of the sea, decorated their pots with patterns impressed with cockle shells. Pottery must have been used for storage, cooking, eating and drinking. Most vessels from this period of early farming have rounded bottoms, and are either bowl or bag-shaped (Pl 27). Handles are usually simple lugs on the sides of the pot, while later on, simple geometric patterns were incised into the wet clay before firing. Although most pottery production was local, at certain causewayed camps, such as Windmill Hill, pottery from distant sources has been found, no doubt carried there by visitors who had travelled from afar. In addition fine pottery made from clays on the Lizard in Cornwall has been discovered on a number of settlements as far afield as Wiltshire and Dorset. In Scotland and Ireland there was an additional range of thick-walled vessels with flat bases which appear to have been a rather coarse type of pottery used for domestic storage.

No doubt there were countless new developments in the arts and crafts at this time, but the axes and the pottery survive best of all. Some of these items were traded over considerable distances. For instance, axes from the quarry at Penmaenmawr in north Wales have been found on the south coast of England, and we have seen that many Irish axes ended up in Scotland. We would be wrong in assuming that all axes were used to fell trees. Some examples are particularly fine and very thin, suggesting that they were ceremonial or prestigious objects. Indeed over 100 jadeite axes have been discovered in Britain, although the source of the stone lies in the French and Italian Alps. Most are very thin and surely were prized as valued objects rather than working tools.

So how did these axes travel? Were they carried around by some enterprising travelling axe-maker from farm to farm and exchanged for food or other desirables? Or were they exchanged between communities and gradually passed from hand to hand away from their place of origin? The latter seems more likely. In so-called primitive societies you are either friend or foe; there is no silent majority of strangers. Exchanging artefacts is an important way of easing tension between communities and of promoting harmony. Even then exchanges are often conducted away from settlements since they can be notoriously fraught affairs, likely to spill over into insult and possibly injury. The objects usually change hands as gifts rather than by barter. Despite this there may be still an element of competition in the exchanges such that communities or partners try and offer more than their neighbours can return, thereby achieving some sort of superiority. Some prestigious objects may be treated like people, with individual characteristics, histories and reputations, again height ening the importance of the exchange. It may also be the custom that if a neighbour asks for a specific object known to be in his friend's possession then that artefact must be given; if not, a grave insult would result, with the possibility of future hostilities. In Britain and Ireland axes were probably exchanged in these ways between communities, and thereby travelled enormous distances from their original sources. In some cases, however, it is clear that unfinished axes were obtained in bulk from a source and then finished in distant settlements. This must be the explanation for the great number of Lake District axes found in the Humber area, and those of Cornish origin found in Essex. From these secondary centres the process of exchange began, axes passing from hand to hand, and spreading out in ever increasing circles.

Pathways of the Past

One area of Britain – the Somerset Levels – is slowly revealing the exceptional wood-working skills of this period (Fig 14). The Levels form a low basin, bordered by the Mendips to the north and the Quantocks to the south, closed by the rising Somerset countryside in the east, but open to the coast on the west. Today it is a managed landscape of lush green meadows, grazing cows, hanging willows and black peat-fields. Excavations over the past twenty years have shown, however, that in 4,000 BC at the centre of the Levels, between the Polden hills and Westhay island, the scene was very different. A network of small streams and ponds separated islands of reed, birch, willow and alder, while dense stands of deciduous trees grew on the bordering dry lands. Crossing the treacherous expanse of boggy ground could not be achieved without constructing a variety of timber pathways across the meres, enabling travellers to tread safely, if a little damply, from island to island. Discovery and excavation of some of these pathways have added considerably to our understanding of contemporary craftsmanship, since timber and associated organic finds have been preserved in the waterlogged peat.

The Sweet Track, named after its initial discoverer, Ray Sweet, has been traced for a distance of over 1,500 m between the Polden hills and the western end of Westhay island. This raised timber walkway was built across a wet reed swamp in ingenious fashion. The construction sequence was both skilful and simple: a wooden pole or rail was first laid down on the surface of the marsh; then angled wooden pegs were driven down from either side across it; finally a flat plank was wedged into these projecting V-shaped supports, usually some 40 cm above the rail. The planning of the operation was so intricate that there was even a preliminary stage before construction began. A roughly built track was positioned to allow access for the materials and builders of the Sweet Track. By such means as these was the marsh crossed. It must have been quite a feat of balance for the less nimble footed, since the track was only one plank's width. One wonders what happened when two parties met in the middle!

The peat has also preserved a remarkable range of

Pl 27. The First Pottery. This round-bottomed pot is from the causewayed camp at Staines in Middlesex. Note the complete absence of decoration, the simple rim, and the mineral inclusions. (Diameter of pot is 23 cm)

Pl 28. The Farmer's Axe. Found at Ehenside Tarn in Cumbria, this flaked and ground axehead is made from rock obtained in the Lake District at Great Langdale. (Length of axehead is 22 cm)

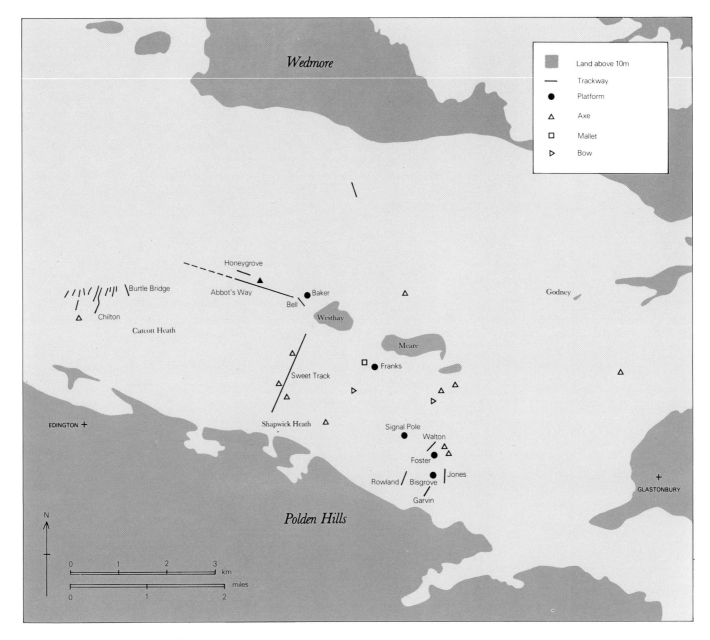

Fig 14. Somerset Levels, South-West England. Prehistoric trackways, platforms and finds in Somerset. Some of the trackways ran between the Polden Hills and raised ground, or islands, at Westhay and Meare. The Sweet Track, named after its initial discoverer, Ray Sweet, was constructed around 4,000 BC.

materials connected with the track. For instance, fragmentary remains of the Raft Spider, which has a body length of 2.5 cm, were located in one place. This awesome arachnid prefers to live by, and on, permanent water and it was across such stretches of water that the track was built of three superimposed planks. Broken hazel nuts were found between the timbers, the remains of snacks taken on the run by travellers in a hurry. Numerous beetles, sensitive to slight differences in climate and therefore useful indicators of minor environmental changes, suggest that at the time of the track winter temperatures were 2-4°C colder and summers 2-3°C hotter than today. The woods from the track itself help to fill out our

picture of the neighbouring dry land forest. Oak, elm, lime and ash were the common large trees, with hazel and holly comprising most of the undergrowth, and alder, willow and poplar on the wetter fringes. The planks for the track were fashioned from trunks of oak, ash or lime, split with wedges of stone or seasoned oak. Tree-ring studies, which can be used to compare the felling dates of individual trees, have proved that timber for the Sweet Track was cut in a single year, which must have been a major communal enterprise for the local settlements. By looking at cross sections of the various timbers the pattern of annual growth rings can be compared;

Fig 15 (*opposite*). Axe-Factories and Flint Mines. Suitable rock for stone axes occurs at a number of locations in north and west Britain. Flint occurs in quantity only in the south and east, and the earliest flint mines are located in those areas. The numbers refer to the individual sources as identified by archaeologists.

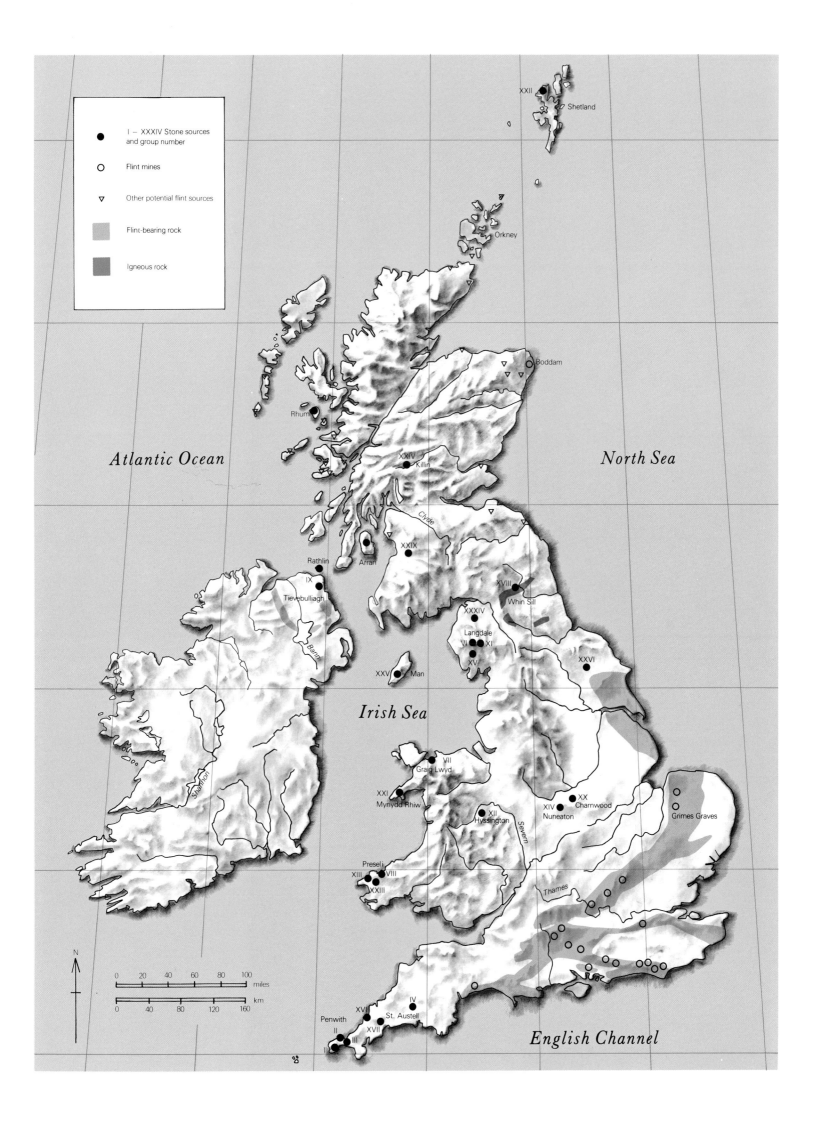

I — XXXIV Stone sources
and group number

Flint mines

Other potential flint sources

Flint-bearing rock

Igneous rock

Atlantic Ocean

North Sea

XXII

Shetland

Orkney

Boddam

Rhum

XXIV
Killin

Clyde

Rathlin

IX

Tievebulliagh

XXIX

XVIII
Whin Sill

XXXIV

Langdale

VI   XI
XV

XXVI

XXV   Man

Bann

Shannon

Irish Sea

VII
Graig Lwyd

XXI
Mynydd Rhiw

XII
Hyssington

Severn

XIV
Nuneaton

XX
Charnwood

Grimes Graves

Preseli

XIII   VIII
XXIII

Thames

N

0   20   40   60   80   100
miles

0   40   80   120   160
km

XVI
Penwith

IV
St. Austell

II

XVII

I

English Channel

such comparisons demonstrate whether all of the timber is contemporary.

The peat has also preserved items that would not have survived on dry-land sites. Two leaf-shaped arrowheads still had the remains of hazel shafts attached, while a third had the residue of a black sticky substance adhering to it, probably the remnants of some birch-bark resin used to fix the point to its shaft. Another arrowhead was bound to its arrow by nettle-fibre thread. Pottery was sometimes dropped alongside the trackway, and once it sank into the muddy waters was not easily retrieved by frustrated travellers. One of the lost pots had a wooden stirrer beside it; another was full of hazel nuts when it slipped from somebody's grasp. Many types of wooden objects have been preserved in the peat. These include bows of yew and hazel, digging sticks, a probable mattock, toggles, pins, a comb, a burnt spoon and a wooden container that may once have held an axe-head. A unique find from close to one of the tracks is the so-called God-Dolly, a roughly carved block of ashwood about 16 cm high and of vaguely hermaphroditic appearance. It was found beneath the timbers of a track. Could it have been a ritual offering or simply a lost toy? The most remarkable find however, was a slender, exquisitely finished green axe of jadeite discovered beside the track. The stone source for this implement lay in the Alpine foothills and this axe-head must have passed through many hands to reach the Somerset Levels. It was not found with any haft and it might have had a ceremonial function. It may have been a ritual offering, perhaps thrown from the track when completed, to placate the spirits of the marsh and ensure a safe crossing for all. On the other hand it may just have been an accidental loss, dropped by a preoccupied owner, and quickly concealed by the brown waters.

The Sweet Track was not the only artificial crossing of the Levels. Sections of a number of other trackways have come to light, some formed by simply laying down brushwood, others by the construction of hurdles and then placing them horizontally end-to-end. At some time around 3,000 BC it may have been possible for people to walk from home on the Poldens north along one track to reach the Westhay island, west along the island then out and across the marsh to Burtle and then southwards to Edington, crossing another expanse of wet ground by a trackway, to return to the Poldens. A final walk eastwards along the slopes of the Poldens and they would be home; a round trip of some 22 km, about half of which was on artificial tracks across wet ground.

Who built the Sweet Track? Almost certainly the occupants of farms, on the Poldens and on Westhay island. These families had been in the area for at least a generation since some of the woods used in the construction clearly came from coppiced woodland, that had been managed for some time. They remained in the locality for at least another ten years since they carried out regular repairs to the track before it became engulfed in decaying marsh vegetation and a rising water table . They probably farmed on the dry hills but they definitely exploited the fish, mammals, birds and wild plants of the Levels. In that sense their livelihoods were gained by a mixture of the old methods of hunting and gathering and the new elements of agriculture. Experimental reconstructions indicate that although the felling and cutting of suitable timber, and its transport to the site, must have taken a year, two groups of at least half a dozen adults could have constructed the Sweet Track in one day.

Houses of the Dead

Tombs and death loom large in our archaeological evidence of the early farming communities (Fig 17). Most of us fear death, be it our own or the death of someone we are close to. There can be little doubt that similar feelings of dread and grief were felt by the generations of farmers who spread across Britain and Ireland. A death in their small communities was not only a loss to friends and relatives, but also an economic blow to the entire group since they were so few in number. These fears were overcome by providing the dead with a role to play in the future of the community as ancestors. In this way the sharp dividing line between the elders of the living and the ancestors of the dead was blurred and softened. The dead were housed in large tombs and looked out over the fields that their sons and daughters would farm, advising and protecting their descendants. For the bereaved, the death of the individual was mitigated by his or her incorporation into a communal tomb, containing a number of ancestors. In due course the bones of the individual became mixed with others in the tomb, so that the deceased's identity was equated with that of the ancestors, just as the individual grief of the closest relative was gradually shared by the whole community.

With this in mind it comes as little surprise that, for the first two thousand years or so of farming in Britain and Ireland, the monumental features on the landscape were a great variety of earth, timber and stone tombs. The houses for the dead were much more important than the homes for the living, and so more time and energy were invested in their construction than on ordinary settlements. There are many different styles of tombs and it is clear that some tribes preferred one kind to another. We must not assume, however, that one particular tomb-type would be the only one constructed by any one community. Just as our society has different methods of burial (e.g. inhumation and cremation), and many kinds of graves, so similar variation might have existed in the past. Most of the thousands of tombs in Britain and Ireland, however, do possess some basic features in common: many have a chamber built either of wood or stone. Often this is contained within a large mound, of earth or stone; sometimes this mound was much larger than was needed simply to conceal or support the chamber. The tombs usually contain the remains of many individuals and are, therefore, communal tombs or vaults used over a long period of time. Frequently the burial rite seems to have involved exposure or cremation of the corpse elsewhere and subsequent depositon of the bones or ashes in the tomb, with earlier burial placements disturbed or pushed to the sides. Finally there is increasing evidence that some tombs were periodically remodelled. We can consider the types of tomb by country.

England

Some of the earliest tombs are elongated earthen mounds, known as earthen long barrows. These usually fall between 4,000 and 3,000 BC and are dated either by the radiocarbon method or by comparing artefacts found in them with similar, more securely dated, objects from other sites. The mounds vary in length from 30 to 122 m, although there is a small group of even larger specimens called bank-barrows, the most famous of which overlies the causewayed camp at Maiden Castle, Dorset, and is almost 0.5 km long. The main concentrations of these monuments lie in Wessex and on either side of the Humber estuary. Usually the mounds are aligned east–west and the burials occur at the higher, eastern end. In many cases a timber mortuary house seems to have held the bones of many individuals before they were finally entombed by the construction of a covering mound of earth. This seems to have been the case at Fussells's Lodge in Wiltshire. A timber mortuary house, whose roof was supported by three posts, held the fragmentary remains of over fifty people. The excavator claimed that the corpses had originally been exposed or buried elsewhere, with the bones being exhumed and placed in the mortuary house. The long mound was thrown up from quarry ditches on either side and buried the house of the dead under its eastern end. At Wayland's Smithy in Berkshire a tent-like wooden structure buried by the barrow housed the partially articulated bones of nine individuals. Post-holes found by the excavators suggest that the corpses may have been exposed to the elements on a platform in front of the mortuary house. At Hambledon Hill a long barrow stood next to the causewayed camp in which bodies were exposed; it is entirely possible that the bones were periodically removed from the camp to the nearby barrow for the final burial rite. The abundance of some types of bone and the paucity of others in certain long barrows has led some archaeologists to suggest that only a selection of bones from any skeleton were buried.

An interesting feature of two Wiltshire barrows, South Street and Beckhampton, was the way in which the mound was built by dumping spoil into a series of rectangular compartments that had been marked out with stake and wattle fences. Was this a device to stabilize the barrow during its construction? Or was it meant to represent the contributions of several different families to a communal monument? At both of these sites, however, the mounds were not graves, since no bones were discovered; they must, therefore, be considered as cenotaphs or memorials, perhaps for dead relatives or companions who died elsewhere, or who never returned from an expedition of some kind. A fascinating variation on the long barrow theme has been revealed by excavation at Loftus in Cleveland. Here a mortuary house stood between a massive timber façade and a rectangular kerbed area. Bodies were exposed within the kerbed precinct and, after a suitable length of time, the semi-articulated skeletons were placed in the house for the dead. The cemetery then appears to have been closed, first by the burning of the façade and mortuary house, then by the infilling of the whole area, resulting in a low rectangular platform of stones.

Certain similarities exist between the Loftus barrow and that at Haddenham in the Cambridgeshire Fens. Excavation here took place in advance of peat shrinkage and uncovered an extremely well-preserved monument. Peat, as we have seen in the Somerset Levels, can preserve a variety of organic remains. At Haddenham parts of the floor, walls and roof of a timber mortuary chamber survived. The timbers were composed of massive oak planks up to 25 cm thick, 1.3 m wide and 4 m long. These planks were created by splitting the timber across the full diameter of the trunk, a difficult, but necessary, process if timbers of this width are desired. Partially articulated bones from at least five individuals were found in the mortuary chamber.

It is clear that the shape of the mound could vary while the burial rite remained essentially the same. There are a number of round mounds or barrows associated with these early farming communities; a principal concentration lies in north-east England. At Calais Wold in Yorkshire a round mound covered an elaborate mortuary enclosure with timber facades containing cremations mixed with disturbed unburnt bones, and a slab pavement on which were found ten skeletons in crouched positions. Broken pottery was found in the foundation trenches for the enclosure posts. At Ayton Moor, also in Yorkshire, a timber mortuary house containing at least two corpses was set on fire, burning with such intensity that one of the bodies was almost totally cremated, before a round mound of limestone slabs was thrown up over it. But a third North Yorkshire example, the well preserved and multi-phase barrow at Duggleby Howe, was constructed at a slightly later date, around 3,000 BC, and suggests that there was a trend away from multiple burials towards single burials. The primary burial, at the bottom of the central grave-pit, was accompanied by a pot, two flint cores and nine flint flakes. In the subsequent phase further burials were placed in the fill of the grave-pit. These included a male, buried with what must have been personal possessions – a flint adze, a lozenge-shaped arrowhead and an antler macehead – hinting, perhaps, at a waning of the power of the ancestors housed in their communal tomb. Further single burials took place in the third phase.

For the period from 4,000 BC until 2,500 BC, however, the influence of the ancestors was generally all-pervasive. In the later part of this period the ancestors ruled over the living from even bigger and more durable monuments now constructed of huge stones, or megaliths. In these tombs the burial chambers were fashioned from massive stones, often linked by dry-stone walling and roofed either by equally impressive flat capstones or by a primitive form of vaulting known as corbelling. These tombs are generally later than the earthen barrows. Megalithic tombs (also called chambered tombs) were not peculiar to Britain and Ireland. They are to be found across western Europe, particularly in the coastal areas of Spain, France, the Low Countries and Denmark. The predilection for constructing such tombs may thus have come from abroad.

The tombs were set into a variety of shapes of covering mounds, made of earth or stone. We might conjecture that whole communities laboured over the construction of these

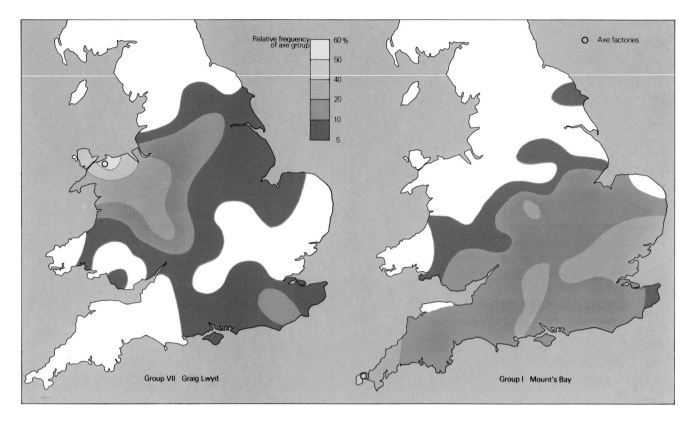

Fig 16. Stone Axe Distributions. Axes were exchanged frequently between communities and travelled far from their source. With Group VII, axes of this rock-type decrease gradually with distance from source. This pattern also occurs with Group I, except for surprising concentrations in southern and eastern England.

tombs in order that the dead could be honoured and encouraged to watch over their offspring; failure to perform the necessary rituals would remove the shadow of their protection from the land of the living. Additionally we can perhaps speculate about what would happen if the ancestors neglected their offspring: crops would wither in the fields, animals would be still-born, and enemies attack when least expected. For it was only through the good wishes of the ancestors that the sun rose every morning and became warmer every summer. It was only because they wanted it that crops ripened on the stalk and cows became swollen with milk and calves. Such a mixture of fear and reverence must have been a powerful driving force in the transport, erection and covering of massive stone houses for the dead.

Perhaps some of these reasons were behind a number of megalithic tombs in the Cotswolds, Somerset and Wiltshire. Even today these extraordinary monuments excite a sense of wonder and mystery at how they could have been constructed, and why they were built at all. These tombs comprised stone chambers of various sizes and shapes incorporated into wedge-shaped long mounds of earth or stones. The most famous monument of this group is that at West Kennet in Wiltshire (Pl 29). Here the two pairs of central chambers flanking the passage contained a total of forty-six individuals. Most of the remains were not articulated and there was some evidence to suggest that long bones and

skulls had been stacked against the sides of the chambers. Not all the bones of every individual were present, which may indicate that some bones were either periodically removed for rituals outside the tomb, or were not buried in the chambers. The tomb was open for hundreds of years, perhaps acting as a mausoleum for a particular family, until, in a final act, all of the chambers and the passage were deliberately filled with chalk rubble containing a mixture of pottery sherds, animal bones and flints. (Such material may have come from offerings made over the centuries and deposited in a nearby shrine). At Wayland's Smithy in Berkshire a stone passage and a pair of side chambers were built into the eastern end of a mound that entirely encompassed the earlier earthen long mound on the site. The perimeter of the new mound was lined by upright stones, while a majestic façade of towering megaliths stood by the entrance to the passage. At Hazleton in Gloucestershire a long mound over 50 m in length, built around 3,800 BC, incorporated two sock-shaped passages and chambers that were placed in opposing long sides of the tomb. In all some 9,000 human bones were recovered during the excavation of the site. These included twenty-three skulls which were mostly found around the

Fig 17 (*opposite*). Houses of the Dead. The first farmers buried their dead either under earthen mounds, both round and long, or in large stone tombs. There are far too many to indicate individually on any one map and a schematic distribution is portrayed here. Comparisons between tombs leads to the identification of regional groups (shown by names in bold).

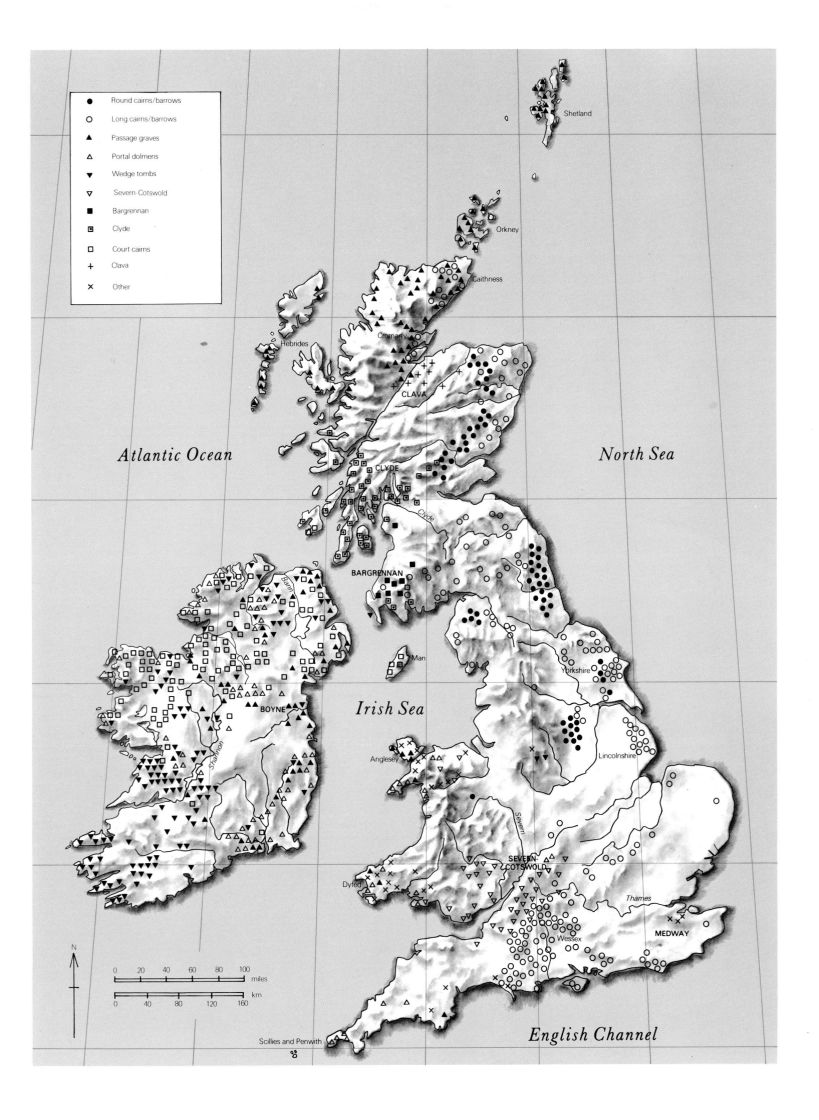

Round cairns/barrows

● Round cairns/barrows

○ Long cairns/barrows

▲ Passage graves

△ Portal dolmens

▼ Wedge tombs

▽ Severn-Cotswold

■ Bargrennan

◙ Clyde

□ Court cairns

+ Clava

× Other

Atlantic Ocean

North Sea

Shetland

Orkney

Caithness

Cromarty

Hebrides

CLAVA

CLYDE

Clyde

BARGRENNAN

Man

Yorkshire

Irish Sea

BOYNE

Bann

Shannon

Lincolnshire

Anglesey

Dyfed

Severn

SEVERN-COTSWOLD

Thames

MEDWAY

Wessex

Scillies and Penwith

English Channel

N

0   20   40   60   80   100
miles

km

0   40   80   120   160

edges of the burial chambers.

There are a number of tombs where all the covering mound has disappeared and only the incongruous, but still impresssive, stone chambers survive. Good examples come from the Medway group in Kent in the form of the ponderous stones from Coldrum and the delightfully named Kit's Coty House, where three colossal uprights in the shape of a letter H support the giant slab of a capstone. This chamber was, at least partially, situated at the end of a chalk rubble mound over 70 m long. But there are other stone chambers, so spectacularly massive, that it is conceivable they were built deliberately to impress the visitor with the technical skill involved, and were therefore not hidden by any mound. The Cornish dolmens – the word comes from two Breton words meaning stone table – at Zennor Quoit (Pl 30), Trethevy Quoit and Lanyon Quoit today cause the same astonishment as they must have thousands of years ago (Pl 37). They are matched by similar tombs in Wales and parts of Ireland. How were these huge stones quarried, transported and erected? Many

stones, of course, may have been lying conveniently near, where they had been deposited during the Ice Ages. Ropes, timber rollers and hundreds of people would have been needed to move them. Their erection would have been achieved using ropes and earth ramps to lever and haul the stones into position.

A very late tomb type, classed as an entrance grave, can be seen on the Isles of Scilly. They occur in remarkable numbers, with over fifty surviving and, no doubt, many more destroyed through agriculture. One of the most striking features of these tombs is that they cluster in groups or linear cemeteries. For instance, seven tombs lie on the slope of Kittern

Pl 29 (*below*). West Kennet, Wiltshire, England. Situated just south of Silbury Hill, this photograph shows part of the façade of the large sarsen stones at the eastern end of the megalithic tomb. Note the original dry-stone walling between the two nearest stones. The entrance to the tomb lies underneath the flat capstone.

Pl 30. Zennor Quoit, Cornwall, England. This collapsed dolmen was originally a rectangle of five uprights supporting a capstone. The latter was dislodged as a result of nineteenth-century blasting to find buried treasure. The farmer responsible for the outrage found a whetstone and a small piece of pottery for his trouble.

Hill, while twelve form a line on the North Hill of Samson. The graves are very similar in plan, most comprising a circular cairn edged by a massive stone kerb, containing a roughly rectangular chamber which opens from the perimeter of the monument. Most of the tombs have been robbed, although there are indications that cremation may have been the principal burial rite. Pottery from the graves generally dates to after 2,000 BC, much later than megalithic tombs on the mainland. Whether this suggests that the tombs were built at this time is difficult to gauge. They could have been constructed much earlier, with the tradition of collective burial surviving much longer here than elsewhere, and pottery coming into use in the funerary rites only at a late stage in the use of the tombs.

Wales

There were clearly some links across the Severn between communities in the Cotswolds and the Black Mountains and other parts of south-east Wales, resulting in some very simi-

lar wedge-shaped mounds. The chamber in the mound at Tinkinswood in Glamorgan was covered by a capstone weighing over 50t, which must have greatly taxed the resources of the 200 people calculated to transport and erect it (Pl 31). The bones from at least fifty people were found in the tomb, while in the monument known as Ty-isaf in southern Powys at least thirty-three individuals were represented. This latter site was very like Hazelton in design, with a wedge-shaped mound containing two passages and chambers in the opposing long sides, and a dummy or blind forecourt. This type of forecourt seems to have been a deliberate attempt to disguise the location of the tomb chambers, whose entrances often lay in less obvious parts of the covering mound. Perhaps hostile communities not only attacked settlements, but also attempted to desecrate communal tombs. The forecourt at Ty-isaf may well have seen periodic rituals when the bones were brought out, since of the thirty-three corpses only three complete long bones, seven skulls and twenty-two mandibles were found. A similar effort at concealment seems to have taken place at Gwernvale in Powys. Excavations have demonstrated that there were three or four lateral chambers, set within a cairn of trapezoidal shape. The

Pl 31. Tinkinswood, South Glamorgan, Wales. The burial
chamber is at one end of a wedge-shaped mound which is edged
with dry-stone walling. The herring-bone pattern of this walling is
also seen in the stalled cairn at Midhowe. The capstone, weighing
some 50t, is the biggest in Britain.

entrances to these chambers were deliberately concealed by
blocking material that closely resembled the dry stone walling around the perimeter of the mound. These blockings
were removed periodically when fresh burials were made,
and were then replaced. The chambers were finally blocked
and the tomb abandoned some time before 3,000 BC. Chambered tombs also occur in the south-west, and a superb example lies at Pentre Ifan, near Fishguard; here a crescentic
façade is situated at the southern end of a cairn unusually
oriented north–south (Pl 41).

There are a number of dolmens in Wales, particularly in
the south and north-west (Pl 32). The usual form of the
burial chamber is a rectangle, composed of four upright slabs
supporting a capstone. In some examples the side slabs pro-
ject beyond the roof to make a sort of porch to the chamber,
although often the entrance is blocked with a large stone.
The capstone frequently slopes down towards the rear. Such

a tomb has been excavated at Dyffryn Ardudwy in Gwynedd. The first structure here was a dolmen enclosed within
its own oval cairn. At a later date this round mound was
covered by a very much larger rectangular cairn with, to the
east of the original chamber, a second dolmen-type tomb.
Some round mounds were also constructed. At around 3,000
BC at Four Crosses in Powys, a round mound covered a pit in
which there was a single, central inhumation, while two
further inhumations were placed in graves dug into the floor
of the pit.

Pl 32 (*opposite, above*). St. Lythans, South Glamorgan, Wales. The
megalithic tomb is situated in beautiful countryside. Three huge
mudstone uprights, weathered to give the stones such an
extraordinary texture, support a massive capstone. The
rectangular chamber stood at the eastern end of a long mound.

Fig 18 (*opposite, below*). Boyne Valley Passsage-Grave Cemetery,
Co. Meath, Southern Ireland. The cemetery has three focal points,
the passage graves of Knowth, Dowth and Newgrange,
constructed about 3,000 BC. Note the enclosure at Monknewtown,
which may be a henge monument.

Large and small passage graves   Large and small enclosures

Large and small barrows   X   Destroyed sites

Standing stones

Monknewtown

Matrock

Dowth

Knowth

Ballinacrad

Newgrange

Boyne

N

0   1 mile

0   1   2 km

Pl 33. Bryn Celli Ddu, Anglesey, Wales. An impressive passage grave comprising a roofed passage, some 7 m in length, leading to a polygonal chamber formed by six uprights, one of which has a spiral carving. The passage and chamber are contained in a mound, 26 m across, with a double kerb of stones around its edge.

Megalithic tombs were developed to their greatest extent on the fertile island of Anglesey. It is here that we can examine one of the final forms of tomb, the passage grave. Barclodiad y Gawres, translatable as the 'apronful of the giantess', is a spectacular example of the developed skills of the designers and builders, who may well have been specialist tombbuilders by this time. Set in a round mound, a narrow passage led to a cross-like central chamber which contained the cremated remains of at least two men, and originally perhaps a good deal more since two of the side chambers had been heavily disturbed. Although the passage and side chambers were roofed by flat slabs, the central chamber would have been covered by a corbelled roof, where stones are tiered in ever narrowing rings until the aperture is small enough to be covered by one flat stone. The most dramatic aspect of the tomb, however, is the decoration applied to five of the stones in the chambers. This decoration was done by pecking the smooth surface of the stones with a harder stone chisel. The designs are abstract in form, comprising a series of zig-zags, lozenges and spirals. Seen in the harsh light of

day they look rather uninteresting, but exaggerated by the flickering flame of a torch they become much more impressive. Similar designs can be appreciated in some passage graves in Ireland and it may be no coincidence that Barclodiad y Gawres is magnificently sited on the south-west coast of the island, facing out across the Irish sea. An equally impressive passage grave on Anglesey is known as Bryn Celli Ddu, which can be translated as the 'mound in the dark grove' (Pl 33). The tomb comprised a passage and chamber in a round mound. After all the cremation burials had been deposited the passage was blocked, apart from a small opening that did not allow access. Platforms of white quartz pebbles, hearths and a structure surrounding the skeleton of an ox, found outside the mound, clearly played a role in the rituals in front of the tomb.

Scotland

There are a number of long barrows or cairns along the eastern coast of Scotland, and a few in the Borders region, which are comparable to the long mounds of southern England (Pl 45). At Lochhill in Dumfries and Galloway a timber and boulder mortuary structure was buried beneath a trapezoidal cairn. This house of the dead, however, had first existed as a free-standing building, complete with a plank floor and timber facade; it received deposits of human bone before being set alight and subsequently covered by the cairn. Contemporary with Lochhill, at around 4,000 BC, a complex timber mortuary building was constructed at Dalladies in Grampian. This was a multi-phase structure, designed as a series of timber uprights at first, then modified to form a light building roofed with birch-bark, inside a wood and stone setting, which was subsequently burnt. There can be little doubt that these houses of the dead functioned as communal repositories for the bones of the ancestors, before their deliberate destruction by fire, and burial by mounds.

Round mounds were also a feature of the landscape in eastern Scotland in the centuries after 4,000 BC, particularly in the Tay valley. The mounds vary from 12 to 40 m in diameter and are anything from 1 to 9 m in height. They have a marked lowland distribution, and the majority occur on the alluvial gravels of the valley floors. At Pitnacree in Tayside excavation revealed a complex sequence of constructions. The earliest structure bears a close resemblance to those from the earlier phases at Lochhill and Dalladies.

An early group of megalithic tombs is scattered around the Clyde estuary, and south to Wigtown. Most have rectangular chambers; their side walls and roofs are formed by massive stones and dry-stone walling, and the interiors are often divided into compartments by lower slabs. Mid Gleniron I in Wigtown is a good example of a modified and enlarged tomb of this type. Two simple rectangular chambers were originally incorporated into small circular cairns, one behind the other. At a later stage these were covered by a wedge-shaped mound with a crescentic stone facade at its wider, eastern end. A stone side chamber was then added between the two earlier cairns. Both inhumed and cremated bones have been found in these tombs, although disarticulated inhumations are the more numerous, with a maximum of over forty individuals from a single chamber. In the Wigtown area there is also a small group of twelve tombs usually covered by round-mounds, and named after the site at Bargrennan.

The zenith of megalithic tomb architecture in Scotland was reached in the passage graves of the far north: the Western Isles, the Orkneys and Shetlands. Some were small chambers at the end of short passages, while others consisted of larger chambers divided by upright slabs into a number of stalls or compartments, as at Camster in Caithness, or Midhowe on Orkney (Pl 34). Undoubtedly the most sophisticated is that at Maes Howe on Orkney (Pl 46). The passage grave was set into a round mound some 45 m in diameter and 7 m high, itself sited in an oval compound surrounded by a ditch. A passage 11 m long gave access to a superbly constructed square chamber of thin slabs of stone, supporting an accomplished corbelled roof. Three side-chambers, or cells, opened off the main tomb. Maes Howe was probably built around 3,000 BC, but continued in use for some hundreds of years. The Vikings broke through the corbelled roof in the 1150s and left runic inscriptions of their visit on the walls of the chamber. At another Orkney tomb, Quanterness, the remains of at least 150 people were found. The bodies appeared to have been temporarily buried nearby, perhaps in sand dunes, until the flesh had decomposed; then they were exhumed and their bones broken into small pieces and

Pl 34. Midhowe, Rousay, Orkney, Scotland. This type of chambered tomb is known as a stalled cairn. Its enormous burial chamber, over 23 m long, is divided by upright slabs into twenty-four stalls, twelve on either side. Unburned skeletons of twenty-five people were discovered in these stalls; only six skulls were found, however.

Pl 35 (*overleaf, left, above*). Creevykeel, Co. Sligo, Ireland. An impressive court cairn with a narrow entrance leading to an enclosed, oval court. Beyond the court lies the lintelled entrance to the burial chambers. The small, circular feature in front of the burial chambers is a much later iron-working hearth.

Pl 36 (*overleaf, left, below*). Newgrange, Co. Meath, Ireland. The famous decorated stone outside the entrance of the passage grave carries the triple spiral, unique to Newgrange. Through the open box above the lintel a narrow pencil of light from the midwinter rising sun creeps along the passage to illuminate briefly the burial chamber deep inside.

Pl 37 (*overleaf, right*). Chun Quoit, Cornwall, England. Silhouetted against the setting sun, the remains of this chambered tomb make an improbable sculpture. Four huge slabs are covered with a tilting capstone, and were once contained in a round barrow some 10.7 m across.

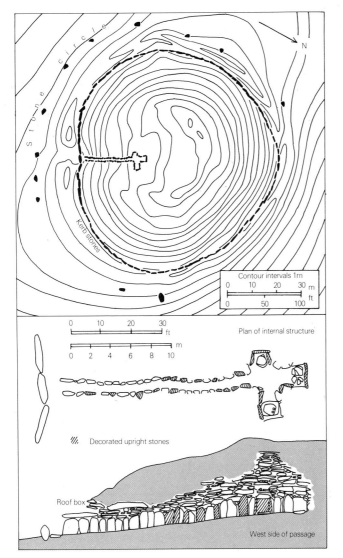

transferred to the tomb. Fires were burnt within the chamber at this stage, while, to judge from the bones of sheep, cattle, fish and birds found alongside the tomb, the mourners shared a meal with their ancestors.

The latest of the megalithic tombs in Scotland are likely to be the eleven passage graves in the vicinity of Inverness and the Spey valley, named after the site at Clava. All have round chambers at the centre of substantial circular cairns with long passages leading to them. Their circular plan links them with the round mounds already mentioned at Pitnacree, and to the numerous burial cairns built in eastern Scotland after 2,500 BC. In addition, some are surrounded by concentric circles of standing stones, which point to a time after 3,000 BC, when a new set of beliefs was sweeping the ancient authority of the ancestors aside, as we shall see below.

Ireland

The earliest megalithic tombs in Ireland consist of the so-called court cairns (Pl 39). These are generally confined to the north of Ireland (with a few outliers in south-west Scotland) and comprise trapezoidal cairns with an east-west axis and a ritual focus at the eastern end. There are 329 court cairns known, of which thirty-eight have been excavated. The mounds incorporated one or two oval courts, open to the sky. Short, gallery-like burial chambers, of two to four cells, opened off these courts. The cells were divided one from the other by low sills and the galleries were roofed with large corbels set in a number of overlapping courses.

The best example of an excavated and restored court cairn is that at Creevykeel in Co. Sligo (Pl 35). An oval court was contained within a trapezoidal cairn 55 m long. A two-chambered gallery some 10 m in length opened off the western side of the court. Five small pockets of cremated bone were discovered in the chambers. Clearly the open court must have witnessed various mourning services. The court could hold about fifty people, and was paved just in front of the burial chamber. A polished diorite axe-head buried at the entrance hints at the sacred ceremonies that the court must have staged. Indeed some argue that the most important function of court cairns was as temples where rituals were performed. Some court cairns did function as communal tombs, however. In a tomb at Creggandevesky, Co. Tyrone, analysis of the cremated bone indicated the remains of at least twenty-one individuals. The affinity between the living and the ancestors is underlined by the building of the

Pl 38. Poulaphuca, Co. Clare, Ireland. There are over fifty wedge tombs on the limestone uplands of the Burren in north Clare. The solid chamber at Poulaphuca (the cave of the spirits) with its well-fitting stones, is in great contrast to the huge capstones so precariously supported in some of the dolmens.

Fig 19. Newgrange, Co. Meath, Ireland. The plans and section of the passage grave at Newgrange. The passage and cross-shaped chamber occupy only a small part of the covering mound. It is possible that other passage graves lie undiscovered within the mound.

court cairn at Ballyglass, Co. Mayo, over the remains of an earlier rectangular house. A type of dual court cairn, with a court at either end and galleries back-to-back, can be found at Carbad More, near Killala in Co. Mayo, at Glenmakeerin in Antrim and at King Orry's Grave on the Isle of Man.

A second type of tomb in Ireland is the portal dolmen. These are concentrated in south-west Donegal, in the Carlingford area, around Dublin, on the Leinster granite of west Wicklow and Carlow, and near Waterford. There are over 160 known examples to compare with the fifty or so similar monuments from Wales and Cornwall. They consist of single-chambered tombs with indications of an entrance porch and facade, and roofed by enormous capstones sometimes in excess of 100t. Only twenty-five show traces of an associated cairn and many may have been designed as free-standing monuments. They present an incredible appearance; huge and ungainly roof stones balanced on slender, uneven side walls. Most have been disturbed long before this century, but there are signs that both inhumations and cremations were originally placed in them. Undoubtedly the most photographed dolmen in Ireland is Poulnabrone in Co. Clare (Pl 40). Excavations within this striking monument produced the jumbled bones of twenty-two people, sixteen adults and six juveniles. The majority of the adults died before reaching the age of thirty, while only one lived past forty years.

A third type of tomb in Ireland is the wedge tomb (Pl 38). There are about 400 of these, with large concentrations in west Cork, east Clare and the adjoining parts of Tipperary, the Burren country of north-west Clare and in Sligo and north-east Mayo. Stone burial chambers, often with porches and end-cells, were frequently covered by oval or D-shaped cairns and faced west rather than east. The tombs were used for communal burial, both inhumation and cremation. In the Lough Gur tomb in Co. Limerick at least twelve people were interred, along with one cremation. Although these tombs are usually associated with the much later period of beaker pottery dating from after 2,500 BC, it is possible that these deposits represent re-use of tombs that were constructed much earlier.

The finest megalithic tombs in Ireland are the passage graves. Many of these were constructed around 3,000 BC and, unlike other megalithic tombs, they were grouped together to form cemeteries. Sophisticated passages and cross-like chambers were covered by round mounds; the chambers contained the cremated remains of the dead with some of their possessions, such as personal ornaments, curious stone and chalk balls, and heavily decorated pottery. The form of the tomb links these people with communities building similar monuments on Orkney, while abstract designs carved on the stones also suggests contact with Anglesey.

The earliest passage grave cemetery has as its principal components three massive tombs at the Bend of the Boyne, near Slane in Co. Meath (Fig 18). After their construction, satellite tombs of later generations clustered around the tombs of the tribal founders. Newgrange is the most elegant of the three (Fig 19). A mound over 80 m in diameter and 15 m high was erected by a labour force of hundreds (Pl 42). The tomb it covered was reached by a long passage and con-

Pl 39. Deerpark (Magheraghanrush) Court Cairn, Co. Sligo, Ireland. Standing on a hill high above Lough Gill, the tomb has an oval central court, with burial chambers opening off at either end.

sisted of a cross-like chamber, roofed by corbelled blocks each weighing up to 1t (Pl 43). Stone basins in each of the recesses of the chamber received each new cremation during the burial ceremony. The ingenuity of the architect of Newgrange is suggested by the open space in the lintel above the doorway to the passage, which allowed light from the rising sun to strike the back of the chamber each midwinter's day (Pl 36). The complex spiral and lozenge designs that adorn the ornamental stone kerb encircling the mound testify to the wonderful imagination of the artist (Pl 44). Neighbouring

Pl 40. Poulnabrone, Co. Clare, Ireland. A portal dolmen with a massive tilted capstone situated in the unusual limestone formations of the Burren. Note the unweathered upright, which is modern, and replaces a cracked prehistoric predecessor.

Dowth and Knowth are the sister tombs of Newgrange and complete the cemetery.

At Knowth the large round mound contains two great passage graves, which were built almost back to back at the same time. They are orientated towards the east and west respectively and it has been suggested that they may be deliberately orientated towards where the sun rose on the 20th or 21st of March and set on 22nd or 23rd of September, the spring and autumn equinoxes. This might link the passage graves with the sowing season and the gathering in of the harvest. Both tombs contain decorated stones, usually displaying abstract or geometrical designs, executed with pecking or with an incised technique. One particular stone, in the passage approaching the burial chamber in the western tomb, carries a stylized human figure with two eyes.

Around the huge mound are the remains of eighteen smaller, round mounds, containing tombs with varying ground plans. Many of these probably post-date the main mound, although at least one pre-dates it.

60 km to the west, one of the early generations of a farming community built focal tombs on the three highest hill-tops in Co. Meath at Loughcrew. More than thirty tombs were constructed by subsequent generations around the graves of their earliest ancestors. A similar cemetery was formed by the concentration of monuments at Carrowkeel in Co. Sligo, while the largest complex of over 100 tombs is that on the plain of Carrowmore, beneath the monstrous Maeve's Cairn at Knocknarea, also in Co. Sligo.

Pl 41. Pentre Ifan, Dyfed, Wales. Part of a chambered tomb, this huge capstone is now precariously balanced on pointed and slender uprights. The chamber was once incorporated in a long cairn, which was unusually orientated north-south, with a crescent-shaped forecourt at its southern end.

Pl 42. Newgrange, Co. Meath, Ireland. Built around 3,000 BC
Newgrange is one of the finest passage graves in western Europe.
The white retaining wall of quartz and granite boulders was
reconstructed and rebuilt from an original wall that had collapsed
outward over the kerb stones.

Not every group adopted communal burial rites. There are a
number of burials concentrated in the area from Dublin to
counties Carlow and Kilkenny which demonstrate individual burials of adult males. The graves comprise massive
stone cists, generally polygonal in shape, set in the centres of
round mounds. The advent of this single-grave tradition may
have weakened the collective rule of the ancestors from their
communal tombs.

Death of the Ancestors

By 3,000 BC we may assume that many different tribes
existed in Britain and Ireland. Tribes contained more people
than bands and were formed by the loose association of
related families and communities who traced their descent
back to a common progenitor. Individual tribes were perhaps associated with particular communal monuments, with
individual causewayed camps or particular groups of megalithic tombs. We must use our imagination, intelligently of
course, to reconstruct their lifestyles. They lived by farming,

indulged in long-distance exchanges of axes and other
objects , and believed in the communal family of ancestors to
protect their farms, fields, kith and kin. Successsive farming
generations placed their dead in these massive megalithic
tombs situated in the tribal homelands. These tombs were
their tombs, just as the lands they stood upon were their
lands; their small world was a safe world providing that they
did not anger the residents of the house of the dead.

But the small world was growing all the time as the number of people in it grew and, conversely, pioneer forest clearings that had been opened up, quickly lost fertility. A crisis
came some time after 3,000 BC when pollen evidence indicates the growth of secondary woodland over some agricultural clearings. It did not affect all areas simultaneously;
changes probably occurred first in southern England and
then spread during hundreds of years to more distant regions. Already there had been signs that burials of single
powerful individuals were becoming more common. Some
late megalithic tombs were grouped in cemeteries where
there was a clear difference between the more massive round
mounds of certain persons and the much smaller affairs of
some of their followers. In addition some tombs showed elements of an early interest in astronomy, with tombs like
Newgrange and the sites around Inverness incorporating
exotic ideas such as stone circles. The blocking of some
graves, like Gwernvale, seems to signal the end of the author-

Pl 43. Newgrange, Co. Meath, Ireland. In an excellent state of preservation, the corbelled roof of the central chamber rises over 6 m above the floor. The builders tried to ensure that the slabs or corbels in one horizontal course overlaid the joints in the course below, so shedding seepage water and keeping the tomb below remarkably dry.

ity of the ancestors. Power over the living was now in the hands of the living – or at least a few of them. The new leaders or chiefs that perhaps emerged combined sacred with secular influence. They built religious centres such as henges and stone circles from which to exercise control. The construction of such monuments close to Maes Howe on Orkney and near West Kennet in Wiltshire show that, in places, there was a deliberate and successful attempt to usurp the power of the ancestors.

The take-over did not go smoothly everywhere. Sometimes the old traditions could not be ignored. At Callanish, on the island of Lewis, a tomb was set in the middle of a complex circle and alignment of stones. But the inevitable probably happened everywhere, sooner or later. We can only really chart the changes through intelligent guesswork. A new generation of chiefs gradually may have come into being. Their sacred rites and knowledge of astronomy put them in touch with the Gods rather than ancestors. They tried to control and learn the mysteries of the movements of the heavenly bodies through astronomical knowledge, just as

Pl 44. Newgrange, Co. Meath, Ireland. The spiral triskele figure is prominent on one of the upright stones in the back chamber of the passage grave. The whole pattern is only 30 by 28 cm. The spirals are picked out by shallow channels, so that the intervening bands stand out in relief.

Pl 45. Clava, Highlands, Scotland. An impressive necropolis of three large cairns, each surrounded by boulder kerb, and a stone circle. Two have passages leading to central chambers which, although now open to the sky, were originally roofed over. The central cairn is without a passage.

they sought to control the minds and bodies of those on the ground. The ancestors were by-passed as the chiefs became mediators between the aspirations of the living and the favours of the divine. But the position of such chiefs was never secure. They could lead by exhortation and example, control by cajoling, but could not overcome the dissent of their followers by force. Their position, therefore, rested on their success with the Gods. Any natural or man-made disaster could quickly lead to the overthrow of those in power. The chiefs managed to persuade their followers not only to lend a hand to construct these inspiring monuments, but also to donate some of their annual agricultural produce to the chiefly coffers. In return they were provided with supernatural protection and perhaps the occasional feast thrown by the chiefs. Such, or something like it, must have been the scenario that encouraged the laborious construction of hundreds of the most enigmatic sites in Britain and Ireland, culminating in the most magnificent of them all, Stonehenge.

Pl 46. Maes Howe, Orkney, Scotland. The passage grave was constructed on specially levelled ground, and surrounded by a circular ditch which provided material for the covering mound. A low, stone bank was built on the outside of the ditch, defining the sacred perimeter of this extraordinary tomb.

Chapter 3

Sunset over Stonehenge

c 2,500–1,100 BC

Stone Circles and Henges

The majority of stone circles and henge monuments were constructed in the thousand years between 2,500 BC and 1,500 BC. Megalithic tombs gradually went out of use, many of them being deliberately blocked and closed off. The new public monuments were circles of stones or earth, not so obviously connected with death and burial. But this transformation in the landscape was itself a slow one. The first phase of Stonehenge, for instance, was completed within two or three centuries after 3,000 BC, yet megalithic tombs were still being used on the Scilly isles, on Orkney and in southern Ireland a thousand years later. The transformation appears to have been an insular phenomenon since, unlike megalithic tombs, very few stone circles occur on the European mainland, one of the nearest being the partly submerged stone circle on the island of Er Lannic, off the coast of Brittany. In the end, however, the new order emerged everywhere.

Why did this change occur and how did it affect the farmer in his field? In order to answer this question archaeologists must go beyond the limits of direct archaeological evidence and construct plausible hypotheses as explanations. There are dangers in this approach, of course. Often the data are capable of supporting more than one hypothesis, and such theories can often be disproved by further excavation. Bearing this in mind, it does seem – as we have already seen – that the early agricultural communities placed much faith in the power of the ancestors for their well-being. There were, of course, leaders in society who organized the construction of tombs, led raids on neighbours and secured good lands for their followers. The ultimate authority, however, was exercised by the collective group of ancestors in the tombs. But, as we saw in the previous chapter, there was an additional element in the construction of these houses for the dead. A great number of the wedge-shaped mounds were aligned in an approximately west-east direction, with the broader and higher end towards the east. Some astronomical influence was incorporated into their design from the beginning. This celestial aspect steadily grew, until some time after 3,000 BC when it eclipsed the power of the ancestors.

The new leaders, now perhaps identified as chiefs, dispensed with the the authority of the dead and instead slowly harnessed power for themselves. Perhaps powerful individuals arose through more efficient farming, producing a surplus with which they assisted the less fortunate. They may have reinforced their position by monopolizing astronomical knowledge and taking it upon themselves to guarantee supernatural safety for their followers through mediating directly with the Gods. Communal rule from the ancestral group, and the more collective decision-making process used by the tribe, was therefore replaced by the individual leadership of the chief. For the farmer in his field the gap between the leaders and the led had widened considerably. Many people could become ancestors but few could hope to acquire the secrets of the heavens and become a chief.

Henges and stone circles were inextricably linked, since stone circles may have been a translation into stone of the idea of an earthen henge. A henge monument is usually a circular earthen bank with an internal (rather than external), ditch enclosing an area of varying diameter, from 14 to 110 m. Banks and ditches are pierced by one entrance or two opposed entrances. Interiors contain a number of enigmatic features such as pits, timber settings and structures, stone settings, and both in earlier and later phases, burials. Some henges were grouped together in clusters and may have comprised not simply ritual locations but sacred landscapes. Such ceremonial complexes are known at Milfield in Northumberland and Balfarg in Fife. These sites were clearly not

Pl 47. Avebury, Wiltshire, England. Set within the ditch of the henge at Avebury was an outer stone circle formed by ninety-eight huge sarsen boulders. These two stand in the south-west quadrant. Behind them is the ditch and bank of the henge, while to the left can be seen the first stones of the Avenue.

Pl 48 (*overleaf*). Castlerigg, Cumbria, England. Set in the midst of the highest mountains in England, the thirty-three standing stones of this fine circle are coloured a warm brown by the rising sun on midsummer morning.

settlement sites and must have acted instead as both sacred and secular centres for chiefdoms, where meetings were held, religious rites staged and goods exchanged. Since the henges performed communal roles, most of the settlements and farms they served were presumably distributed in the immediate region, although relatively few sites of this kind are known. It is highly unlikely, however, that all henges had the same functions. Stone circles were built by erecting a number of stones in an approximate circle. Again the size of the individual stones, the area circumscribed and, no doubt, their original use or uses may have differed considerably. But the two types of site were somehow associated. At Avebury a massive henge incorporated one large and two smaller stone circles, while the stone circle which we now know as Stonehenge itself began life as an earthen henge.

Those areas in which there is a concentration of large stone circles invariably contain henges; the Mendips, Wiltshire, the Peak District, Cumbria (Pl 48) and the Orkneys are good examples. The distribution of stone circles, however, is almost exclusively an upland, western and northern one, no doubt related to the availability of suitable stone found lying on the landscape as glacial erratics. The distribution of henges is more widespread and there are a few in eastern England where no stone circles are known. There are some sites in Ireland that may well be interpreted as henges, and stone circles can be certainly found there in abundance. In all there are about sixty-six henges which are easily outnumbered by almost a 1,000 surviving stone circles (Fig 21).

The evidence suggests that, as with the henges, not all stone circles had the same range of functions. One obvious distinction is that the circles of north-west Britain, Ireland and Dartmoor generally contain human burials, while those of western and southern England usually do not. It may be that the association of burials with some of the earliest stone circles in Cumbria was a way of using the still powerful influence of the ancestors to sanction the emerging authority of the new chiefs. Another distinction lies in shape. There are two principal forms, circular and ovoid, with a widespread minor rectangular group in Scotland known (rather incongruously) as four-posters.

The astronomical significance of stone circles and henges (and related sites such as stone alignments and long ditched enclosures known as cursus monuments) continues to be hotly debated. On balance, it is probable that some settings and designs had astronomical sight-lines built into them. Trying to find where these lines might have been at a particular site is altogether problematic. If we imagine a stone circle with twelve separate stones there exist sixty-six possible lines between stones; as these can be sighted in either direction the total number is doubled. Turning to the possible targets, the risings and settings of the sun at midsummer, midwinter and the equinoxes provide six different possibilities, while the much more complicated cycles of the moon add a further forty. If we combine these with stars and natural features the chances of finding one good alignment in a stone circle are quite high. But would this have been an important sight-line in the past?

Accepting the likelihood of solar and lunar alignments in some of the henges and stone circles, it is easy to perceive how the knowledge of such alignments would have become very important. One obvious way would have been for the chiefs to use such knowledge to provide a simple calendar, marking the correct days for festivals or the prediction of seasonal changes vital in a farming community. More speculatively, the full moon and the setting sun may have been personified as Gods. The connection between the summer sun and the ripening crops would be self-evident, while the twenty-eight day cycle of the moon could have been linked to the menstrual cycle and thus to human reproduction. But it would not at all have been clear how both sun and moon were controlled. The immutable physical laws of the universe were discoveries of the distant future. It was entirely conceivable that the next day the sun would not rise and crops would stay green on the stalk. Or that the waning moon would disappear forever leaving women cold and barren. Only the chiefs through their sacred rites could ensure that the sun would be turned back from its extreme southerly rising or that the new moon would once more fill the sky. Only the chiefs could talk to the Gods.

Statistical proof of lunar alignments has now been provided by an exhaustive study of 276 sites in western Scotland. The monuments concerned are not stone circles but free-standing lines formed of usually two or three stones. The analysis showed a strong preference for lines to the southeast. This implies that the structures were deliberately aligned on the southerly limit of the rising moon in its monthly cycle. Such directions could be decided upon by simply observing the rising of the full moon nearest to the summer solstice. Through such devices were the prehistoric chiefs or priests of the Western Isles able to control time itself.

In England the henges cluster into several major groups, which include concentrations around Dorchester-upon-Thames in Oxfordshire, on the Mendips, around Ripon in Yorkshire, near Penrith in Cumbria and in the Wessex region. Apart from Stonehenge the best known of the Wessex henges is the great monument at Avebury in Wiltshire (Pl 47). Here a bank just under 365 m in diameter was pierced by four opposing entrances. A massive ditch separated the bank from the circular interior, which originally had a stone circle of about 100 undressed sarsen blocks around its edge. At least two smaller stone circles lay inside. An avenue of paired stones ran from the south-east entrance of the henge to another ceremonial site, the Sanctuary, on Overton Hill, where a stone circle replaced an earlier timber circle. Circular settings of timbers have also been located in three very large Wessex henges, those at Durrington Walls, Marden and Mount Pleasant. Some of these may have been roofed, but alternatively they can be interpreted as the timber equivalent of stone circles. However, the balance of opinion suggests that the Durrington structures, at least, were roofed buildings (Fig 20).

The stone circles concentrate in Cumbria, Derbyshire, Wiltshire, on the Mendips and in the Cornish peninsula. Some of the earliest circles are to be found in Cumbria and a spectacular example is Long Meg and Her Daughters. Long

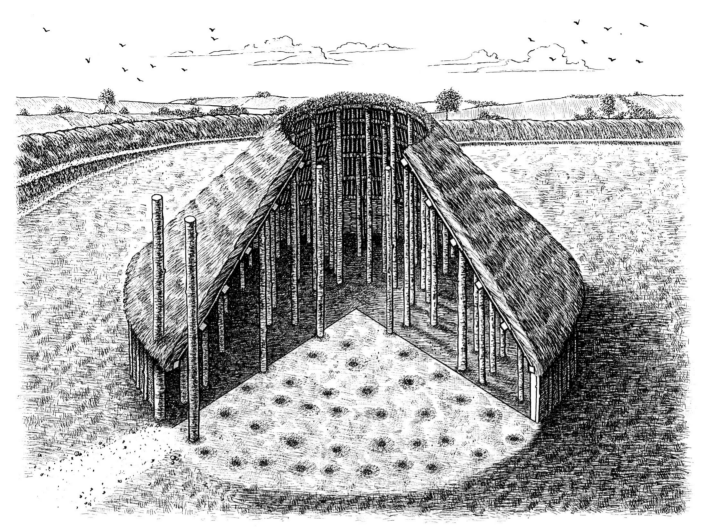

Fig 20. Durrington Walls, Wiltshire, Southern England. A reconstruction of one of the structures within the henge monument. There is an element of doubt in any archaeological reconstruction however, and it is possible that this concentric setting of timbers was never roofed.

Meg is a 3.7 metre high slab of red sandstone that lies outside and to the south-west of the circle. Circular stone engravings on the side of Long Meg, facing the stone circle, underline the connection between the solitary upright and the remaining stones. Anyone standing in the centre of the ring would have seen the midwinter sun set behind Long Meg. Her daughters, members of the circle, form a flattened circle of over 100 m diameter. Not all were as slim as their mother and the fattest daughter weighed in at about 28t and would have required some 120 people at least to set her up! Close to the stone circle, aerial photography has revealed previously unsuspected evidence for this ritual complex. A large, ditched enclosure, containing a pear-shaped area 220 m by 190 m, lies to the north of Long Meg, while at least three other enclosures are situated to the east and west. This is a typical example of how repeated aerial photography can provide novel information about a seemingly well known site.

In Wales the best known henges are two which now lie beneath an industrial estate at Llandegai, opposite the isle of Anglesey. A stone axe from the Langdale quarry was found buried blade downwards, beneath the bank and near the entrance of one of the henges. Such a position seems to suggest that the axe might have been an offering planted in the ground during the construction of the monument. Other associations of axes and henges underline the possibility of a link between the use of axes and the function of some henges. At Stonehenge and Woodhenge in Wiltshire, ceremonial chalk axes were found, while at Mount Pleasant in Dorset a freshly cast bronze axe, one of the earliest metal tools from Britain and Ireland, was discovered in the main ditch. And, of course, there are the famous axe carvings on the sarsen uprights at Stonehenge. Could the exchange of axes have taken place in henges?

The stone circles of Wales are few in number and comparitively small. The circles concentrate in Gwynedd, south-west Dyfed, the Shropshire border and on Mynydd Epynt in central Wales. One of the most emotive sites is the Druids' Circle, high up on a flattish plateau overlooking Penmaen-mawr and the Irish Sea, and not far from the stone axe quarry. Thirty pillars, some nearly 1.8 m high, form an oval of some 25 m diameter. The stones still stand in a low, circular bank, which has a well defined entrance in its south-west quadrant. Excavations in the interior produced three cremations, at least two of them of children.

In Scotland henge monuments are scattered throughout the east of the country. At Balfarg, in Fife, around 3,000 BC, a timber circle of sixteen uprights was set up inside, and concentric to, a henge ditch. The timbers were eventually replaced by two stone circles. There is a magnificent henge containing a circle of massive stones at the Stones of Stenness, Orkney (Pl 60). When the sections of the encircling ditch close to the entrance were excavated, bones of ox and sheep were found, for the most part mandibles and extremities of limbs, hinting at rituals that must have played a role in the ceremonies within. The site lies only a few 100 m from the impressive henge and stone circle at Brodgar (Pls 61 & 62), and only a stone's throw from a settlement at Barnhouse. Stone circles are located in a number of areas: the south-west, Arran, the Western Isles, the north-east and Perthshire. On Arran excavations have demonstrated that at least two of this important group of stone circles were preceded by concentric settings of timber uprights. Perhaps the most emotive circle, however, is the spectacular arrangement of tall, thin stones at Callanish, on Lewis (Pl 1). Sitting on a ridge overlooking East Loch Roag, a cross-shaped pattern of stones radiates from a central circle. As has already been mentioned, a small megalithic tomb was squeezed into the central circle, seemingly as part of the original design. This hints that in some places the ancestors were capable of making a comeback. An idiosyncratic collection of stone circles is concentrated in Grampian. These are known as recumbent circles since they incorporate a horizontal slab generally flanked by the two tallest uprights and frequently in the south-west quadrant. Other types of stone circle from Perthshire have been labelled four-posters because of their rectangular settings. Whatever their range of functions it is noticeable that both henges and stone circles seem to incorporate burials as secondary and later features.

No definite henges are known from Ireland, although there are possible candidates in the Boyne Valley, close to the complex of megalithic tombs at Newgrange. One site has been partially excavated at Monknewtown. An earthen bank enclosed an area some 96 m in diameter. Inside twelve burials in pits were discovered, while at the opposite side of the enclosure an irregular pattern of post-holes and a hearth probably suggest some sort of roofed structure.

Stone circles, on the other hand, abound in the southern counties of Cork and Kerry, and in mid-Ulster, with a few examples in central Ireland (Pl 59). The Cork-Kerry type consists of a ring of free-standing stones arranged so that the so-called axial stone (usually the lowest or recumbent stone) always lies in the south-west quadrant of the circle, facing the entrance which is situated in the opposing north-east quarter. A particular characteristic of this group is that the uprights decrease in height as they approach the axial stone. About half of the eighty-eight sites in this area have an average of a dozen stones per circle; the other half, however, possessed only five stones each. In some excavated circles cremation burials have been discovered. The purpose of these monuments is as enigmatic as elsewhere. Certainly the stone circles of Ireland are sometimes associated with other types of site, such as standing stones and stone alignments. The consistent north-east:south-west axis has led most people to suggest astronomical functions connected with the midwinter sunset. We must not imagine, however, that precise astronomical accuracy was achieved or aimed for; indeed the variation in alignments of these sites shows that this was not a requirement. It was enough that the chiefs or priests conducted their rituals and monitored the positions of sun and moon with respect to the stones. What mattered most was the implicit faith the people had in the God-given ability of their leaders to control both heavenly and human movements.

The circles of northern Ireland are quite different from their cousins in the south. The most spectacular cluster in these northerly sites is in the Sperrin mountains, at Beaghmore in Co. Tyrone. Here three pairs of circles and a further isolated example have been unearthed beneath a covering blanket of peat. Four rows of standing stones converge on a mound sandwiched between two of the circles; the mound was found to contain a stone axe. In mid-Ulster the circles are of irregular outline and are constructed of quite small stones.

A blind faith, or rather just a blurred one, was enough, therefore, to bind together the circle-building communities of Britain and Ireland. Given the widespread distribution of such sites it is tempting to imagine that there must have been some similarity of beliefs. This, of course, would not imply that religious homogeneity led automatically to social, economic or political unity. Indeed a glance at many modern conflicts around the world proves that there is no correlation. It does seem, however, that success with predicting such things as the days of festivals or the solstice enabled the powerful influences of the priests and chiefs to pervade every aspect of daily life. Yet there was one place where chiefly charisma was not enough; where astronomical prediction meant precision; where the faithful needed proof as well as promises. This site may have become the most important location in southern Britain, the sacred, if not secular, capital of the region, the foundation of all ritual authority – Stonehenge (Pl 68).

The thousands of worshippers who built the first phase of Stonehenge began digging the ditch and bank that circled the site around 3,000 BC. There are some reasons to think that the place had already been chosen by the leaders as a result of astronomical observations carried out over a number of years. Four stones were eventually set up within the bank defining a rectangle, the long axis of which was aligned on the northerly setting of the midwinter moon, while the short axis was directed at the midsummer sunrise. The midsummer

Fig 21. Stone Circles and Henges. The map illustrates certain concentrations of stone circles, such as the Cork-Kerry type in southern Ireland and those in the north of the same country. Henges can be found in eastern England, where stone circles are few, and also show a tendency to cluster into groups.

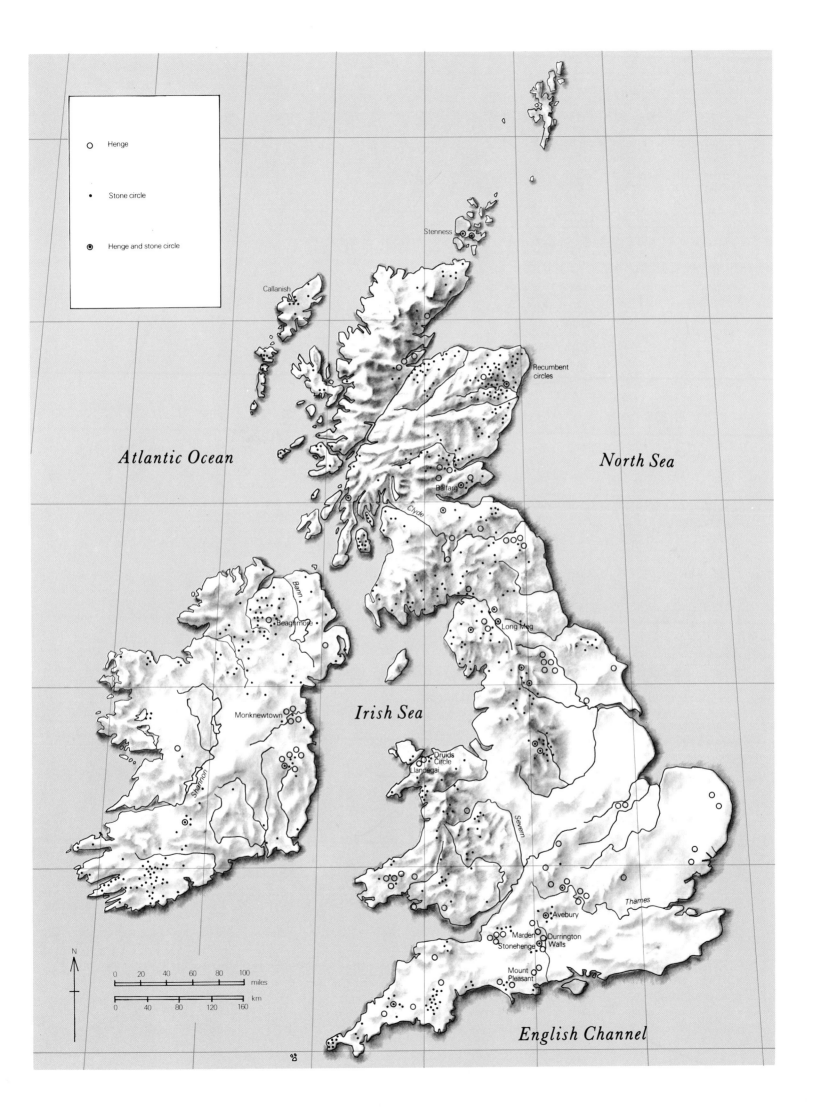

Henge

Stone circle

Henge and stone circle

Atlantic Ocean

North Sea

Stenness

Callanish

Recumbent circles

Balfarg

Clyde

Long Meg

Bann

Beaghmore

Irish Sea

Monknewtown

Druids Circle

Llandegai

Shannon

Severn

Thames

Avebury

Marden   Durrington Walls

Stonehenge

Mount Pleasant

N

0   20   40   60   80   100
                                    miles
0   40   80   120   160
                                    km

English Channel

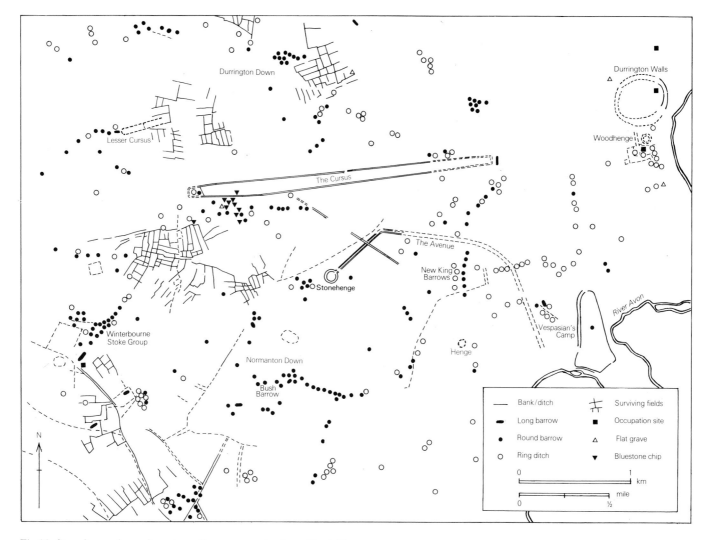

Fig 22. Stonehenge Area. An extraordinary concentration of burial
and ritual sites lie close to Stonehenge. Notable here are the
Avenue, the cursus, the henge at Durrington Walls, the Bush
Barrow and the groupings of barrows.

sun and midwinter moon thus rose and set approximately at
right angles to one another. Stonehenge must surely have
been sited deliberately at this junction. In such a way the
priests emphasized their control and communion with the
Gods. At the entrance to the henge, two stones were set up,
one on each side, while beyond the gap a line of four timber
posts perhaps functioned as a ceremonial gateway. A little
further out the so-called Heel Stone was put up. In the interior of the henge, just inside the bank, fifty-six pits were dug
and then almost immediately backfilled.

For nearly a 1,000 years this relatively standard henge
remained an important monument, though perhaps rivalled
in status by several other sites. Around 2,100 BC, however, it
was transformed into a unique centre, with architectural
modifications that at once set it apart from every other henge
or stone circle in Britain and Ireland. We do not know the
identities of the new line of powerful chiefs who are assumed
to have impressed upon thousands of followers the need for
such an undertaking. Yet around the site were to cluster
some of the richest burials in prehistory which is surely no

coincidence (Fig 22). The changes that were carried out were
dramatic indeed. The entrance to the old henge was
widened, and a ditched Avenue was laid out in a straight line
some 530 m in length running away from the entrance. Some
of the fifty-six backfilled pits now had human cremations
placed in them. But the major revolution was the design of
the centre. Work began on laying out a double circle of bluestones; whether these came from the Preseli mountains of
south-west Wales, or were found as isolated and scattered
stones on Salisbury Plain is still being argued about. What is
not a matter for debate is the fact that the bluestone circles
were never completed. The monument was about to enter its
final and most fantastic form (Fig 23).

This ultimate metamorphosis was achieved by dragging
seventy-seven blocks of sarsen sandstone, each on average
26t, from the Marlborough Downs, across stream and down
dale to Salisbury Plain. Creaking rollers, straining ropes,
brusied backs and shoulders, chanting, coaxing, cursing and
coercion all combined in a massive display of manpower and
muscle. The chiefs directed, the old and the young watched
and wondered while the Gods inspired. Towering uprights
were linked by stone lintels, held in place by mortice and
tenon joints, a technique borrowed from wood-working.

There had been nothing, and there would be nothing like it again in Britain or Ireland, or indeed any where else. This final transformation was itself carried out in stages. First five trilithons (two uprights joined by a lintel) were erected in a horseshoe setting, with an open end towards the Avenue. This setting was surrounded by a complete circle of lintelled sarsens. The bluestones were then reused both as an oval arrangement within the horseshoe and as a double circle outside the lintelled circle. But these modifications were yet again never completed and the final reorganization, at about 1,500 BC, involved the erection of another bluestone circle between the horseshoe and the ring of sarsens. Even then there was a postscript. About two centuries later the Avenue was extended, not in a continuation of its original line, but at an angle.

Stonehenge was a focus of activity for over 1,500 years. As we have seen above, it was apparently taken over by new groups of people from 2,100 BC onwards and changed into a centre from which earthly influence and divine direction spread across Salisbury Plain and permeated perhaps as far as the mountains of Wales. It was with little doubt seen as the centre of the universe for numbers of different tribes and chiefdoms in southern Britain, separated by distance, language, dress and culture, yet somehow united in common beliefs associated with the sun and moon. As if to emphasize the magnetic aura of Stonehenge, it attracted to its vicinity a large concentration of ritual and burial sites. It was the nodal point in a ritual landscape peppered by burial monuments and other henges. Similar ritual centres containing complexes of major monuments must have existed in the Boyne Valley in Ireland, on Orkney, at Balfarg in Fife, at Milfield in Northumberland and elsewhere.

Magic Metals

The first appearance of gold ornaments, of copper and bronze tools and weapons, must have made a tremendous impact on the stone-using peoples of Britain and Ireland. It must also have left a magical impression. The magic, of course, lay in the production of these exotic metal implements . The whole process must have appeared mysterious to communities who had lived for generations with a stone technology. There were a great many stages involved in its manufacture. First the prospection for ores of copper and tin, followed by their subsequent collection through time-consuming processes like quarrying and mining. Then the smelting with or without a flux (depending on the type of ore) and secondary smelting to obtain a purer metal. The final stages involved the combination of copper and tin to produce bronze prior to pouring it into a mould to form the finished artefact. If we add to these technicalities the manufacture of stone or clay moulds, the construction of hearths and furnaces, and the trimming, hammering, annealing and occasional decorating of the object, then we can appreciate how difficult it might have been to comprehend.

What was not difficult to understand was that metal artefacts were more efficient and could be more decorative than their stone equivalents. We do not know how metals were first introduced into Britain and Ireland. The beginnings of metallurgy are to be found in faraway south-east Europe, in Romania and Bulgaria. Whether it was folk movements, new ideas, or ore prospectors that introduced the technology is uncertain. In Britain the earliest metal objects are often found with pottery beakers, and archaeologists used to think that the Beaker Folk had migrated to these islands and brought the knowledge of metal with them. What is known is that metal objects were being manufactured in Britain and Ireland before 2,000 BC. The earliest objects were of pure copper, but arsenic and tin were soon added to produce bronze and give a tougher product. As with any new technology, whoever managed to control it would inevitably have gained influence and prestige. The chiefs and priests who had exercised power through access to the Gods by way of monumental communal undertakings, such as the stone circles were now challenged. The new source of influence was the process of metal production, secretive and individual compared with the communal efforts involved in stone circle construction. Authority could now be grasped by anyone capable of cornering its production and directing its distribution.

The ore sources for the metal industries were widely scattered in the uplands of the west and north, while Cornwall possessed a valuable concentration of tin. Some of the earliest copper mines were located on the slopes of Mount Gabriel, Co. Cork, where a total of twenty-five mineshafts have been found. The mines consist of low, narrow approach galleries which lead down into chambers. The copper ores were extracted by means of fire and pounding with stone mauls. Around the entrances to the galleries there are dumps of waste which show where the ores were brought out and broken up by pounding. Claims for early copper mines have also been made for shafts on the Great Orme and Parys Mountain, both in north Wales, and at Cwmystwyth, a short distance inland from Cardigan Bay. The first metal artefacts were axes, daggers, halberds and spearheads. The oldest axes were thick-butted flat examples, cast in one-piece stone moulds. The medium of molten metal, however, allowed for easy experimentation and soon thinner butts with hammered and cast flanges were produced. Further elaboration led to the introduction of stop bevels, and recurving cutting edges as seen in the axes from Arreton Down on the Isle of Wight (Pl 49).

Daggers display a similar technological development, from simple flat specimens to larger blades which have midribs and grooving that are both strengthening and decorative. Halberds are curious blades, shaped like daggers, yet mounted to wooden shafts almost at right angles; they were vicious weapons but not all metal artefacts were functional and many must have been ceremonial. Some daggers found with rich burials clearly never possessed sharpened edges and were thus used solely for display, while some massive axeheads were so large that they could never have been used for chopping wood. Sometimes appearances seem to have been all important. Two axes from Sluie, Moray, for instance, had their surfaces enriched by the addition of so

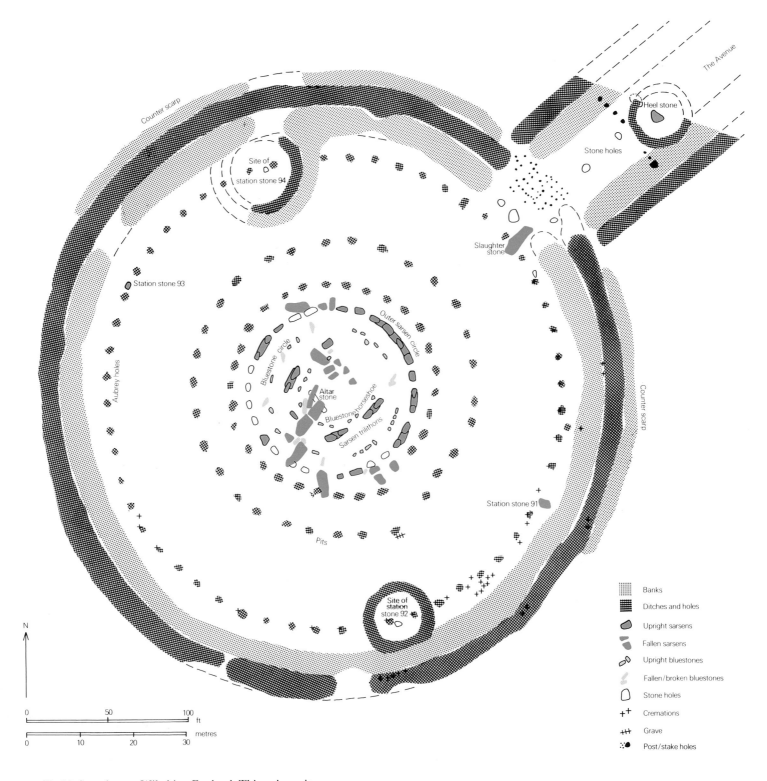

Figure labels (clockwise/as positioned):
Counter scarp
The Avenue
Heel stone
Stone holes
Site of station stone 94
Slaughter stone
Station stone 93
Outer sarsen circle
Bluestone circle
Altar stone
Bluestone horseshoe
Sarsen trilithons
Counter scarp
Aubrey holes
Station stone 91
Pits
Site of station stone 92
N

0   50   100 ft
0   10   20   30 metres

Legend:
Banks
Ditches and holes
Upright sarsens
Fallen sarsens
Upright bluestones
Fallen/broken bluestones
Stone holes
Cremations
Grave
Post/stake holes

Fig 23. Stonehenge, Wiltshire, England. This unique site was a focus of activity for 1,500 years, spanning the period from 3,000 to 1,500 BC approximately. Not surprisingly, the monument was modified and redesigned several times during these centuries. The four so-called station stones defined the astronomical significance of the site's location.

much tin that they must must have shone like silver. Spearheads were cast with an integral socket, which was fastened to the shaft by means of a transverse rivet.

Most of the copper and bronze objects from Britain and Ireland have been found either with burials or in hoards – caches of artefacts deliberately placed in the ground. It can be conjectured that as the new class of chiefs arose, their authority was not based on communication with the Gods, but on the patronage of these mysterious craftsmen and their products. But such magical items were not allowed to be manufactured and exchanged at will. The amount of supply was definitely not governed by the degree of demand. Supply was instead artificially restricted by the disposing of some metal in rich graves, and the burial of more in hoards. (Not all hoards were concealed for this reason; some smiths may have buried old and broken bronze tools with the intention of reworking the metal at a later date.) Ostentatious display of the precious material in public ceremonies by the leaders, and minimal access to functional tools and weapons for the followers, was the framework of the new order. Certainly the

Pl 49. Bronze Tools and Weapons. A selection of objects from Arreton Down on the Isle of Wight. At the bottom is a halberd with three rivets, which would have been mounted at right angles to a wooden haft; to the right are spearheads with tangs and sockets, while to the left are axes with cast flanges, stop bevels and geometric decoration. (Length of halberd is 23.9cm)

Pl 50. Blessington Lunula. Ireland was a great centre of prehistoric gold-working. This is a sheet gold lunula, or neck ornament, from Blessington in Co. Wicklow. The abstract, geometric decoration is typical, both in its execution and in its position on the collar. (Overall width is 22 cm)

number of axes in Irish rivers and bogs suggests that some quantity of finished artefacts were taken out of circulation to preserve the imbalance in their use and distribution.

Bedecked with gold, either in life or in death, the chiefs came into their own. Large gold earrings, gold collars, gold belt buckles, gold buttons and, at least in one case, a gold cape marked them out from the masses. The precious metal was available from two sources: alluvial sediments in the streams of Cornwall, Wales, Scotland, and west and north

Ireland; and the drift source in the Wicklow mountains of eastern Ireland. In addition, imported ornaments could augment the supply. These spectacular accoutrements were fashioned from highly burnished sheet gold, and decorated with linear geometric motifs. The handiwork of unsung craftsmen can now be detected in some of the pieces. For instance, in the Wessex area, it is clear from studies of toolmarks and the like that the self-same goldsmith fashioned the Bush Barrow chest plate and belt hook, the gold covers for the shale button at Upton Lovell, Wiltshire, the lozenge plate from a burial at Clandon in Dorset and the gold-bound amber discs and button cover from Wilsford in Wiltshire.

Gold was used for the manufacture of elongated, basket-shaped earrings, as well as gold discs (like those from Knowes of Trotty, Orkney) that seem to have been fastened to clothing. But all these objects are surpassed in beauty by the magnificent gold collars or lunulae which contain the greatest volume of gold in use at this period in western Europe (Pl 50). The concentration of these splendid items lies in Ireland, with a total of eighty-one examples. Undoubt-

edly this attests the superiority of Irish craftsmen over their counterparts in England, Wales and Scotland. The sophistication of work in sheet gold was not confined to Ireland, however, and was highlighted in two very individual masterpieces. One is a gold cape, from Mold in Clwyd, which was found placed with a burial (Pl 52). Lined with some sort of felt, this must have hugged the shoulders of a very influential individual. The second object is a superb gold cup from Rillaton, in Cornwall (Pl 51). Whatever special liquid it contained, it must have only been drunk on extremely important occasions.

.Compared with the exuberance of the goldwork, contemporary pottery seems fairly restrained. Whatever the number of different tribes and chiefdoms within Britain and Ireland at this time, it is clear that a similar set of conventions dictated the form and decoration of pottery everywhere. In particular, decoration is confined to geometric patterns rather than any more individual or naturalistic design. Purely domestic pottery must have been fired locally using a simple hearth, while more sophisticated vessels, used as burial urns, as grave goods, as ritual containers or specialized drinking cups, were perhaps fired in specially prepared bonfire kilns at more distant locations. A typical example of the latter is the various forms of grooved decoration which adorn the sides of bucket-shaped vessels commonly discovered in the henge monuments. Another form of decoration can be found on the numerous beakers, zonal arrangements of motifs made using toothed bone combs. Similar beakers are found all over Britain and Ireland, and in western Europe. It was for long the opinion that the migrating Beaker Folk might have been responsible for the introduction of metallurgy, and incidentally for the transportation of the bluestones to Stonehenge. Scholarly opinion has now swung away from this idea and beakers have been linked to the spread of some prestige cult practice, no doubt associated with fermented drink of the kind possibly identified in residues in pots from Ashgrove in Fife and North Mains in Tayside; perhaps, by analogy, akin to the spread of clay pipes after the introduction of tobacco. Large pottery vessels and urns, again with impressed and geometrically arranged decoration, were increasingly used for cremation burials.

From funerary deposits also come some rather more unusual items made from jet and amber. These resinous and lustrous materials were prized not only for their beauty, but also because they possessed the magic property of static electricity. Jet occurs rarely in Britain, only in narrow strata amidst the fine-grained cannel coals exposed in cliff falls and exposures along the eastern coast of North Yorkshire. Other jet-like substances may have been used from time to time, such as cannel coal itself, lignite and some varieties of shales. Amber, on the other hand, could be picked up from the beaches of East Anglia, where it is still cast up by the tides today. Both amber and jet were worked into precious items that roughly fall into three categories: jewellery, including beads, necklaces (Pl 53) and bracelets; clothing accessories, such as buttons, belt sliders and pulley rings; and finally display objects like cups, maceheads, dagger pommels, plaques and wristguards. Although amber and jet had discrete

Pl 51. Rillaton Cup. This gold cup was found in 1837 at Rillaton in Cornwall accompanying a single burial. The body of the cup is a single piece of gold, while the handle has been attached by rivets. Did the cup contain a reviving beverage for the world beyond? (Height of cup is 8.3 cm)

Pl 52. Mold Cape. This superb sheet gold cape was found at Mold in Clwyd, around the bones of a skeleton contained in a stone cist. The decoration on the cape is formed by lines of raised bosses separated by plain ridges. The cape may have been lined with leather and stiffened at the base with a strip of thin bronze. (Height of cape is 23.5 cm)

Pl 53. Jet Necklace. This necklace comes from Melfort in Argyll. A mixture of perforated beads and rectangular panels produce an interesting composition, while the abstract, geometric decoration on the panels can also be seen on contemporary beaker pottery. (Average length of panel is 5 cm)

centres of origin and production, it is clear that these much sought after materials were widely exchanged between groups, since they have been discovered in burials and occupation sites in distant regions of Britain and Ireland.

Where the substance itself was not intrinsically exciting then something remarkable could be done to it, in order to make it more prestigious. Such must be the case with a class

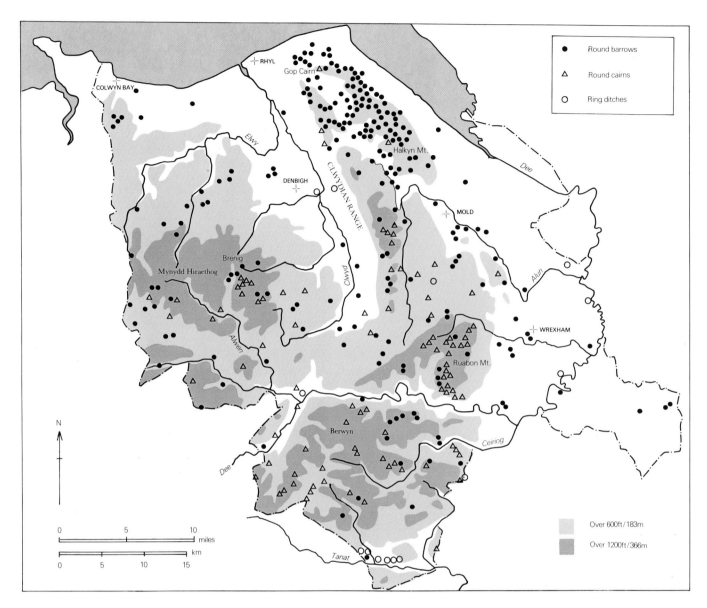

Fig 24. Round Barrows, Cairns and Ring-Ditches in Clwyd, North Wales. Individual sites are plotted on this map showing how the earthen barrows and stone cairns are related to lower ground and higher, stonier ground respectively. Round barrows, flattened by the plough, are detected in the valley bottoms as ring ditches on aerial photographs.

of curious carved stone balls, of which the specimens from Fyvie and Turriff, both in Grampian, are excellent examples of two different types. Then there are three chalk cylinders or drums which accompanied an inhumation burial beneath a round mound at Folkton, in Yorkshire (Pl 54). These carry incised and geometric designs, and also schematic facial motifs outlined by eyebrows, eyes and nose. Unless future discoveries reveal more figurative representations of the men and women of the time, these three caricatures are the closest we will come to a contemporary portrayal of the faces from that long-distant time.

As the later phases of Stonehenge were being planned, and while the amount of metalwork in circulation was still fairly small, the use of stone for tools entered its most sophisticated

stage. Intensive mining for flint occurred, as at Grimes Graves in Norfolk. Here shafts up to 15 m deep and 5 m wide were sunk to reach the fine floorstone. This was mined first, and then radial galleries were driven off the main shafts to exploit it more widely. The entire site might have produced in excess of 14,000t, enough to fashion some 28,000,000 axes. Not all went into the production of larger tools, however. Some beautifully finished barbed and tanged arrowheads have been discovered in burials, especially those with beaker pottery. Some of the long-lived stone quarries continued to be worked too, including those of Cornwall and the Lake District. In addition fresh sources were quarried, for example in

Fig 25 (*opposite*). Burials: 2,500–1,100 BC. Most burials of this period were placed underneath round mounds and cairns or in stone boxes, or cists, themselves sometimes covered by round mounds. Schematic distributions are shown here, and one symbol on the map usually indicates several sites on the ground. More cists are known outside Ireland, although the published data is insufficient for mapping purposes.

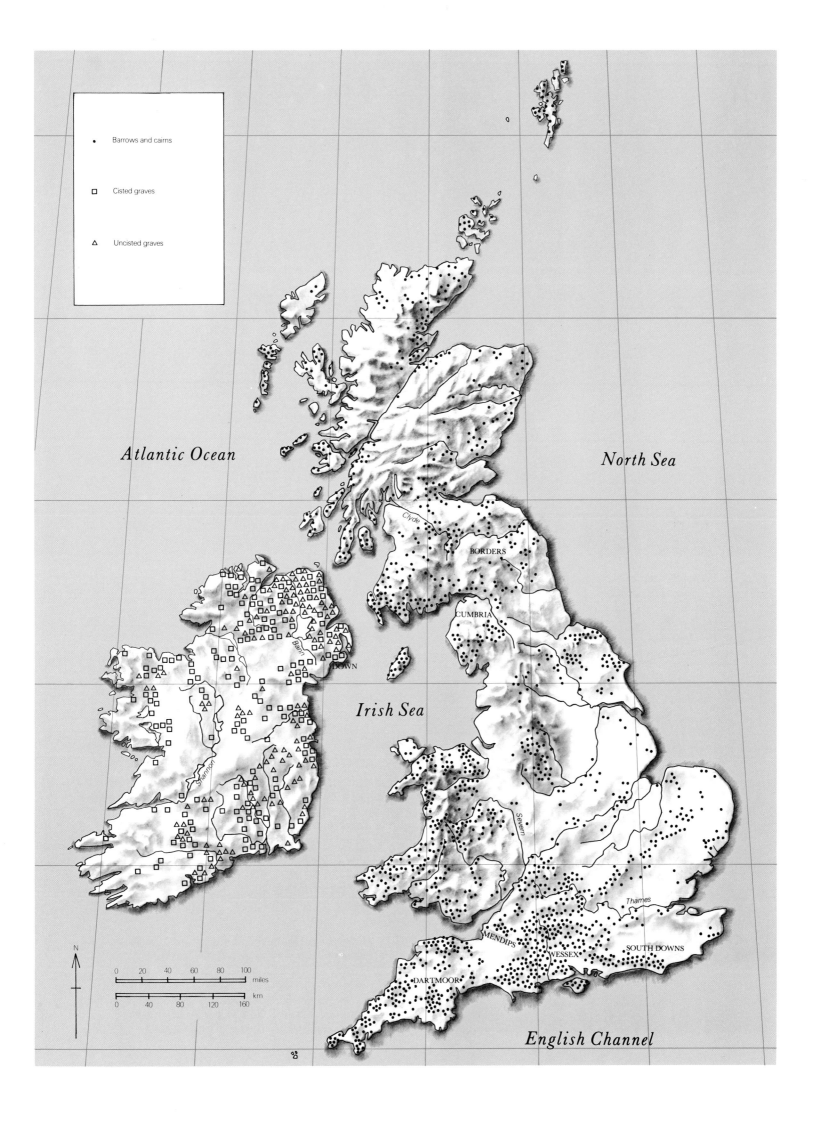

Barrows and cairns

Cisted graves

Uncisted graves

Atlantic Ocean

North Sea

Clyde

BORDERS

CUMBRIA

Bann

DOWN

Shannon

Irish Sea

Severn

Thames

MENDIPS

WESSEX

SOUTH DOWNS

DARTMOOR

N

0   20   40   60   80   100
                              miles

0   40   80   120   160
                         km

English Channel

Pl 54. Folkton Drums. These are from North Yorkshire and unusually carry stylized eyebrow-and-eye motifs. Their function is quite unknown. On the largest one, the geometic panels underneath the eyes may suggest a mouth, and it is possible that the abstract panels may represent the type of body decoration painted on individuals. (Diameter of largest drum is 14.8 cm)

the Preseli mountains of Dyfed. Many stone axes were now perforated for hafting. This must have been a laborious task using flint-tipped bits, perhaps turned by bow-drills, and with sand as an abrasive. But the results were, in many cases, spectacular, culminating in the manufacture of some very impressive examples, the so-called battle-axes, some of which were ceremonial items rather than weapons (Pl 55).

Stone implements, of course, withstand the passing of time much better than those made from organic materials, such as bone, antler, wood, or animal products. There must have been a tremendous variety of such items as as can be seen from rare survivals like some bone pins from Skara Brae, Orkney, or an antler macehead from Watnall in Nottinghamshire. Moreover, in looking at these items now, we must never forget that stone axes (for instance) were attached to finely crafted wooden hafts, that some bronze daggers were held in horn handles, and that, most important of all, their proud owners were no doubt dressed in exquisitely dyed garments of linen and wool.

Pl 55. Macehead and Battle-Axe. These two stone implements from Ireland show the developed craft of the prehistoric stone-worker. On the left is a battle-axe from the river Bann; the central perforation is emphasized by the concave depressions rimmed by a raised border. On the right is a beautifully finished macehead from Lough Gur in Co. Limerick. Both objects are likely to be ceremonial. (Length of macehead is 10.5 cm approx.)

Pl 56. A Burial with Beaker. Sometime after 2,500 BC single burials
accompanied by beakers and other grave goods appear in Britain.
This is a grave-group from a burial at Lambourn in Berkshire.
Note the heavily decorated beaker, the barbed and tanged
arrowheads and the jet button. (Height of beaker is 19 cm)

Death and Burial

Although the sun, moon and the stars loomed ever larger in
the lives of men and women during the long history of Stonehenge, death still continued to have a strong hold on people's
imagination. While the old communal tradition of mass
burials in megalithic tombs persisted for a considerably long
time in some areas, in other regions a bewildering variety of
burial monuments came to be constructed. Usually the
deceased were now buried individually, either as inhumations, often in a crouched position, or as cremations. The
burials were not isolated, however, and were usually grouped
together either in flat cremation cemeteries or in cemeteries
underneath mounds of earth or stone, called barrows/
cairns. Each barrow or cairn, if it covered and contained
multiple interments, might have been considered as the
burial ground of a family. And, although some barrows occur
as individual monuments in the landscape, more often than
not they are associated with other barrows, either in pairs or
triplets, in linear arrangements or as concentrated groups of
barrows. It is thus possible to interpret such clusters as the

cemeteries of entire communities over a number of generations. However, archaeological interpretation is never
straightforward. There is a distinct possibility that barrow
burial was reserved for a minority of the population, presumably those of high status. If this was the case we can only
speculate on the nature of the burial rites for the unseen
masses. Perhaps their ashes were scattered in the winds, or
their bodies exposed above ground until nothing remained to
be found by future generations of archaeologists.

The types of barrow or cairn were numerous (Fig 25). Barrows could form round mounds some up to 60 m in diameter
and 6 m high, with or without a surrounding ditch. Stone
cairns, too, varied enormously. Some were mounds of stone,
others low stone platforms, while a third type consisted of a
flat stone ring. Many were modified and enlarged at later
dates. Some started out relatively small, covering a central
cremation or inhumation. Later on the mound might be
increased in size by the addition of extra layers, and many
further cremations or inhumations might be inserted into the
upper part of the monument. Excavation shows that some incorporated more complex timber features. They began life,
perhaps, not as mounds at all but as timber mortuary houses
that contained the remains of the deceased. These small
structures were sometimes surrounded by timber fences, perhaps screening the deceased from the mourners. Later in the
ceremony mounds often incorporating circular banks of
earth or stone, were piled up occasionally in more than one

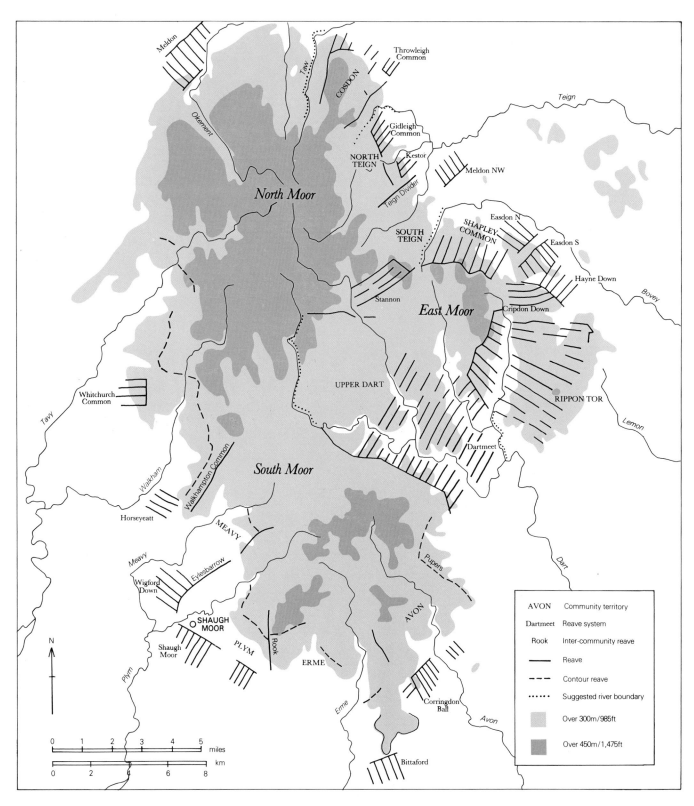

Fig 26. Reaves on Dartmoor, South-West England. Dartmoor was divided up after 1,500 BC into ten or so farming units of unequal size by a system of stone banks or reaves. The largest identifiable unit is that around Rippon Tor, on the east side of the moor. The excavated settlement at Shaugh Moor is on the south-west part of the moor.

Fig 27 (opposite). Farms, Fields, Resources and Ritual Sites: 2,500–1,100 BC. There are few dated settlements of this period. The inferred distribution of farms and fields is primarily an upland one and is shown here schematically. The upland bias in the map is because the archaeological sites survive in greater numbers beyond the limits of modern intensive farming, not because there was an absence of similar settlements in the lowlands. The map also illustrates major mineral and metal resources, and a few important ritual monuments.

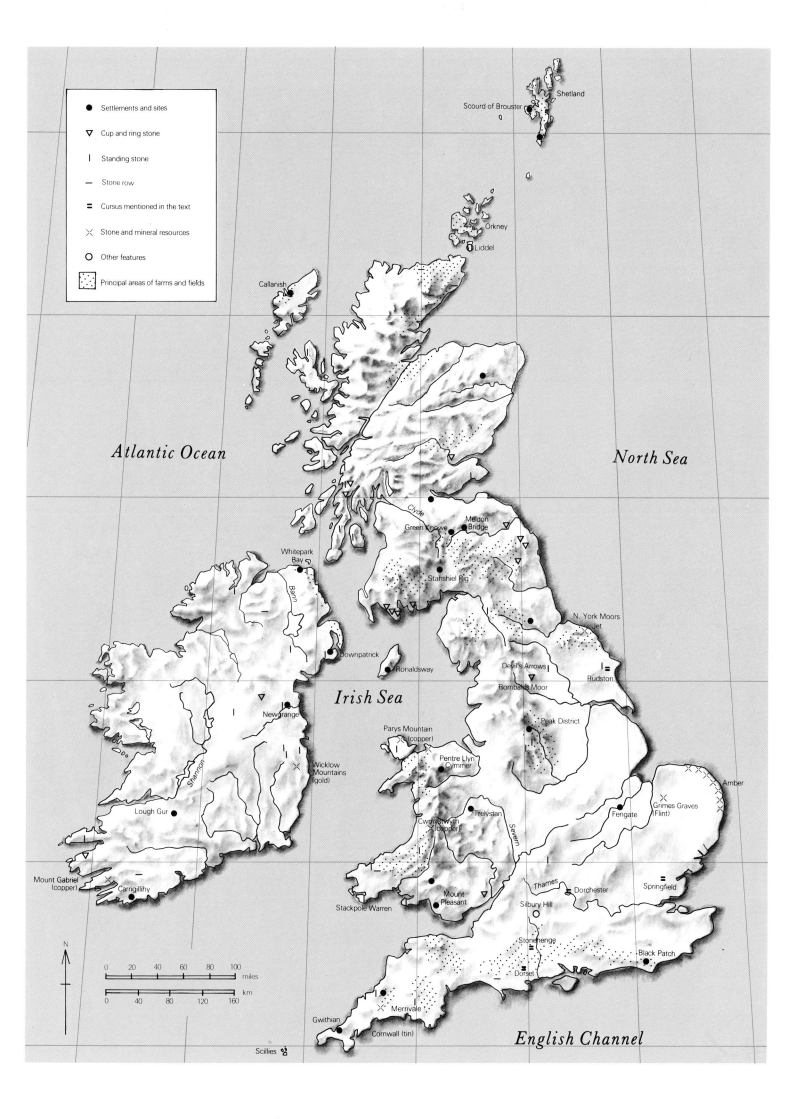

Legend

- ● Settlements and sites
- ▽ Cup and ring stone
- | Standing stone
- — Stone row
- ＝ Cursus mentioned in the text
- ✕ Stone and mineral resources
- ○ Other features
- ⬚ Principal areas of farms and fields

Atlantic Ocean

North Sea

Irish Sea

English Channel

Shetland
Scourd of Brouster
Orkney
Liddel
Callanish
Clyde
Meldon Bridge
Green Knowe
Stanshiel Rig
Whitepark Bay
Bann
N. York Moors Jet
Downpatrick
Ronaldsway
Devil's Arrows
Rudston
Rombalds Moor
Newgrange
Peak District
Parys Mountain (copper)
Pentre Llyn Cymmer
Shannon
Wicklow Mountains (gold)
Amber
Grimes Graves (Flint)
Trelystan
Fengate
Lough Gur
Cwmystwyth (copper)
Severn
Mount Gabriel (copper)
Carrigillihy
Thames
Dorchester
Springfield
Mount Pleasant
Stackpole Warren
Silbury Hill
Stonehenge
Black Patch
Dorset
Gwithian
Merrivale
Cornwall (tin)
Scillies

N

| 0 | 20 | 40 | 60 | 80 | 100 |
miles

| 0 | 40 | 80 | 120 | 160 |
km

Pl 57. Normanton Down, Wiltshire, England. Burial mounds sometimes occur in linear cemeteries, and this is clearly the case at Normanton Down, 1 km south of Stonehenge, where round barrows of different shapes and sizes were constructed.

episode, around and over both mortuary house and fences to form a more orthodox looking barrow or cairn. Both barrows and cairns must have been striking features in the landscape. Some of them seem to have been deliberately sited on high ground or ridges to command extensive views and to be seen from afar. The gleaming white chalk mounds of the southern English counties, or the rain-washed sparkle of quartz-capped cairns in the uplands of Wales must have been prominent reminders for contemporary communities of the brevity of their lives.

The containers that the deceased were buried in were also varied. Some were placed in simple pits, stone boxes or cists, others in coffins; while cremations could be placed in different types of burial urn or leather bags. Some had grave goods placed with them, including beaker pots and archery equipment (Pl 56): others were buried without possessions. That the living may have believed in an afterlife is apparent from the nature of some cremations. Often these were placed in an inverted pot with a lid sealing the mouth of the pot and sometimes with a stone covering the base. The most obvious interpretation of this procedure is to presume that the mourners feared the potentially malevolent return of the dead. Of the few generalizations that we can make about burial customs one is that cremation, especially where burials are clus-

tered together in flat graves, became more popular. Cremation had always been more frequent in Ireland, Scotland and Wales than in England. In upland areas, too, burials in stone cists were more prevalent. A stronghold of inhumation burials, however, accompanied by beaker pots, was northeast England and eastern Scotland. The total number of barrows and cairns has never been accurately counted; it is estimated, however, that there are between thirty and forty thousand in England and Wales alone.

England

The most famous barrows from England are those 100 or so examples that make up the Wessex group. These cluster in Wiltshire (Pl 57), Berkshire, Hampshire and Dorset (Pl 65) and are characterized by unusual barrow forms and grave goods of sophisticated metalwork. They have sometimes been seen as the burials of a group of warlord-chiefs who might have been responsible for the final phases of Stonehenge. The barrows tend to concentrate in cemeteries, sometimes clearly expanding from a founder's barrow. The structure of these barrows usually includes a stack of turf covering the central burial, and in some cases a pre-mound arrangement of wooden fences. The burial itself was generally an inhumation, placed in a grave pit and contained in a wooden coffin. Notable among the Wessex burials is that from the Bush Barrow, in the Wilsford cemetery south of Stonehenge (Fig 22).

The body in the Bush Barrow was that of a male, laid out on his back on the surface of the ground beneath the barrow. The body was accompanied by metal daggers and a bronze axe; one dagger was of copper, the other of bronze while the third disintegrated on discovery. In addition, on the chest lay a lozenge-shaped plate of sheet gold, perforated at each end of the long axis, and decorated with a carefully executed geometric design. Further gold items included a miniature version of the lozenge-shaped plate and a belt hook, which was again perforated. Beside the right arm was a perforated stone macehead, no doubt a symbol of the man's authority and prestige. Women appear to have been given equally rich burials. At Manton, near Marlborough in Wiltshire, a female was buried with a rich series of grave goods which included a gold-bound amber pendant, a small halberd, perhaps also a pendant, with a gold shaft and bronze blade, a gold-bound shale bead and a small knife with an amber pommel. There is no consensus among scholars about the reasons for the sophistication of these Wessex burials. Some archaeologists have interpreted them as the result of a migration to the area of warrior-chiefs and their followers; others have imagined that this group managed to control the supply and movement of gold and became all-powerful as a result; yet another school of thought sees the Wessex chiefs leading a dominating band of pastoralists across Salisbury Plain.

Apart from Wessex there are a great number of barrows on Bodmin Moor, Exmoor, Dartmoor and the Mendips. There are about 650 cairns on Dartmoor, with at least 130 of the smaller specimens revealing evidence of a central stone cist. The cists are large enough to have contained crouched

Pl 58. Brenig, Clwyd, Wales. A focal point in the cemetery of round barrows at the Brenig in about 2,000 BC was the ring-cairn. A timber setting and low stone bank enclosed an area for ritual purposes connected, no doubt, with the burial of the dead. One of the round barrows can be seen beyond the ring-cairn.

inhumations, although cremations were certainly placed in some of them. Additional features on many of these sites are the presence of a retaining kerb around the base of the mound, and the remains of stone rows or avenues leading downhill from the cairns, most often following the gentlest slope. Good examples of linear barrow groups are Priddy Nine Barrows and Ashen Hill Barrows on the Mendips.

Not all barrows contained burials. A group of nine mounds at West Heath, West Sussex, was excavated in advance of sand extraction. Mound III was the focal point of the group and was constructed around 2,100 BC. A large turf mound, some 20 m in diameter, was faced with wooden fences, indicated by stake-holes. The mound and fences were, in turn, surrounded by a ditch. Several centuries later, and after the first ditch had silted up, a second ditch was excavated around the mound. No burials were located with either phase of the monument. Six other turf mounds were investigated at West Heath, all without evidence of burials. Only two of the mounds contained cremation burials. Mound VII covered a pit in which was found an urn containing a cremation. Mound VI also sealed a pit which held five urns, of which only one contained a cremation. In addition, two urns with cremations were inserted into the mound during its construction.

Other concentrations of barrows or cairns tend to survive on high ground, or in areas of less intensive farming. Many specimens can be found in the southern Pennines, as well as large numbers on the wolds of Lincolnshire and Yorkshire, and the moors of Yorkshire, Cleveland and Northumbria. Whether this upland bias is an acccurate reflection of their geographical extent at the time of Stonehenge is debatable. Certainly, aerial photography, now revealing many levelled barrows in low-lying areas, is beginning to redress the balance. In the centuries after 1,500 BC, it seems, fewer and fewer new burial mounds were constructed, and additional burials were either placed in the tops of existing mounds or dug into other types of monument such as stone circles, or were arranged in flat, moundless cemeteries. Examples of the latter include sites like Pokesdown in Hampshire, Steyning in Sussex, and, in the north, Garlands, Aglionby and Urswick in Cumbria.

Wales

The distribution of cairns and barrows in Wales shows that human settlement and burial practices were now commonplace throughout the uplands, whereas in the first millennium of farming activity they were largely confined to coastal locations and the Black Mountains of southern Powys. Amongst other things, this must surely indicate that population levels were steadily rising. In England it is usual to discover that a round mound covers a single burial, whether or not additional burials have been inserted into the barrow once constructed. The situation in Wales is different in that barrows and cairns are often found to cover four or more cremations and, where excavation evidence allows, it is possible to demonstrate that these multiple burials have been interred during a single ceremony. The Welsh material also suggests that many of the different styles of cinerary urn, in which the cremated remains were placed, may have been contemporary with one another. For instance, three very different types of pot were found in an apparently single-phase burial mound at Treiorwerth, on Anglesey.

Excavation has also shown that the construction of burial mounds or cairns could be a lengthy affair, with several different stages. The complex of burial monuments at the

Pl 59. Lough Gur, Co. Limerick, Ireland. One of the most impressive stone circles in Ireland, formed by contiguous stones. It has a well-marked entrance and is enclosed by a circular bank. Other stone circles and archaeological sites lie in the vincinity.

northern end of the Brenig reservoir in Clwyd shows that superficially simple barrows may hold the traces of timber mortuary houses, concentric fence lines, palisade slots, stone walls or different mound cappings (Pl 58). This may indicate that some cemetery sites were perhaps dedicated as such before the first burial, and modified and reused for further burials over a number of generations. Wales is also fortunate in having a large number of well preserved upland stone monuments, some comprising an open central space surrounded by a circular kerb or platform of stones. Many of these are close to more orthodox cairn or barrow clusters and a possiblity is that these special sites were locations where ceremonies connected with the funerals, but not actually burials, took place. The area of Halkyn mountain in northeast Clwyd has the largest concentration of barrows in Wales (Fig 24), together with the second largest prehistoric mound in Britain and Ireland, the enormous Gop cairn near Prestatyn (Silbury Hill is the largest). The Gop site is usually assumed to have acted as both a cenotaph and focal site for the great concentration of barrows to the east and south.

Wales possesses a number of burial monuments that incorporate stone cists. These are more commonly a feature of burial sites in Scotland and Ireland. In Wales, cairns can include multiple cists (four or more) and single cists; there are examples, too, of cists without any apparent covering cairn or barrow. South Wales appears to be a centre of the multiple-cist type. An excavated round cairn near Oystermouth, West Glamorgan, had three contemporary cists, while we know that at Plashett, near Laugharne in Dyfed, there was once a cairn with seven or eight cists. The cists could contain either flexed inhumation burials or cremations.

Scotland

The burial tradition in Scotland included a mixture of stone cists, round cairns and flat cemeteries, with round cairns and barrows in the minority. These were either inhumations or cremations, but cremation seems to have become more popular with the passage of time. Numerous incidences of cist

Pl 60 (*opposite*). Stones of Stenness, Orkney, Scotland. Like the Ring of Brodgar, this monument was originally a henge. The stone circle, of which only four out of twelve uprights survive, was made with unshaped slabs of local flagstone, some over 4 m high but only 30 cm thick.

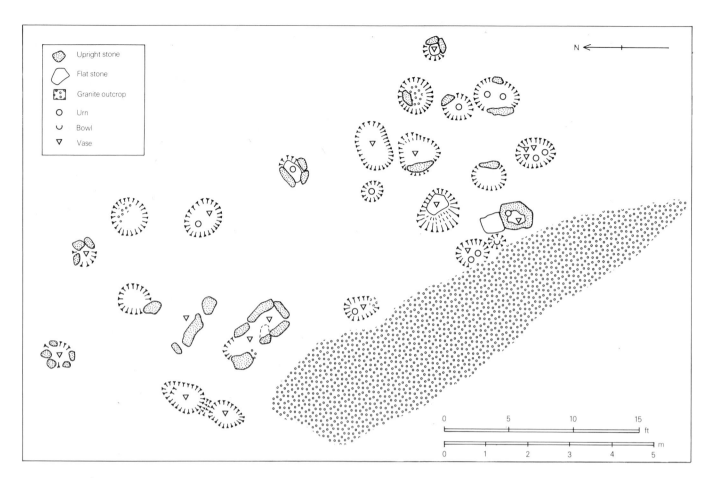

Fig 28. Cloughskelt, Co. Down, Ireland. This small cemetery reveals the complexity of burial traditions. Some graves are formed by stone cists, others are simply pits. There is no coordination, however, between the type of grave and the pottery vessel placed with the deceased.

burials have been excavated. Some are multiple interments in one cist, like the mother and child burial placed with three beakers at Dunnottar in Dumfries and Galloway; or the cist at Horsbrugh Castle Farm, Borders, which contained the bones of a male of about eighteen years of age, covered by a filling of earth which included the cremated remains of three other people. Others are of single individuals, like the crouched skeleton from a cist at Aberdour Road, Dunfermline, Fife, accompanied by a flint knife and a flint strike-a-light. Some of the cists were covered by round mounds or cairns, while others may have been dug into the ground and left unmarked by a covering mound.

Round cairns do constitute an important percentage of burial monuments. When excavated they, too, show structural complexity and stages of enlargement that make them comparable to their counterparts in England and Wales; in eastern Scotland they can be over 40 m in diameter and 6 m high. A group of cairns which rarely contain pottery are the so-called kerb cairns. These are low, round mounds of some 3 to 5 m diameter, frequently edged by large stones taken from the immmediate vicinity. Such cairns may be more numerous in the highland areas of Scotland than was once imagined. Examples include those from Logie Newtown, in

Grampian, Monzie in Tayside, and Claggan in Strathclyde which held central cremation deposits. Several round cairns seem to be associated with standing stones, and there is a remarkable series of standing stones and adjacent cairns near Kilmartin village in Strathclyde. Indeed, close by, an older megalithic tomb at Nether Largie South clearly acted as a focus for a linear cemetery of round cairns, rather like the linear cemeteries built adjacent to long barrows in the Stonehenge area. A massive barrow, of considerable complexity, was constructed at North Mains in Tayside. Six phases of construction were identified by excavation, beginning with a circular timber enclosure that was buried by a mound which incorporated radial fences, boulders, a circular bank and a capping of turf.

Flat cist graves are a striking feature of the regions north of the Tees. These comprise box-like compartments formed by stone slabs, roofed with cap-stones, sunk into pits in the ground and covered over with the upcast. Many seem to be short cists, designed to contain a crouched or flexed body, on its side with the knees drawn to the chest; some also contain cremations, including groups of eight or more individuals in one cist. South of the Tees some graves held wooden coffins, perhaps the wooden equivalents of the stone cists north of the river. There are also numerous flat cremation cemeteries. Extensive examples are to be found on the gravel terrraces of the river Clyde, in north-east Fife and in Grampian. Adjacent to the recumbent stone circle of Loanhead of Daviot in

Grampian, thirty-five individuals were buried within such a cemetery. The burial ground was marked by two shallow ditches, with causeways in the north-east and south-west; the central area contained burials in inverted cinerary urns and in grave-pits.

Ireland

Burials in Ireland during this period appear to be dominated by the practice of burial in individual stone cists or pits, sometimes underneath round mounds, where more than one burial can be found, but also in flat cemeteries, as at Church Bay, Rathlin Island, Co. Antrim. At least three different varieties of funerary pottery are associated with these burials. (Beaker pottery is generally not located in burials in Ireland but rather on settlements.) Both inhumation and cremation were in vogue but, as in England, cremation finally became the more popular rite. The distribution of these graves is much more in evidence on the east side of the country, with concentrations in north-east Ireland. It is tempting to suggest that the new burial tradition was brought into the country by groups sailing from lands further east and settling in the east of Ireland. Contemporary with these arrivals the older type of tomb, as exemplified by the wedge-tomb of western Ireland, may have continued to be built and used by communities resident in the west and undisturbed by the immigrants.

By the time that heavy rimmed urns come into fashion, around 2,000 BC, cremation is the principal form of burial. Instead of the pottery accompanying the deceased, the urns were inverted over the cremated remains and thus became a container for the ashes. Grave goods were now sometimes included, and could comprise miniature pottery vessels, stone battle-axes or bronze razors. The majority of burials were either in pits or in cists; they could be isolated, or form cemeteries, and be both inserted into mounds or comprise flat areas. Occasionally the mounds covered a single burial, but more often they covered more than one, and are thus comparable to contemporary burial mounds in Wales.

An important cemetery that has illustrated the complexity of contemporary burials is that at Cloughskelt, Co. Down (Fig 28). The cemetery is a mixed one, containing both cisted and uncisted graves in a small area less than 15 m in length. In the southern half of the cemetery the graves contained urns while the graves in the northen half produced a different type of grave vessel. However, this did not coincide with the distribution of uncisted and cisted graves. Looking at Ireland as a whole, cemeteries (i.e. more than one grave) with cists account for fifty-three per cent of all cemeteries, those without cists amount to twenty per cent, while the mixed variety, like Cloughskelt, account for nineteen per cent. The cisted graves and cemeteries are generally distributed all over the east side of the country, while the uncisted types occur mainly in the north-east. Some of the differences in burial practice in Ireland must be due solely to popular styles, some to chronological differences, and some to the preferences of separate communities. The break with the previous communal tradition in large stone tombs, and its

replacement with burials in smaller, individual containers, however, is very apparent.

Farms and Fields

The many burial mounds that spread like a rash over the face of the landscape had mostly been built by about 1,500 BC. Their very profusion suggests that the distribution of settlements, of farms and their fields, and even villages, must have been equally dense (Fig 27). Indeed, the picture is slowly emerging of a gradual increase in settlements. Relatively few farms are known from when the first stone circles were being set up, but by about 1,500 BC there are examples of houses and fields, from coastal locations right up into the uplands of Wales. Some of the farms are enclosed within palisades or walls, others are open groups of huts; the majority do not seem to have been constructed or sited with any special

Fig 29. Shaugh Moor, Dartmoor, Southern England. The stone enclosure at Shaugh Moor was occupied from about 1,400 BC until 600 BC. Circular stone huts were probably the main domestic buildings, with ancillary structures formed by the smaller rectangular units. The internal lay-out of the enclosure was altered through the centuries.

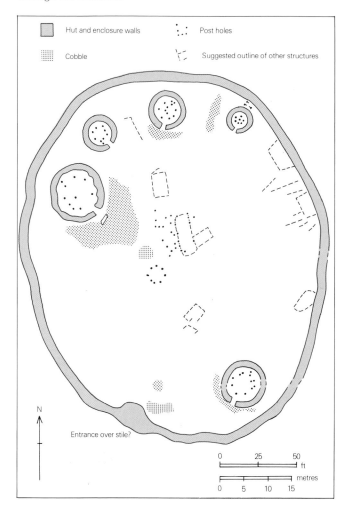

Pl 61. Ring of Brodgar, Orkney, Scotland. This is the finest and biggest stone circle in Scotland. It lies within the bank and ditch of a henge monument, which is 142 m in diameter and has two opposing entrances.

defensive need in mind. There is enormous variety in the form and layout of the settlements, although round-houses are particularly common (Pl 66). (Round-houses, circular roofed structures of timber and stone, are a common occurrence on settlements of the later prehistoric period. Not all of them were houses, however. Some may have been used for storage, or for ceremonial purposes, while others may have been for specific purposes, such as eating or sleeping). In southern England some of the farms are associated with blocks of rectangular fields, each on average about 0.4 ha in area, the whole sometimes covering as much as 9 ha. The following examples give some idea of the different types.

England

In the coastal sands of Gwithian, Cornwall, two superimposed houses were discovered, containing fragments of beaker pottery. The earlier structure was circular in shape, with a diameter of 4.5 m and wall lines defined by individual post-holes; a central post may have supported the roof, which covered an off-centre hearth. The later house was 7.6 m in diameter. Both houses had been positioned within palisaded enclosures, and the evidence suggests that there may have been an interval of no more than fifty years between them. The resident farmers seem to have supported themselves by mixed farming and shellfish collection.

The extent of agricultural organization and landscape division is exemplified by Dartmoor after 1,500 BC (Fig 26 & Pl 63). Here the landscape was divided into ten or so units of unequal size. Each block contained valley land, hill-slope and upland grazing. The largest identifiable unit is that around Rippon Tor on the eastern side of Dartmoor. It covers some 3,300 ha (about 6 by 6 km) and incorporates several settlements. The divisions were carried out by building stone walls, or reaves, across the land to separate one area from another. These have been dated by the radiocarbon method. This incredible feat of partition seems to have been carried

Pl 62. Ring of Brodgar, Orkney, Scotland. The Comet Stone lies some 150 m to the south-east of the henge and stone circle. Even from here you can appreciate that there are numerous different sight-lines between the Comet Stone and particular stones in the circle.

out as a result of one planning decision, not as the outcome of organic growth of land enclosure. Farms within the system are either single circular houses or groups of round and rectangular structures within enclosing walls (Fig 29). Other major areas of contemporary upland farming were in the Peak District of Derbyshire and on the North York Moors.

Some of the best-known farms, constructed after 1,500 BC, are situated on the chalk downs of Wessex and Sussex. Typically such farms might contain four or five circular timber buildings, sometimes sited on terraces cut back into the downland slopes. The huts were occasionally grouped within an enclosing bank and ditch, outlining an area up to 50 m across. These farms were often associated with groups of fields, sometimes separated by field banks, droveways and trackways. In some cases round burial mounds lay close by

and it is possible to conjure up a coherent picture of agricultural life and death. One location where this is feasible is at Black Patch, Alciston, in East Sussex. In the vicinity of a group of burial mounds, five round-houses have been excavated, with attendant storage pits containing a considerable quantity of primitive emmer wheat and hulled barley. Cattle and sheep were kept and deer hunted for venison. Weaving was obviously carried out in one of the huts since a number of clay loom weights were discovered. This is one of the earliest examples of the evidence for weaving in a domestic context. It must be presumed, however, from the presence of pins and cloth fasteners in graves, that woven cloth was present in Britain well before 2,000 BC. Not all habitation sites were enclosed, as is suggested by the open huts at Chalton in Hampshire.

The importance of livestock can be demonstrated by the extensive fields revealed at Fengate, near Peterborough. Once again deliberate and large-scale planning can be illustrated. The system of rectangular enclosures and droveways extended for at least 2,500 m along the fen edge, and for some

Pl 63. Grimspound, Devon, England. This village, on the edge of Dartmoor, has a dry-stone wall perimeter which probably stood to a height of 2 m. The stone foundations of two dozen round-houses are visible in the interior. Each house contained a hearth, and several had raised areas that were probably sleeping benches.

1,500 m inland. Some of the enclosures contained wells and seem to have been used as flood-free paddocks for the pasturing of livestock during winter. The focus of the settlement was a circular ditch within which was a house. The farmers at Fengate seem to have indulged in a certain amount of hunting, as the bones of deer indicate.

Wales

The uplands of Wales are littered with the stone remains of field walls, clearance cairns and small rectangular and circular huts. There is a long tradition of pasturing cattle and sheep in the uplands during the summer, and wintering on lowland farms. It is, therefore, quite possible that some of these date from the time that stone circles were being erected on adjacent hills. Many examples of potentially early sites, as yet unexcavated, lie in the area between the Great Orme and the Lleyn peninsula in Gwynedd. The most typical complex is at Cwm Ffrydlas, near Llanllechid, at an altitude of some 440 m above sea level. The settlement consisted of nine circular or oval huts and five round clearance cairns, small piles of stones gathered to clear areas for pasture or cultivation, together with a well developed arrangement of irregular fields. A similar complex is that at Pentre Llyn Cymmer in Clwyd, where an upland hut and associated enclosure have been securely dated by radiocarbon samples to before 1,000 BC. A different, and much earlier, architectural tradition is demonstrated by the discovery of two small and roughly square timber huts beneath adjacent burial mounds on a ridge-top at Trelystan in Powys. Each hut had a central hearth with pits dug into the floor and was built before 2,000 BC. The presence of only wild plant remains in the huts may suggest seasonal occupation.

Lowland equivalents of these upland farms are more difficult to find. At Mount Pleasant in Glamorgan a stone and post structure was discovered beneath a later burial mound. The house was rectangular in shape, measuring 5.7 by 3.3 m and was presumably covered with a pitched roof. Not everyone, however, even by 2,500 BC, had come to rely on farming as a way of life. Just as there are pockets of hunters and gatherers surviving today in isolated parts of the world, so too little bands of hunters clung tenaciously to their old ways in the later prehistoric period. A collection of stone tools and a midden or rubbish heap containing limpet shells and animal bones at Ty Mawr on Anglesey would appear to be evidence for one survival, comparable to other sites of similar date in the Western Isles of Scotland.

Scotland

Many unenclosed round-houses have been located by field work on the northern and eastern sides of the Cheviot hills in

Scotland, at altitudes up to 380 m, complementing those already known from the upper Clyde and Tweed valleys. The number of houses in individual settlements varies from one to about eighteen, (although not all need be contemporary), with the average being about four or five. Some houses are strung out along the contours, while others form more tightly-clustered groups. Often the settlements are associated with some indication of land clearance, either in the form of small clearance cairns or linear field banks. Whether these fields were for arable or simply used for grazing is difficult to ascertain. Most unenclosed hut groups with land clearance are sited on south-facing, and warmer, slopes. A key excavated site of this type, dating from about 1,200 BC, is that at Green Knowe in the upper Tweed valley in Tweeddale. An earlier, but altogether different site, lies just east of Green Knowe at Meldon Bridge. Here, at some time before 2,000 BC a massive timber wall, over 500 m in length, cut off a gravel promontory between two river valleys, enclosing ritual sites, burial areas and possibly a settlement. This is one of the relatively few examples of apparent defence works from this period, although an enclosure for ritual purposes cannot be discounted.

In the north of Scotland, particularly in Caithness and Sutherland, unenclosed platform settlements are a feature of the upland landscape, again concentrating on south-facing slopes. Huts seem to have been small in size and, in the absence of visible stone remains, built of timber. Further north, on the western side of Shetland, an agricultural landscape of six irregular fields, three houses, a burial cairn and numerous clearance cairns lies at Scourd of Brouster. Generations of farmers seem to have occupied this site between 3,000 and 2,000 BC.

In the Western Isles, on Arran, excavation at Machrie Moor has shown that the area within and around the stone circles was divided, more than once, by wooden fences, and ploughed. At Callanish on Lewis narrow spade or hoe dug cultivation ridges of this period have been found. How extensive these fields and plots were is difficult to determine, given the limited areas excavated. Ridges for cultivation may have been used to improve drainage and raise soil temperatures for cereal cultivation.

Ireland

By 2,500 BC the great mound at Newgrange had started to slip over the decorated kerbstones surrounding it. After these first signs of decay, a small settlement grew up in the shadow of the monument. The inhabitants built rectangular houses of wood and wattle, with roofs of thatch. The newcomers used beaker pottery, and left behind for archaeologists a variety of stone tools, including axes, and a bronze axe.

Pl 64. Rudston, Humberside, England. The tallest standing stone in Britain towers to some 7.8 m and weighs 26 t. It was fashioned from gritstone and hauled from Cayton Bay some 16 km away. Three cursuses converge on Rudston and this pillar was clearly a focal point in a ritual landscape.

Pl 65. Maiden Castle, Dorset, England. Half a kilometre north of the later hillfort stands a conical chalk round barrow, surrounded by fields. If not protected, barrows like these are gradually levelled and spread by annual ploughing.

Numerous animal bones were retrieved, predominantly those of cattle and pig. Horse bones were also located and it is about this time that horse riding may have become a form of transport.

Some time before 2,000 BC a number of settlements had also become established on the sand-dunes of north-eastern Ireland. When excavated, these show up as black layers of organic refuse against the light-coloured sand. On the sandy spit of Murlough, Co. Down, within 200 m of the modern shore, two post-built structures were uncovered. More permanent signs of occupation were located in Co. Antrim at Whitepark Bay (Pl 24). Twenty circular timber huts were uncovered at the centre of the bay; fourteen of these were in a rough line some 500 m long and parallel to the shore; six others stood behind. The economy of the inhabitants of these coastal sites seems to have been one that utilized shellfish, such as oyster, mussel, periwinkle, limpet and cockle. Beach and cliff flint was used for the manufacture of implements. Similar pottery has been found on both the Irish sites and settlements on the Isle of Man. A post-built structure at Ronaldsway, for instance, was located a short distance above the line of the raised beach, and measured some 7.3 m by 4 m, with a central hearth. Another connection with the Isle of Man is demonstrated by the number of elongated flint flakes found at sites in the lower Bann valley, between Lough Neagh and Kilrea, and also at several Manx settlements. These are thought to be for arming fish-spears, used during the summer in the temporary camp sites of fishermen.

In south-west Ireland, the light limestone soils around Lough Gur, Co. Limerick, continued to be attractive for settlement. At one location, on the promontory of Knockadoon, three circular timber houses were discovered, each about 5 m in diameter and containing a central hearth. The limestone soils had preserved many animal bones, of which ninety-five per cent were of ox, four per cent pig and the few

Pl 66. Merrivale, Devon, England. The stone foundations are all that survive of this prehistoric round-house. Thousands of similar sites can be found in the uplands of Britain suggesting agricultural expansion in these areas around 1,500 BC

remaining either of sheep or goat. Other approximately contemporary settlements have been excavated at Downpatrick in Co. Down. Two round-houses, with diameters of 4 m and almost 7.5 m respectively were uncovered there. Futher south, at Carrigillihy, Co. Cork, an oval house measuring 11 by 7.2 m, made of earth and stones and faced with boulders, and standing within an oval walled enclosure, may also have been in use at this time.

Excavating Enigmas

Whatever advances are made in the future in archaeological excavation techniques, certain sites will always stubbornly refuse to yield satisfactory answers about their function and purpose. This is not altogether surprising. After all, archaeological remains are usually incomplete, with any organic elements long since decayed; nor is there any contemporary literature to tell us about their use . The task of explanation is therefore considerable. Imagine trying to work out the rules of cricket simply from the holes in the ground where the stumps last stood. Here are five such archaeological enigmas (Fig 27).

Silbury Hill is an enormous circular mound of chalk, covering an area of some 2.2 ha and standing 40 m high (Pl 70). It lies close to the stone circle and henge at Avebury, and is the largest prehistoric man-made mound in Europe. Its construction took place in three stages and started around 2,500 BC. First a small primary mound of turf and gravel about 36 m in diameter was constructed. This was subsequently covered in a mound of chalk rubble quarried from an encircling ditch. Before many years had elapsed another and larger ditch was dug to provide chalk for the massive mound seen today. The final mound had a stepped profile during construction, presumably to prevent collapse, each step later being filled in with soil to give a smooth profile. The top step was never concealed in this way, and is still visible. The changes in design of this monument seem to echo those that occurred at Stonehenge. Its purpose, however, is unknown. Despite tunnelling, both horizontally and vertically, no burials have been located in it. It has been calculated that its varying stages of construction would have involved 500 men working every day for ten years. Whatever the purpose of their labours, Silbury Hill still guards their secret.

Standing stones and stone rows are among the more enigmatic stone monuments (Pls 64 & 69). Standing stones are distributed over western Britain and Ireland, often as single stones, but sometimes in groups. No convincing explanation can yet be suggested for them, and it is likely that not all had the same function. As we have seen, some stones in the west of Scotland are claimed to have significance for astronomical sighting, while others have been suggested as markers indicating the lines of prehistoric cross-country routes. A rare excavated example is that at Stackpole Warren in Dyfed,

Pl 67. The Badger Stone, West Yorkshire, England. A large coarse-grit rock on Rombalds Moor is finely carved with cup and ring marks. The decoration, which occurs on more than one face, totals some ninety-five simple cups, three cups with two rings and fourteen cups with one ring.

which was partially surrounded by a setting of hundreds of tiny vertical stones. Some standing stones may have marked boundaries, others undoubtedly were like gravestones. At the base of a standing stone at Try, near Penzance in Cornwall, a burial accompanied by a beaker was located; at Onvell in Fife cremation burials have been found in the sockets of standing stones. It is exceedingly difficult to date a standing stone just by looking at it. Some may even be cattle-rubbing posts set up quite recently by farmers for their itchy livestock. Stone rows present similar problems. They share the same distribution, and some of them are associated with henges or stone circles, as at Avebury or Callanish. There are at least seventy known in south-west England, the majority on Dartmoor. They occur as single rows or double or more complex patterns. Some of the rows are of considerable length, running to more than 2 km. Again, functions are difficult to ascertain, but boundaries or processional ways are the best hypotheses. They may have something in common with a type of long monument known as a cursus, to which we now turn.

The cursus monument comprises a pair of parallel linear ditches with internal banks, closed off at the ends. There are over thirty examples known, mostly from southern England. The longest is the Dorset cursus, which runs for nearly 10 km across the chalk downlands and was laid out some time after 3,000 BC. Close examination of this cursus has revealed that it is really two monuments joined end to end. The Springfield cursus, in Essex, is more typical, being some 700 m in length, with ditches about 40 m apart. Often the cursus seems to incorporate earlier burial monuments in its design. At Stonehenge one end is aligned on a long burial mound. The Dorset cursus incorporates two long mounds, while that at Dorchester-on-Thames, Oxfordshire, crosses a small rectangular mortuary enclosure. At Rudston, Humberside, three cursus monuments surround the modern village, suggesting a carefully delimited ritual area or landscape. The name cursus derives from the nineteenth-century idea that they were prehistoric racing tracks. More recently the possibility of processional ways has been aired. It seems more likely, however, that the carefully aligned rectangular enclosures were in some way utilized for astronomical observations. Probably related to the cursus are the double alignments of pits (often closed at one end) known from southern Scotland.

Burnt mounds occur in increasing numbers after 2,000 BC, and indeed continued to be used in Ireland into the early centuries AD. They are distributed thickly in Ireland, and there are concentrations in southern England, the Midlands, parts of Wales and the Northern Isles; they are being found in increasing numbers in south-west and northern Scotland. The sites are characteristically marked by heaps of burnt stones which adjoin areas where activity took place, the focus of which is a large trough. In Ireland these troughs are made of wood, in the Northern Isles of stone. They appear to have held water which was heated by dropping hot stones into the trough. Some of the complexes are quite substantial. At Liddle, on Orkney, just such a trough, 1.6 by 0.62 m deep, was incorporated in an elaborate oval building. This still retained many of its fittings, including a large hearth and

Pl 68. Stonehenge, Wiltshire, England. Sarsen blocks were dragged from the Marlborough Downs and arranged into trilithons (two uprights joined by a lintel). The lintels were held in place by stone mortice and tenon joints, a technique borrowed from wood-working.

slab-built boxes and compartments, some of which may be beds. Excavation of a burnt mound at Cob Lane, in south Birmingham, uncovered a vertical-sided pit 0.8 m deep and an adjacent oval hollow. The pit was interpreted as the water tank, and the hollow as a hearth in which stones were heated. This mound was in use around 1,500 BC. Different explanations have been put forward for these fascinating sites. Some have argued that they were temporary cooking places, although the Orkney examples look more like structures associated with permanent settlement. Another hypothesis suggests that they are the prehistoric equivalent of the Scandinavian sauna and steam bath, or the North American Indian sweat houses.

Cup and ring is a general term for carvings on rock which are composed of small hollows (cups), with or without surrounding grooves (rings) (Pl 67). They are most common in northern Britain and Ireland, with particular concentrations in Derbyshire, Yorkshire, Northumberland, south-west Scotland, the Forth-Clyde isthmus, Argyll, Inverness, south-west and north-west Ireland. The majority seem to have been executed between 2,500 BC and 1,500 BC. Cup and rings were pecked into the surface of rock outcrops, often over large areas, and then rubbed smooth. Although the essential design element is simple, the cup and rings appear in a variety of different combinations. Cup and ring markings, and even more so cup marks on their own, are also found on the stones of some stone circles. This particularly applies to the stone circles around the burial mounds near Inverness, and to the recumbent stone circles and related ring monuments of eastern Scotland. Some idea of the great numbers of cup and ring markings can be provided by the survey of Rombalds Moor in West Yorkshire, which recorded some 286 rocks carved in this way. No conclusive explanation has yet been proposed for these carvings. Given the simplicity of the principal motif and the complexity of their varying combinations this is perhaps to be expected. Among the more likely suggestions are that they represent astronomical diagrams, maps and plans of settlements, or records of families and burials.

Culture Crash

Picture, then, Britain and Ireland in the centuries before 2,000 BC. The population was ruled by priests who guaranteed its welfare through communication with the Gods. Stone circles and henges were the great centres where the mystical rites of astronomical observation and prediction were demonstrated by successive generations of the priesthood. The old order was challenged, however, by some powerful secular leaders who managed to grasp temporal control and secure their positions by controlling the production and distribution of the new technology – the mining, smelting and casting of copper and bronze. The new chiefs controlled the use of this novel technology by their domination of a caste of magic men who could turn stone into liquid, and back again into something much harder. The burial mounds of such chiefs and their successors shone chalk-white on the warm, rolling landscape of southern England. For the masses life was spent on the farm, building and repairing round timber houses, and tending stock and

Pl 69 (*above*). Merrivale, Devon, England. Dartmoor contains around sixty stone rows, and three of them can be seen at Merrivale.

Pl 70. Silbury Hill, Wiltshire, England. This is the largest man-made prehistoric mound in Europe. The slight shoulder near the top of the mound shows the stepped nature of its construction.

crops in small, rectangular fields. The mild climate meant that mixed farming was viable in the uplands well beyond 300 m, and beyond the normal limits of farming today.

After 1,100 BC, however, climatic conditions began to deteriorate sharply, intiating a decline which continued for the next few centuries. A colder, wetter, more unsettled period began in which mean temperatures fell nearly 2°C, reducing the length of the growing season by more than five weeks. The agricultural base of the society began to disintegrate, and upland farms and their fields became deserted. Soils began to acidify; peat encroached and gradually buried many upland settlements. Absolute population levels must have fallen and the economic surplus, which had supported the chiefs, dwindled. Immigrants or traders introduced new types of bronze weapon and the position of many existing leaders must have been eroded. Stone circles lay abandoned in the uplands. The new society that was taking shape would be radically different from its predecessor. Economic security would now be provided by strong defence and new weapons. Religious welfare would become the prerogative of a class of priests who communicated with the underworld through springs and rivers. Prestige was there to be won by the warrior. The age of the heroes was about to begin.

Chapter 4
Homes of the Heroes
c 1,100 BC–AD 43

Troubled Times

The two centuries either side of 1,100 BC were ones of crisis and change, so much so that the communities that eventually emerged were of a fundamentally different character from their predecessors. The causes of this transformation are difficult to assess. Clearly Britain and Ireland were not unaffected by events taking place further afield. The eastern Mediterranean had been thrown into turmoil by the raiding of the Peoples of The Sea. These pirates were mentioned in Egyptian records, for they were the maritime enemies of the Egyptians. A great famine had struck Turkey in the thirteenth century BC, resulting in emigration westwards over the sea; Sicily, Sardinia and Etruria are all named after contemporary Middle Eastern peoples. Mycenean collapse had plunged Greece into the Dark Ages. In addition, the eruption of Mount Hekla on Iceland in around 1,150 BC released an estimated 12 cubic km of volcanic dust into the atmosphere, reducing sunlight and having a major impact on the growth of trees. The effect was felt in Ireland where the widths of oak tree-rings decreased significantly around 1,150 BC. Reverberations of these upheavals must have spread throughout central Europe as folk migrations led to a widespread uniformity of burial rite: cremation in extensive cemeteries of urns. It is quite possible that some refugees from the mainland crossed the Channel to settle in Britain.

The growing need for bronze in lowland Britain, where deposits of both copper and tin are few, had led by this time to increased trade with Europe, both to secure finished artefacts and to acquire quantities of scrap metal for recycling. The discovery of a shipwreck in Langdon Bay, Kent, just outside the modern port of Dover, is a remarkable example of such links. The vessel had probably been bound for England carrying a cargo of bronze implements and scrap metal; the objects were French in origin and of a type rarely found in Britain. These rare finds afford a glimpse of a prehistoric activity that is easily forgotten, given the number and diversity of archaeological sites on land. Maritime amd riverine traffic must have been commonplace in the later prehistoric period, yet little of this aspect of daily life survives.

Britain and Ireland suffered their own equally catastrophic disturbances through changing environmental factors. In the preceding five hundred years both islands had experienced a spread of pioneer farming into both upland and lowland zones, so much so that population levels had probably risen considerably. New settlements were often founded on marginal lands where agriculture and pastoralism could just be sustained given stable climatic conditions. But the conditions did not remain stable for long. Slowly, the climate began to worsen, not by much and not suddenly, but disastrously all the same. Annual average temperature fell by about 2°C; and there was more rainfall and wind. Farming in the uplands became gradually more and more difficult. The growing season became shorter; the ground became waterlogged – a natural consequence of greater precipitation, compounded by the felling in the previous centuries of so many of the trees which would have helped reduce waterlogging through transpiration. Soils which had previously been fertile brown earths, similar to the good garden soil of today, now became leached, losing mineral content, some of which formed a hard iron pan layer beneath the topsoil. The sodden surface could not break down the growing carpet of leaf and grass litter, which slowly rotted down into peat and bog. The pioneer farmsteads and fields, that had been built with high hopes and laid out with care, constructed from boulders gathered in from the fields where the last ice-sheets had stranded them, were now deserted. Their roofs fell in, the walls collapsed, rushes colonized what once had been nutritious pasture; in time, some disappeared altogether, covered by a blanket of acid peat.

Flood-water, by contrast, was the greatest threat to low-lying settlements. Increased rainfall in the uplands meant rivers running at full spate, exacerbating the difficulties of lowland drainage, depositing layers of alluvium and silt, meandering uncontrollably. Once-fertile farmland now lay permanently or seasonally under water, and hapless communities were forced to retreat onto more elevated ground. The extent of habitable ground had therefore contracted, with progressive abandonment of the uplands and the extreme lowlands, and a retreat to the higher and drier sides

Pl 71. Bury Ditches, Shropshire, England. Low sunlight helps to pick out the arrangement of multiple banks and ditches that defend the fort interior. The in-turned entrance at the top of the fort can be seen clearly, while, in the foreground, note how the defensive ramparts are carried on past the entrance, preventing any direct approach to the gates.

of river valleys. Water was the malevolent spirit, the curse of the displaced and the cause of the disaster. Little wonder, therefore, that in the succeeding centuries of the first millennium BC it was to the Gods of Water that placatory offerings were made. Sacred springs, wells and pools became places of veneration, and offerings were made in appeasement. Great quantities of costly metalwork were thrown into some rivers, no doubt at the ecstatic culmination of seasonal and annual ceremonies. Perhaps these offerings were designed to show the strength of the community's reverence for its particular water deity, to ensure his or her continuing powers of intercession on the community's behalf. Most of the religious fervour and ritual endeavour seems to have been channelled in this direction, so much so that the thousands of burial monuments containing the ashes and bones of the distant ancestors became neglected. In fact, for several centuries from about 1,000 BC formal burial disappears almost entirely from the archaeological record. We cannot be certain that a widespread burial practice which would leave no material trace – such as corpse exposure in trees or disposal in rivers – was not adopted, but on balance it seems reasonable to suggest

that concern with the living had in some ways replaced caring for the dead.

The most obvious indication of these troubled times was the gradual appearance of hill-top settlements, on sites chosen for their natural defensive possiblities and augmented through time by the construction of large, artificial defences. A new breed of warriors arose, who were capable of defending territories and their followers, and who inhabited fortifications whose defences were periodically strengthened or elaborated. As the population level gradually rose again, increased population density in the more limited area for farming must have heightened the possibilities of friction, and raiding may have become an endemic characteristic of society. Some of the new warrior-chiefs seemingly ruled over large tracts of ground, criss-crossed or delimited by linear earthworks superimposed on an earlier pattern of much smaller fields. Cattle ranching, supplemented by rustling, would appear to have become the mainstay of farming in some areas. Warriors needed weapons and very soon a range of new types appeared, including round shields, swords, spears and various kinds of horse fittings. Some of the weaponry was not just for display. At Tormarton, in Avon, the remains of two young men were found buried in a pit or ditch. The pelvis of one had been pierced by a bronze spearhead. The second body had a similar hole through the pelvis, traces of a severe blow to the head and a bronze spearhead embedded in his spine.

Pl 72. Old Oswestry, Shropshire, England. Formidable defences of ramparts and ditches surround the slight rise on which sat the hillfort. The first settlement of timber round-houses was undefended, but the later stone huts were protected by these impressive earthworks.

Homes of the Heroes

One of the most distinctive traits of the archaeology of the ten centuries before the Roman conquest is the appearance of fortified hill-top settlements, or hillforts (Fig 35). These evocative sites, often set in rugged or undulating countryside of considerable beauty, and ringed by commanding and impressive defensive earthworks, are unevenly distributed over Britain and Ireland. Where they occur, they hint at the underlying insecurity of these times, the warlike nature of the leaders of society, and the heroic apsect of raiding and warfare. For some hillforts surely were the homes of the heroes.

There are more than two thousand hillforts in Britain. These fortified enclosures are normally not less than 0.2 ha in area. The fortifications usually comprise a defensive bank or rampart with an external ditch. There can be a single line of defences (univallate) or a concentric arrangement of two or more banks and ditches (multivallate). The banks are generally constructed of earth or stone, dug or quarried from the ditch, and sometimes faced or strengthened by the use of turf, timber or dry-stone walling.

Hillforts can be divided into minor forts (those enclosing less than 1.2 ha) and major forts (those larger than 1.2 ha). Minor forts are predominantly found only in Cornwall, south-west Wales, northern England and southern Scotland. Major forts occur in a dense band from the Dorset coast to the Mersey estuary, with another concentration in the Cotswolds. It is clear, however, that factors other than the avaiablity of suitable hills affected the distribution of hillforts. There is, for example, a relative scarcity of forts on the Pennines. Small and large forts occur together in some areas, especially, for instance, in the central Welsh borders (Pl 72).

Hillforts can be divided into three principal groups on the basis of differences in siting:

1. Hillforts which rely on natural defences, in the form of cliffs or steep slopes, for most of their perimeter, with only short stretches of man-made defences. These include cliff-edge forts, promontory forts and ridge forts.

Pl 73. Mam Tor, Derbyshire, England. One of the earliest dated hillforts lies deep in the heart of the Peak District at Mam Tor. At some 500 m above sea-level the site seems unlikely to have been occupied all year round.

2. Hillforts which are completely enclosed by man-made defences which follow the contour of the terrain and improve its natural advantages. These can all be termed contour forts.

3. Hillforts where man-made defences extend around the whole perimeter, but where the siting does not seem to exploit natural advantages for tactical strength very effectively, if at all.

In Ireland the number of hillforts is surprisingly small, amounting to about fifty sites. Irish hillforts can also be divided into three main categories:

1. Simple univallate sites of earth or stone, with or without an accompanying ditch.

2. Sites on hill-tops or cliff-tops with widely spaced, multivallate defences.

3. Inland promontory forts.

The use of stone in some of the Irish forts is broadly comparable to the general stone-building traditions of hillforts found in western Scotland, parts of Wales and Cornwall.

115

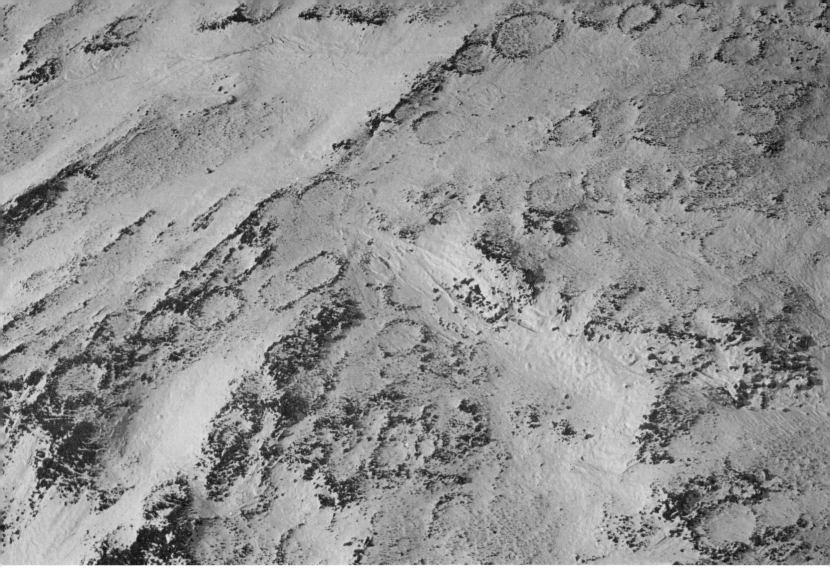

Pl 74. Craig Rhiwarth, Powys, Wales. A covering of snow over the interior of this hillfort highlights the numerous stone foundations of round-houses. Note that some of the houses are larger than others, while some seem to have been rebuilt over earlier examples.

Defences around hillforts could take the form of wooden palisades, dump banks or wall-ramparts (whether with a stone facing, or merely with a timber frame filled with rubble or compacted earth). On many sites ramparts were rebuilt in different forms over several centuries, producing a complex sequence of defence development. Often wooden palisades represent the first period of construction; these are sometimes superseded by a more elaborate vertically-faced wall-rampart which in turn may give way to a sloping-faced dump-rampart. The archaeologist excavating the defences of a hillfort must therefore be prepared to encounter and unravel the different phases of modification. To that end a reasonable length of rampart, say 15 m or more, must be investigated if all the constructional details are to be recovered.

The weakest point of any defensive circuit is the entrance, and considerable efforts were made to protect hillfort gateways. These included the provision of additional outer earthworks so that any would-be attacker was forced to take an oblique or serpentine course towards the gate, at the same time exposing himself to flanking fire from defenders (Pl 71).

Guard-chambers also became a standard feature of some hillfort entrances. Indeed, the sophistication of design suggests that hillfort architecture may have been a specialist occupation. Generally, wall-ramparts are associated with short, narrow passages leading to timber gates which constrict the approach of an attacker. Such entrances can be tactically linked to the use of short-range defensive weapons such as the sword, axe and spear. On the other hand dump ramparts are breached by entrances set back behind the rampart and approached by long, in-turned passages where the attacker has to run down a narrow corridor flanked on both sides by the rampart before reaching the gates. This fundamental change in design seems to be correlated with the development of long-range missile weapons, such as slings, in the last centuries BC.

Interiors of hillforts, when excavated, usually produce evidence of one or more of the following features: rectangular buildings, round buildings (Pl 74), open spaces, pits and four-posters – small square or rectangular structures usually presumed to have had raised floors. The function of these features cannot always be determined by excavation. However, a consensus holds that some of the circular and rectangular timber buildings must have been for habitation, while others may have been for storage. The pits and four-posters are often interpreted, albeit with some reservations, as storage units for grain or other agricultural produce. As we shall see below, some hillfort interiors show elements of formal planning in their layout, which suggests that the skills of hillfort architects were not confined to the defences.

Who lived in hillforts? This most important question is one of the most difficult to answer. We have speculated that warrior-chiefs and their warlike followers must have made up one class of the the resident population. But did such powerful figures only occupy the larger forts, or the smaller ones too? Did they live there all year round, or just for some of the year? Did priests, craftsmen and nobles also reside in hillforts, at least part of the time? And did the surrounding populace take refuge inside the fortifications, fleeing there from outlying farms, in times of trouble? The problem is compounded by the great differences in the sizes of hillforts, and the fact that some developed through the centuries, while others were built, occupied for varying lengths of time and then abandoned early on, say around 300 BC. Clearly each hillfort may not have fulfilled exactly the same function. What can be demonstrated is that some hillforts protected a food store that must have been gathered in, or given by, the surrounding population; a food store that in quantity was far in excess of the needs of the hillfort occupants. Others may have been places of trade, while others were chiefly seats or communal centres of power. We can now turn to some individual hillforts in each country.

England

One of the earliest dated hillforts lies deep in the heart of the Peak District, the 6 ha site at Mam Tor (Pl 73). Lying at some 500 m above sea level and snow-covered for much of the winter, the fort does not seem ideally suited for year-round occupation. Yet within the simple ditch and dump constructed rampart the remains of two timber round-houses have been located, along with some coarse bucket-shaped pottery, fragments of shale bracelets, whetstones and part of a bronze socketed axe. Dating evidence suggests that this hill-top refuge was in use some time before 1,000 BC, although the defences may have been constructed at a later date, since the many unexcavated hut-platforms which mark its interior also occur in smaller numbers outside the defensive line.

Another early fortified enclosure of similar date lies at Rams Hill in Berkshire. Here, an early sequence of defences started with a stone-faced rampart, followed by a timber facing and palisade, with an in-turned timber entrance. In the interior of the fort were shallow pits, a trackway and traces of huts, indicating domestic occupation of a seasonal duration. Pottery from the site represented such a diversity of fabrics, drawn from a wide hinterland that it has been suggested that the enclosure also acted as a regional exchange-centre. It is possible that Rams Hill controlled the adjacent open grassland which was divided by long, linear ditch systems.

The promontory fort of Crickley Hill in Gloucestershire is a good example of an early hillfort. Here, possibly before 600 BC, defences were constructed across the neck of the promontory. In the interior a series of long, rectangular buildings was erected, surrounded by the more common four-posters.

However, these structures only stood for a century or so, before the hillfort was attacked and taken. It seems that a new group of people took over the site and remodelled both the interior and the defences. The newcomers built timber round-houses inside, while the defensive ramparts were enlarged, and the principal gate protected by the addition of an outwork pierced by a separate entrance. A particularly large round-house, perhaps for the chief, lay just inside the entrance. Many of the smaller hillforts in Britain seem to have been abandoned in favour of large, developed forts which continued in occupation until the Roman conquest. Certainly this appears to be the case at Crickley, which became deserted some time before 400 BC.

On the Downs in Sussex there are three developed hillforts: Cissbury, Torberry and the Trundle, with internal areas of 20, 2.5 and 4 ha respectively. At Cissbury and the Trundle the circuit of the defences comprised a massive rampart and ditch. At Torberry the hillfort defences were remodelled at least three times. The first phase consisted of a rampart, with a single gap entrance, which cut off the neck of the promontory and defined the original defended area. In the following phase the defences were continued around the summit of the hill. The third phase saw the extension of the defences to include an additional 1.5 ha. The ramparts were now equipped with a more sophisticated entrance which involved a defended corridor. This entrance was later rebuilt on a more massive scale, perhaps anticipating hostilities, since the gate was deliberately slighted, in a seemingly violent end to the site.

Modification of the defences can also be demonstrated at Hembury, in Devon. The first phase of the defences took the form of a wall-rampart, faced at front and rear by vertical timbers. The width of this barrier was over 6 m, and the filling material was composed of sand, earth and stone from the ditch. Using comparisons with other hillforts, these defences probably date to between 600 and 450 BC. The later defences at Hembury consisted of a dump rampart nearly 9 m wide, retained by a low stone wall at the front. Any attacker unfortunate enough to find himself in the bottom of the ditch outside the rampart, would have had to look up a towering 18 m to the defenders on top of the defences.

Another fine example of a developed hillfort is that at Danebury in Hampshire (Fig 30). Here a large-scale, open-area excavation within the interior and on one of the entrances, over a number of seasons, has revealed the most complete picture yet of the lay-out of such a fort. In both early and late periods of occupation at Danebury, the number of round-houses was small compared with the enormous quantity of pits and four-posters that indicate a storage capacity far outstripping the needs of the occupants of the site. In the early fort, around 500 BC, rows of four-posters in the northern half of the interior were replaced by a concentration of deep, circular pits cut into the chalk subsoil. The defences at this stage comprised a single line of bank and ditch. In the later fort, built around 400 BC, the southern part of the site was divided by parallel lateral roads into areas lined with four-post and six-post granaries, with round-houses and ancillary structures clustered in smaller numbers

Pl 75. Tre'r Ceiri, Gwynedd, Wales. One of the most spectacular hillforts in Britain. Two lines of stone defences can be seen on this side of the hill, with the stone huts and compounds in the interior of the fort. It may have been a stronghold of the Ordovices.

in the sheltered spaces immediately behind the ramparts. During this stage additional defences were constructed all around the perimeter, while the two gateways were protected with extra earthworks to provide defence in depth. The excavator assumed that seed corn for the following season's sowing was probably stored in the pits, while grain that was to be used immediately was placed in the granaries. These four- and six-post buildings would support raised timber floors on which the corn would be stored, so protecting it from the damp and vermin. It may be, therefore, that in the early period Danebury was used primarily to store the seed corn from surrounding farms, while in the later period surplus grain for exchange was collected in quantity. Danebury may have had an important economic function, trading some corn to distant communities in return for other prized materials such as bronze, iron, amber and glass, which were in turn distributed to surrounding farmers.

But not all hillforts need have operated in the same way. The spectacularly sited hillfort at Ingleborough, Yorkshire, high up in the Pennines and only accessible after an arduous climb, cannot have served the local and lower-lying villages and farms in quite the same manner (Pl 101). Nor could the 2.1 ha hillfort at Carrock Fell in Cumbria, defended by a stone-walled rampart, but in a remote and exposed position at some 650 m above sea-level. It is probable that the fort, like Mam Tor, was never permanently occupied. Presumably these fortifications functioned as temporary refuges.

Wales

High up in the Welsh Marches in Powys a hillfort known as The Breiddin dominates the skyline west of Shrewsbury. It continues the tradition of the early occupation of hill-top locations. Evidence has been uncovered both for domestic occupation and for bronze working from about 900 BC, within the first timber-faced but unditched defences of the hilltop. This first phase of occupation apparently ended in a firing of the defences – whether by attack or otherwise. Several centuries later, wider stone-faced multiple ramparts

Pl 76. Hambledon Hill, Dorset, England. An area of 12.5 ha is enclosed by two ramparts and ditches. The fort appears to have grown in size in three separate stages. Inside the fort, at its highest point, is an earlier earthen long barrow.

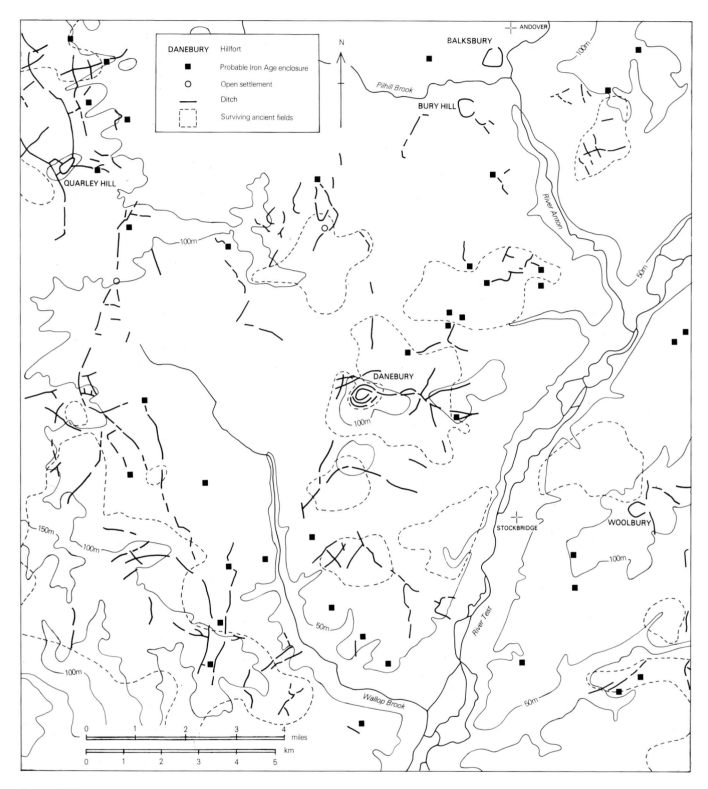

Fig 30. Hillforts and Enclosed Farms in Hampshire, Southern England. Survey evidence shows that hillforts (like Danebury, Quarley Hill and Bury Hill) are surrounded by enclosed farms. A relationship is presumed to have existed between the two types of site, such that hillforts may have controlled territories and dependent farms. Long ditches, dividing up the landscape, also radiate from some hillforts.

enclosed a seemingly permanent settlement which included both circular buildings and four-posters. In this stage the hillfort, whose rugged interior spread to almost 30 ha, may have constituted something akin to a hill-town, with a substantial population running into hundreds, if not thousands.

The value of large area excavation has been admirably demonstrated in Wales by work at the site of Moel y Gaer,

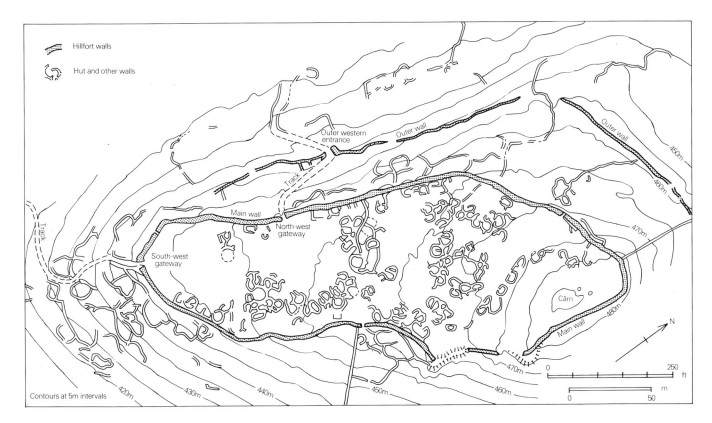

Fig 31. Tre'r Ceiri, Gwynedd, North Wales. Superbly preserved stone hillfort on the Lleyn peninsula. An impressive circuit of defences survives, with the addition of a second line of defence on the north side. A mixture of circular and rectangular huts can be seen inside. The internal areas devoid of stone huts may conceal traces of timber buildings.

Rhosesmor, in Clwyd. Here, on a fairly low hill within site of the Dee estuary, three phases of defensive works and internal arrangements have been revealed. The earliest defence was a timber palisade erected about 650 BC. This enclosed a settlement which consisted, at least in the part excavated, of round-houses, constructed with a ring of timber posts forming the framework for the walls. Not very long afterwards the site was remodelled. The defences were strengthened by the construction of a vertically-faced timber, earth and stone wall rampart. A series of round-houses was located inside, this time the wall framework was constructed of many, closely spaced stakes. In both phases, most of the round buildings possessed a porch which faced roughly eastwards, probably to escape the worst of the weather coming from the west or to catch the morning sun. In the second phase, however, a new element had appeared. Rows of four-posters lined the area behind the ramparts and to the south of the excavated huts, suggesting deliberate planning of the interior, and reminiscent of the ordered layout within Danebury. In the final phase, the defences of Moel y Gaer were overlain by a dump rampart, and irregularly spaced rectangular timber buildings, with compounds divided by fences, were constructed inside the fort.

A question that is often raised about hillforts is the availability of water, since most sites do not possess a natural water supply. There can be little doubt that clay-lined ponds and pits within the forts must have acted as cisterns to collect rainfall. Such a supply would have been supplemented by water transported in pottery or leather containers from nearby springs or rivers, either using animals or humans to carry the load. It must also be appreciated that the standard form of warfare in the period was the quick surprise raid. It is unlikely that many hillforts ever had to withstand a siege, where an enemy would lie in wait until diminishing supplies of water within a fort had become critical.

A superbly preserved hillfort lies on the Rivals in Gwynedd and is known as Tre'r Ceiri (Pl 75). Here local stone was the major building material. Given this fact, and the fort's remoteness from later centres of habitation (which has lessened the chances of subsequent robbing for building stone), the defences and stone-built huts and compounds in the interior have survived remarkably well (Fig 31). The extent of the surviving dry-stone walling presents a particularly difficult challenge for archaeologists trying to conserve the monument. Too many visitors will gradually destroy the very thing they have come to see. Any prehistoric attacker attempting to take this fortification by force would have had a long and arduous climb up to the summit, while the defenders enjoyed spectacular views across to Anglesey, down the Lleyn peninsula, and south towards Harlech.

Scotland

The pattern of hillfort settlement between the rivers Tyne and Forth, in Borders and Lothian, is similar to that of southern England and the Welsh borders. Over ninety per cent of

Pl 79. Gurness, Orkney, Scotland. The site was occupied for some 900 years. Its principal feature is a massive broch, with a gallery inside the wall, and a central courtyard containing slab-built cubicles, hearths and a well. Two outer ramparts and a rock-cut ditch defend a village of terraced houses and the broch.

Pl 77 (*left, above*). Dun Carloway, Lewis, Scotland. One of the best-preserved brochs, still standing up to a height of 9 m. The construction formed by a double wall can clearly be seen, and inside the wall galleries were linked by staircases.

Pl 78 (*left, below*). Clickhimin, Shetland, Scotland. This is a complex site with fortification and domestic occupation over a number of centuries. In the foreground can be seen a house with a central hearth, while in the background stand the lower courses of the broch.

Scottish hillforts are concentrated in the south-east of the country. Hillforts with timber-laced ramparts were built from 600 BC onwards, and it would seem a few of them reached a considerable size in population as well as area. At Eildon Hill North, Borders, it is estimated that there are over 300 houses within the enclosed area of 16.2 ha.

The complex development of a small hillfort is well demonstrated at Hownam Rings in the Borders. An area of approximately 0.6 ha was enclosed by a single palisade set in a bedding trench. This was eventually superseded by a contour fort delimited by a single dry-stone wall, some 3 m wide. This defence was subsequently partially dismantled and material from it re-used in the construction of the innermost of four ramparts. This multivallate stage of the defences marked the final defensive formation of the site. Another fort at Broxmouth, East Lothian, contained timber and stone

Pl 80. Dun Carloway, Lewis, Scotland. A broch showing the characteristic double wall. Staircases within the main wall gave access to horizontal galleries. The principal gateway into the broch was protected by a guard-chamber giving access to the central courtyard. Four doors opened off the courtyard into rooms within the walls.

houses, with a small inhumation cemetery outside the defences and four burials within the defended area. The clearest evidence for the early settlement of hill-top locations comes from the impressive site of Traprain Law, East Lothian. The earliest fortification here may be a stone wall supporting a possible stockade and isolating some 4 ha of the summit. Certainly bronze artefacts found on the west side of the hill are an indicator of occupation at the site prior to 700 BC.

In north-east Scotland some of the hillfort defences illustrate the process of vitrification. Sites like Tap o'North in Grampian and Finavon in Angus were defended by drystone walls interlaced with horizontal timbers. These timbers seem to have been set on fire, either through accident or attack, so that the resultant heat fused some of the stones together. Excavations at Finavon indicated that the defensive wall, which contained vitrified material, had stood to a height of 6 m. Occupation within the fort was concentrated in the area immediately behind the rampart.

In the west, hillforts are much rarer. One of the few large examples is the site of Burnswark in Dumfries and Galloway.

Here it is likely that a double stockade, revealed by twin rows of closely-set post-holes, enclosed an area of some 7 ha. The defences were rebuilt only a short time afterwards and comprised a rampart of earth and rubble with an outer face of stone.

Ireland

At least fifty hillforts are known in Ireland. Univallate forts, on low, rounded hills overlooking agricultural land, occur in the east of the country. Multivallate forts, often built of stone and possessing massively constructed central citadels, have a more westerly distribution. Rather less excavation of hillforts has taken place in Ireland than in England, but there is some evidence to demonstrate a similar sequence to the development of British fortifications in the thousand years before the coming of the Romans. At Rathgall in Co. Wicklow extensive occupation in the earlier part of the first millennium BC was probably comtemporary with the concentric defences around the site. Remains of a circular wooden building were located in the interior. Even more important was a rectangular timber structure that seems to have been used as a metal workshop. Over 400 fragments of clay moulds for the casting of bronze swords, spearheads and socketed axes were discoverd around it. At Downpatrick, Co. Down, early occupation material was again revealed, although its relationship to

Fig 32. Springfield Lyons, Essex, Eastern England. The drawing shows the reconstructed farmstead, sitting inside its bank-and-ditch defences which are pierced by no fewer than six gateways. Defended farms such as this must have been commonplace in the late prehistoric period, although not all would have had so many entrances.

the defences is not clear.

Despite the similarities, Irish hillforts differ from their counterparts in Britain. Their smaller average size, the frequent presence of a central, and possibly later, citadel, the occurrence of internal ditches inside the defences and their uncomplicated entrances give them a distinctive character. In addition, at least three sites – Tara in Co. Meath, Navan in Armagh and Dún Aillinne in Co. Kildare – are mentioned in early Irish literature as important royal sites and may have acted as places of assembly in prehistoric times. Indeed the excavator at Dún Aillinne discovered considerable quantities of burnt animal bones, interpreted as the remains of feasts, and suggests a largely ceremonial role for the site.

Within the hillfort at Navan, a round-house was built next to a circular stockade in about 700 BC; both were enclosed by a circular ditch. The house seems to have been rebuilt no fewer than nine times, and the stockade six times, during the period from 700 to 100 BC. The person or family that lived in this building must have had considerable influence, since the skull of a Barbary ape, which must have come from Spain or North Africa, was found during the excavations. Presumably

the animal was presented as a special gift to the exalted occupants at Navan. Even more spectacular were the developments here around 100 BC. A massive circular structure, perhaps roofed, and some 43 m in diameter, was constructed over the remains of the earlier houses. Not long after completion it was deliberately burned and then covered by a cairn of stones, turf, and topsoil, the whole being some 50 m in diameter and reaching a height of some 6 m. There must be a ritual explanation for this extraordinary construction. As we have seen Navan was to become an important royal foundation in early christian Ireland and perhaps the origins of its importance are to be found in this building.

Forts and Farms

Hillforts, of course, formed only one element in the range of settlements in Britain and Ireland (Fig 37). Even in areas where hillforts dominated the landscape, there was often a variety of smaller forts or defended farmsteads, and undefended farms, set amongst a pattern of trackways and field systems. These sites usually occupied lower-lying ground, from where farmers could tend their stock or gather in their crops more easily. In other areas hillforts were extremely rare. There are few hillforts in eastern England, for instance, or along the coast of north-west Scotland. In both these

Pl 83. Craggaunowen, Co. Clare, Ireland. A full-scale reconstruction of a crannog in its typical lake-setting. Inside the crannog are two round-houses, while a more controversial gate-tower stands over the entrance. Practical problem-solving connected with reconstruction projects can produce valuable insights into everyday life in prehistoric environments.

Pl 81 (*left, above*). Tara, Co. Meath, Ireland. Looking from Cormac's House over the earthworks of the Royal Seat. These two small adjacent ring-forts sit inside a low hillfort with extensive views over the upper Boyne Valley. Several features at this location point to the important ritual significance of Tara continuing over many centuries well into the Christian period. Most of the numerous ring-forts or raths in Ireland were fortified homesteads dating from early Christian times although some are likely to be prehistoric.

Pl 82 (*left, below*). Staigue Fort, Co. Kerry, Ireland. Secluded near the top of a peaceful valley, this is one of the finest stone forts in Ireland. The massive stone wall of the fort was surrounded by a bank and ditch, and stairs at regular intervals inside the walls gave access to the wall-walk.

regions, however, small defended farms and unenclosed sites are just as evident, although the extent and form of the structures may be very different.

England

At Springfield Lyons in Essex a substantial enclosure over 60 m in diameter was defended by a bank and a ditch, in which were found many discarded mould fragments; the defences were pierced by no fewer than six gateways (Fig 32). Several round-houses and a range of farmyard features were located in the interior. At Lofts Farm, also in Essex, a sub-rectangular enclosure contained a single central round-house opposite the only entrance. Further north, at Thwing in Humberside, a settlement first occupied about 800 BC was surrounded by circular defences. The rampart was braced with timbers and a wide and deep ditch ran outside it. In the centre of the site stood a large circular building some 28 m in diameter. Objects found during the excavation indicate domestic, occupation of fairly high status; they included a quern, rubbing stone, loom-weights, spindle whorls, pottery, animal bones and bronze weapons and personal ornaments. Flag Fen in the Cambridgeshire Fens was also occupied about this time. A wooden platform containing thousands of worked timbers, and edged by a boardwalk, originally lay within a shallow lake or lagoon. On top were probably several rectangular buildings, at least one having a central nave and flanking aisles.

In central southern England both sub-rectangular and circular enclosures are known. One famous site is that at Little Woodbury in Wiltshire where about 1.6 ha was enclosed. Two round-houses, numerous pits and four-posters were found in the excavated part of the interior, although other structures may lie in the unexcavated areas. At Gussage All Saints in Dorset both iron-working and bronze-working took place within the enclosed farmstead during the second century BC. The bronze-working concerned the manufacture of horse harness and cart or waggon fittings. A great deal of insight into the local economic practices of these farms has been gleaned from the experimental work at the Butser Ancient Farm in Hampshire. Full-scale reconstructions of round-houses and ancillary agricultural buildings have been built at Butser, and a model farm is open to the public. In addition there has been much experimentation with livestock and crops that are thought to compare closely with late prehistoric types.

The most common type of farm in Cornwall is known as a round. These are circular or sub-circular enclosures usually less than 0.8 ha in area containing a few houses built against the enclosure wall or bank. An excavated example at Trevisker was occupied in the second century BC and produced a possible iron sickle, and a structure with a slab-lined drain that may have been an animal shelter. Courtyard houses are also found in Cornwall. These have a paved central courtyard surrounded by stone huts and byres, the whole enclosed by a compound wall. The sites at Chysauster (Pl 97) and Carn Euny (Pl 98) are good examples of the type. Carn Euny also possesses an underground chamber and passage known as a fogou, meaning cave. There are many of these in the Cornish peninsula and they are related to the souterrains, commonly found in western Brittany, northern, eastern and western Ireland and northern and eastern Scotland. The fogou at Carn Euny is a structure of some architectural sophistication, being constructed in stone and incorporating a corbelled chamber and a passage over 20 m long. Many such underground structures are thought to have been for storage of such commodities as grain, salted meat, fruits, vegetables, cheese, milk and even gulls' eggs. In the Somerset Levels trackways were again constructed out into the marsh from the dry islands, two apparent marsh-settlements being known from Glastonbury and Meare, although there are no definite structures known from the latter site. Concentrations of small palisaded enclosures are known from the Yorkshire Wolds and Northumberland.

Unenclosed, or open, settlements are being located in increasing numbers on valley floors, often through the successful application of aerial photography. On the Thames estuary at Mucking, Essex, a spread of over 100 circular houses has been excavated, dating to the period from 400 BC until the Roman conquest. Similar complexes have been uncovered further up the Thames in Oxfordshire and in the Trent valley of Staffordshire and Nottinghamshire. At Wetwang Slack in Humberside over eighty round-houses have been revealed on the valley floor, along with four-posters and pits for grain storage. Nearby existed a major cemetery; tracks and lanes provided links to adjacent villages, and access to fields. At Roxby in north-east Yorkshire, round-houses lay both within and outside of a ditched enclosure. Further south, at Beckford in Gloucestershire, a series of adjacent enclosures probably constituted a village; each enclosure held round-houses and storage pits and may have been individually owned by a single extended family.

Wales

In south and central Wales settlements similar to those in Devon and Cornwall can be found. The Welsh rath, densely concentrated in the south-west peninsula, is the equivalent of the Cornish round. Walesland Rath in Dyfed was totally excavated, revealing signs of prolonged occupation, with at least six round-houses and a range of timber buildings within the enclosing bank. The main entrance lay in the south-east and was constructed around six massive posts, no doubt supporting an impressive entrance structure. Occupation seems to have started late in the prehistoric period and continued after the Roman conquest, although whether there was continuity of possession by the same community is problematic. Other excavated examples of defended farms in Dyfed include Dan-y-Coed and Woodside, two small hill-slope enclosures which lie within 300 m of one another near Llawhaden.

In the upper Severn valley many defended farms have been found through aerial photography and major excavations in advance of ploughing have taken place at Collfryn, in northern Powys. Here, four roughly concentric lines of deep ditches were again pierced by what must have been a series of impressive gateways. Inside, there were round-houses and four-posters and the site was occupied from the fourth to the first centuries BC. In north-west Wales, on the lower flanks of the mountains of Gwynedd, there are numerous well-built stone farms, consisting of circular and rectangular structures set in stone compounds and often associated with field systems. When excavated, these sometimes show evidence of continuity of use from the prehistoric to the Roman period, as was the case with the farmstead at Cefn Graeanog in Gwynedd. Some upland sites, like Moel y Gerddi and Erw Wen near Harlech, were initially built in timber and then rebuilt in stone. In north-east Wales there are about sixty examples of small enclosures, none of which has been excavated, but some of which, at least, might well prove to be late prehistoric defended farms.

Not all farms were defended, of course, or even enclosed. Excavations at Craw Cwellt in Gwynedd are revealing substantial round-houses, containing evidence for small-scale iron working, set amongst irregular patterns of fields. In

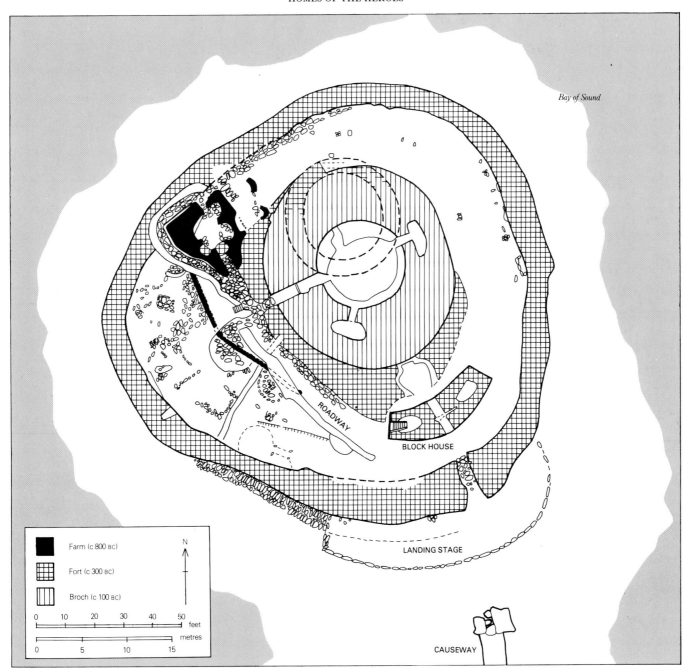

Bay of Sound

BLOCK HOUSE

ROADWAY

LANDING STAGE

CAUSEWAY

Farm (c 800 BC)

Fort (c 300 BC)

Broch (c 100 BC)

N

| 0 | 10 | 20 | 30 | 40 | 50 |
feet

metres

| 0 | 5 | 10 | 15 |

Fig 33. Clickhimin Broch, Shetland, Northern Scotland. This complex site began as an undefended farmstead which was then enclosed by a stone wall. A Blockhouse was subsequently constructed behind the entrance to the enclosure, while in the next phase a broch was built. Further modifications were made to the site at a later date.

Clwyd, at Prestatyn, apparently unenclosed round-houses were located underneath a later Roman industrial site.

Scotland

Distinctive types of undefended and defended farms and set-tlements have emerged in the far north of Scotland and the outer isles. Two famous excavated examples are those of Jarlshof and Clickhimin (Fig 33 & Pl 78), both on Shetland. At Jarlshof the first undefended village of stone houses was established around 1,000 BC (Pl 85). This was eventually

engulfed in sand and a second village of round-houses was constructed by an iron-using community. Souterrains or underground passages, (found also in Cornwall and Ireland) were added to some of the houses, probably to serve as ad-ditional storage areas to maintain a surplus of food. In the following phase a broch was constructed on the site. There are almost 500 such brochs, mostly in the far north and west of Scotland, and in the Northern Isles and the Hebrides; they consist of dry-stone walled towers, usually circular and sometimes towering to at least 15 m.

At Clickhimin, too, where the excavation evidence is cap-able of more than one interpretation, the sequence of deve-lopment begins with an early, undefended farmstead that is later fortified, after 500 BC, with the addition of a massive stone ring-wall (Pl 84). Subsequently a sophisticated block-house was constructed behind the entrance to the earlier ring-wall. In the final phase some of the defensive wall was

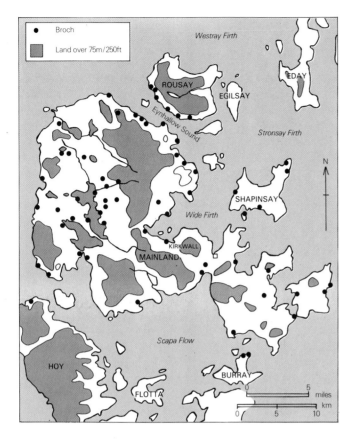

Fig 34. Brochs on Orkney, Northern Scotland. This map of Orkney shows the concentration of brochs on these islands. The distribution is primarily a coastal one, most noticeable on either side of Eynhallow sound, between Orkney and Rousay, where lines of brochs face one another across the water.

robbed to provide material for a broch.

Much debate surrounds the origins of brochs, particularly so since they are such sophisticated structures (Pl 77 & 80). These massive dry-stone towers usually have a base diameter from 12 to 25 m. The walls are thick at the bottom, but taper inward towards the top (Pl 79). Galleries and chambers were left within the thicknesses of the walls. Most brochs may have possessed wooden floors in the circular central courtyard, and they may have been roofed over. There is considerable variation in the type, however. There are over fifty brochs on Orkney, with overall diameters from 12 to 22.5 m, wall thicknesses from 2.75 to 5.2 m and courtyard diameters from 7.3 to 13.7 m (Fig 34).

Another type of defended farm is the dun, a Scottish version of the rath or round. Duns are small, enclosed sites defended by dry-stone walls. They are to be found on a wide variety of uneven terrain, from coastal promontories to inland ridges. They, too, display elaborate architectural features which sometimes include an outward batter to the wall-face, galleries and staircases within the thickness of the walls, and guard chambers at the entrances.

Crannogs – timber houses built on artificial or partly artificial islands – are known from many lochs from the south-west to the Western Isles. A crannog in Milton Loch con-

sisted of a platform-like sub-structure on which a circular wooden house with internal wattlework partitions was constructed. This was surrounded by a boardwalk, set on a series of piles, which led round to a small harbour marked by two jetties of piled stones. Access to the mainland was by way of a wooden causeway. The crannog was occupied from about 400 BC.

In southern and eastern Scotland many homesteads and settlements enclosed by palisades, low stone walls or bank-and-ditch combinations are found, more directly comparable to similar sites in northern England. A bank and ditch enclosed an area of some 40 m in diameter at Boonies, near Dumfries. Traces of a gateway structure and several timber round-houses, some obviously rebuilt, were located in the interior. Unenclosed settlements can also be found throughout most of Scotland. The evidence for these are the foundations of circular, stone or timber huts, either isolated or in groups. Few have been excavated, but many can be assumed to date from the last millennium BC; the distribution of such open settlements is being rapidly expanded by the application of aerial photography, the most prominent indications from the air being the dark marks left by the accumulation of soil in collapsed souterrains associated with many of the huts in Tayside, Grampian and Highland. At Newmill, Tayside a stone-built souterrain lay partly under a timber round-house; it had two entrances – one outside the house, presumably for filling the storehouse, and the other inside the round-house.

Ireland

The form of the typical late prehistoric farm in Ireland is problematic. It may be represented by the ring-fort or rath, a circular enclosed area protected by an arrangement of earthen banks and ditches. Raths do not normally occupy commanding positions, except in badly drained regions where an elevated area was the only suitable place for habitation. Even then they do not attempt to encircle a hill-top with their defences, preferring to retain their small size and basic circular shape (Fig 36). No full listing of these sites has been published but their number is enormous, possibly amounting to more than 50,000 examples. In some parts of Co. Clare characterized by a great number of low, rounded hills, nearly every one is crowned by a rath. Only a few of them are likely to be prehistoric, however. Their use in Ireland – undisturbed by the interruption caused by the Roman conquest of Britain – began during the first centuries AD and the majority were perhaps constructed at much later dates, up to and including the middle ages. Indeed, all the examples exca-

Fig 35. Oppida, Hillforts and Tribal Names. Major hillforts occur in southern England and the Welsh borders, while smaller hillforts are found in the peninsulas of Cornwall, Wales and in Scotland. Few hillforts are known from eastern or northern England. The more sporadic distribution of the Irish hillforts underlines their different character. The five oppida are all in south-east England.

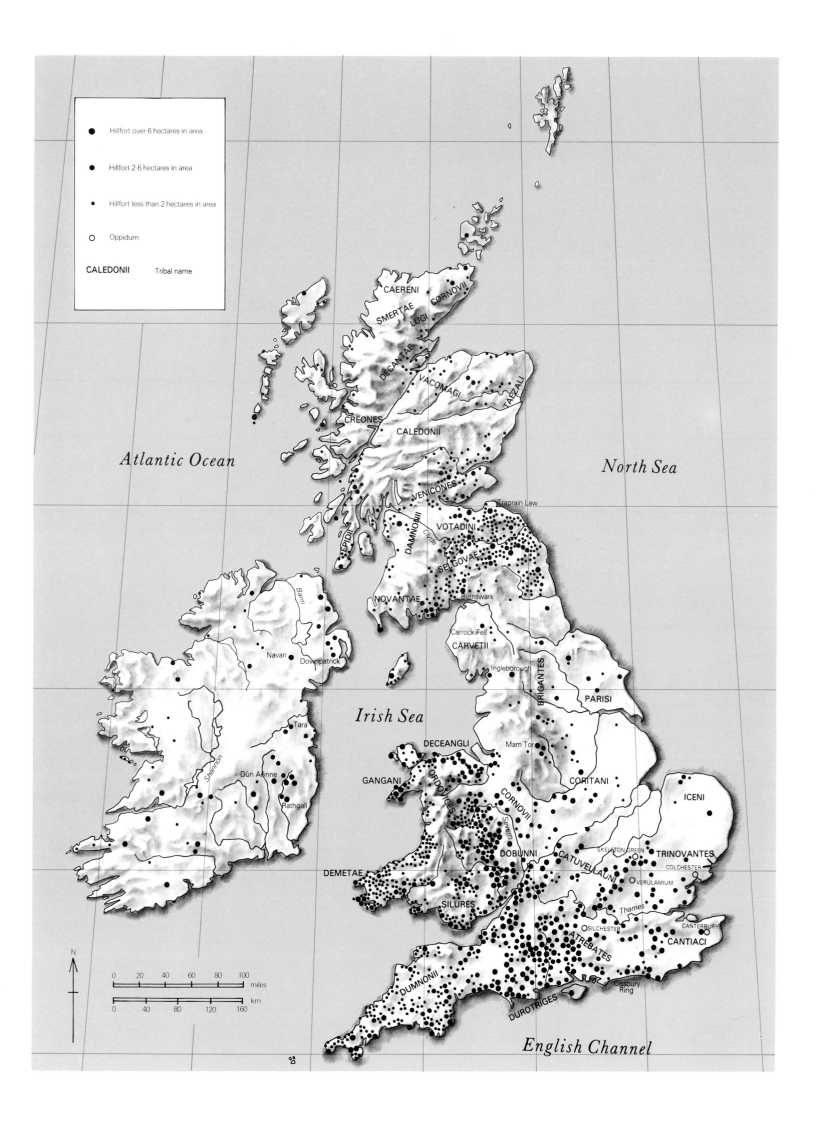

Hillfort over 6 hectares in area

Hillfort 2·6 hectares in area

Hillfort less than 2 hectares in area

Oppidum

CALEDONII   Tribal name

Atlantic Ocean

North Sea

CAERENI

SMERTAE   LUGI   CORNOVII

DECANTAE

VACOMAGI

TAEZALI

CREONES

CALEDONII

VENICONES

Traprain Law

DAMNONII   VOTADINI

EPIDII

SELGOVAE

NOVANTAE

Burnswark

Carrock Fell

CARVETII

Ingleborough

Irish Sea

Bann

Navan   Downpatrick

BRIGANTES   PARISI

Tara

Mam Tor

DECEANGLI

Shannon

GANGANI   ORDOVICES   CORNOVII   CORITANI

Dún Ailinne

Severn

ICENI

Rathgall

DOBUNNI   CATUVELLAUNI   SKELETON GREEN   TRINOVANTES

DEMETAE   COLCHESTER

SILURES   VERULAMIUM

Thames

SILCHESTER   CANTERBURY

ATREBATES   CANTIACI

DUMNONII

Cissbury
Ring

DUROTRIGES

English Channel

N

0   20   40   60   80   100
miles

0   40   80   120   160
km

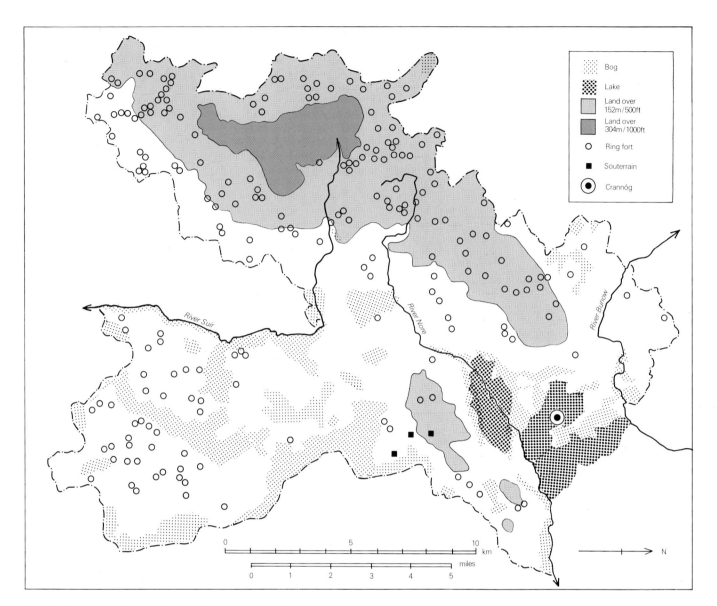

Fig 36. Ring-Forts, Souterrains and Crannogs in the Barony of
Ikerrin, Co. Tipperary, Ireland. This large-scale distribution map
shows the extremely dense concentration of raths or ring-forts in
this part of Ireland. Most of these sites were probably constructed
after the advent of Christianity, although a small percentage are
probably prehistoric.

Pl 84 (*left, above*). Clickhimin, Shetland, Scotland. The central
courtyard of the broch is approached by a long passage through
the massive wall. Two rooms in the walls were entered from
ground level. All the other rooms and galleries were reached by a
wooden ladder up to the first-floor level.

Pl 85 (*left, below*). Jarlshof, Shetland, Scotland. A particular type of
house, wheel-houses, were built at Jarlshof in about AD 200. These
comprised a central court, containing the hearth, seen in the
middle of the photograph, surrounded by roofed compartments.
The compartments were separated from the court by a stone kerb.

vated so far, with one or two exceptions, appear to be early
historic in date. Some well-preserved raths can be seen on the
Hill of Tara in Co. Meath (Pl 81). Tara developed into an
important royal foundation in the early christian period.
Small, defended settlements, linked by ditches and tracks,
are also known from the Isle of Man; a bivallate farmstead at
The Dog Mills is a good example.

Stone forts or cashels also occur in south and west Ireland,
as at Staigue, Co. Kerry and Caher Ballykinvarga, Co. Clare
and demonstrate sophisticated architectural features; their
prehistoric date is still a matter of debate, however. At
Staigue the defensive wall is tapered inward and rises to a
height of some 5.5 m (Pl 82). Internal steps lead onto terraces
and the entrance is formed by a narrow, lintelled doorway.
Small cashels are often sited on the summits of steep-sided
rocky outcrops like Cashlaungar in Co. Clare and Leacama-
buaile in Co. Kerry. There is also some evidence for the occurrence of crannogs in late prehistoric Ireland (Pls 83 &
86). At Ballinderry in Co. Offaly, a short phase of occupation

Pl 86. Craggaunowen, Co. Clare, Ireland. A pair of reconstructed round-houses are situated within the reconstructed crannog at Craggaunowen. The thatch on the roofs of these houses sheds water efficiently, whilst being easily permeated by smoke from indoor hearths. The presence or absence of smoke-holes in such structures is hard to establish from archaeological remains.

on such a site was interrupted by flooding. At least two separate groups of structures were erected on superimposed layers of brushwood. Cattle bones predominated among the faunal remains, although sheep, pigs and goats were also represented. The diet was supplemented by some corn-growing, fowling and red deer hunting. At Rathinaun crannog in Lough Gara, Co. Sligo, a foundation of brushwood and peat was supported by wooden piles. A number of hearths were uncovered lined with clay, but no definite house plans. The hearths had surrounds of plastered woven twigs, giving them a basket-like appearance. Crannogs, two dug-out boats and a smithy for making bronze swords and axes have also been located at Lough Eskragh in Co. Tyrone.

Fighting and Feasting

The last five hundred years of the prehistoric period are centuries that are associated with the spread of Celtic customs across Britain and Ireland. The Celts comprised numerous warrior-like chiefdoms which emerged from central Europe. They were so aggressive that they troubled the Mediterranean powers of the Classical world, at various times sacking both Rome and Delphi. How many waves of Celts there were, and exactly when they reached Britain and Ireland is a matter of debate. At present the literary evidence from Clas-

Fig 37. Late Prehistoric Forts, Farms and Fields. For England and Wales this is a schematic map. In Scotland individual sites are marked by symbols, while in Ireland only a very small fraction of ring forts are shown, since most of this category of site may belong to the early Christian period.

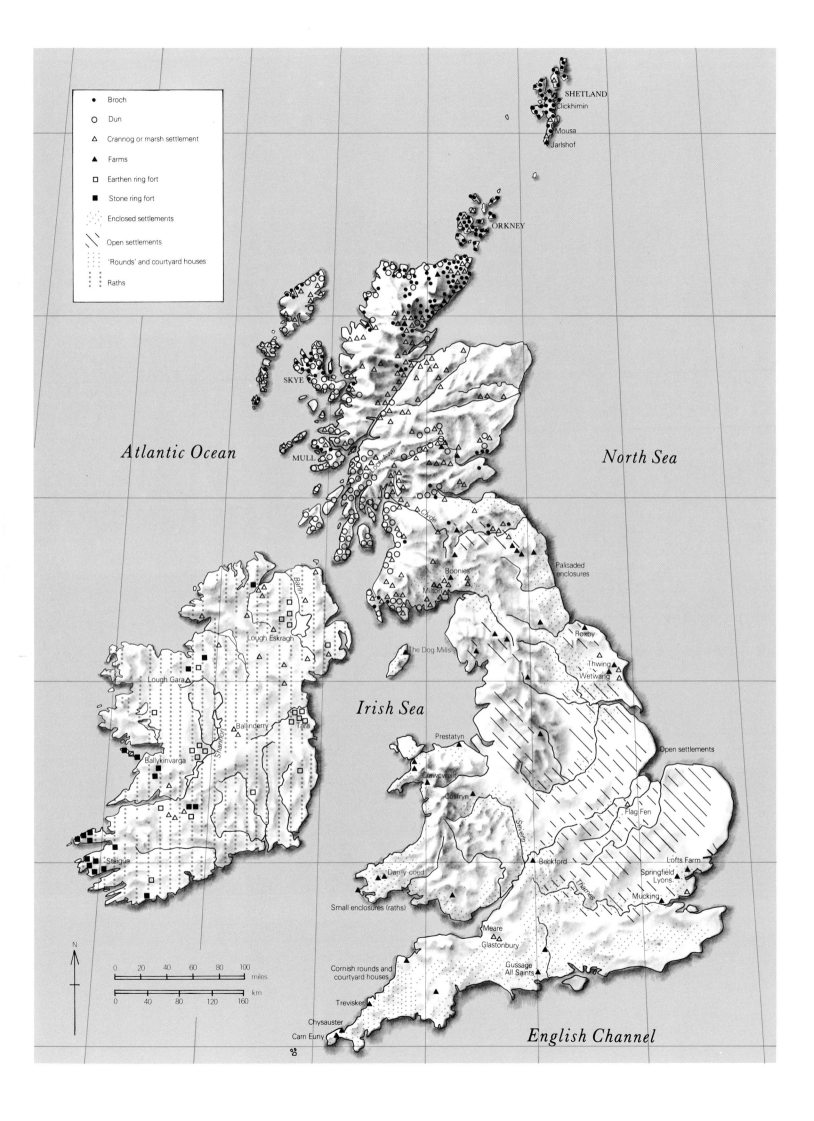

Broch
Dun
Crannog or marsh settlement
Farms
Earthen ring fort
Stone ring fort
Enclosed settlements
Open settlements
'Rounds' and courtyard houses
Raths

Atlantic Ocean

North Sea

SHETLAND
Clickhimin
Mousa
Jarlshof

ORKNEY

SKYE

MULL

Loch Awe

Clyde

Bann

Lough Eskragh

Lough Gara

Ballinderry

Tara

Shannon

Ballykinvarga

Staigue

Irish Sea

Boonies

Milton

Palisaded enclosures

The Dog Mills

Roxby

Thwing

Wetwang

Prestatyn

Crawcwellt

Collfryn

Dan-y-coed

Small enclosures (raths)

Beckford

Severn

Thames

Flag Fen

Open settlements

Lofts Farm

Springfield Lyons.

Mucking

Meare

Glastonbury

Gussage
All Saints

Cornish rounds and
courtyard houses

Trevisker

Chysauster

Carn Euny

English Channel

N

0   20   40   60   80   100
                                miles

0   40   80   120   160
                        km

Pl 87. The Waterloo Helmet. This magnificent horned helmet was dredged from the river Thames near Waterloo Bridge before 1866. This is the only horned helmet of bronze to survive from the Celtic world. Note the typical curvilinear decoration on the helmet proper. (Height of helmet is 24.2 cm)

sical authors, and the archaeological data, are not easily reconciled.

But something can be learnt of the attitudes and practices of these peoples from Classical writings, and from the literature and poetry of early medieval Ireland and Wales. The agricultural economy in Britain and Ireland obviously varied from region to region. Wheat and barley were grown; cattle, sheep and pigs were reared. Cattle were especially prized and formed the medium of compensation when redress was sought by an aggrieved party. Pork, too, seems to have played a special role at feasts. In early medieval Wales surviving documents tell us that the pigs would be fed on acorns in woodland and tended by swineherds. Cattle would have had their herdsmen too and, under a transhumant regime, might have been pastured on unenclosed upland grass at some distance from the lowland winter settlement. Storage of food was essential for survival. Products most commonly specified as dues to be rendered to the chief include beer, bread, meat and honey, and very occasionally,

milk products like cheese or butter. Some Celtic communities also used horses for transport, to pull chariots or for controlling herds, and these needed tending and pasture.

With Celtic attitudes to warfare, we have to recognize that fighting and feasting formed complementary and essential facets of Celtic aristocratic life: fighting during the day and feasting at night when the exploits of the day would be recounted. In Ireland aggression was the prerogative of the *fianna*; oganized bands of young noble warriors who spent part of their lives in hunting and fighting away from their own territories. Much of this fighting seems to have been more akin to sport, since prestige and honour were the aims rather than territorial or material aggrandizement. The Classical authors clearly thought that the Celts had a strong predisposition towards warfare. The geographer Strabo remarked in the first century AD that the whole nation, 'is war-mad, both high-spirited and ready for battle, but otherwise simple and not uncultured'.

In some types of conflict, such as raiding or the more rare pitched battles, social and ritual elements were involved. When the Celts fought the Romans at the battle of Telamon in northern Italy in 225 BC, some warriors stood in front of the whole army naked, except for their weapons and ornaments of gold neckrings or torcs and armlets. Often single combat between two opposing chiefs or noble warriors seems to have been preferred to a mass engagement as a way of resolving a dispute; formulaic boasts or ritual threats often preceded the contest. Another Celtic custom, mentioned by Polybius, was the decapitation of enemies. Head-hunting appears to have been the accepted goal of many encounters. It was usual for noble warriors to ride to battle in magnificent chariots and then to dismount to fight on foot. On the continent, chariots were no longer in fashion when Caesar was conquering Gaul, and he was surprised to find them in Britain. The heroic nature of combat is underlined by the predilection for weapons that could be deployed in hand-to-hand fighting, such as spears, daggers, swords (Pl 88) and shields (Pl 89). Slings were used too but in Britain at least they are never found in the few graves that we know of from this period, perhaps indicating their low status as the weapon of the common man rather than the noble warrior. The Celts also used horses, but again, at least to begin with, as a means of transport to battle rather than to ride during it. It is obvious that Celtic warriors resorted to aggressive behaviour and fighting very easily; any alarm or any fancied insult might result in an instant seizing of weapons. The mode of fighting must have been essentially anarchic; the deafening blasts of untuned horns and the drumming of swords against shields combined with the shouts and confusing feints and advances of the warriors, must have created a terrifying spectacle.

Often ostensibly hospitable occasions, such as feasts, turned hostile. An Irish saga of the ninth century AD is an excellent example of a kind of event that Posidonius must have seen or heard about in Gaul a thousand years earlier. Here one warrior after another, apparently from different chiefdoms, claims the right to carve a pig at a feast, on the basis of his achievements as a warrior. Each claimant's boasts are met with abuse by the audience, and each in turn has to yield to a rival who establishes a better claim. Eventually Conall, an Ulsterman, takes the best part of the pig for himself and gives only the fore-legs to the Connachtmen. Tempers flare and the result is a bloody free-for-all. Likewise in the folklore of early medieval Wales, there is a direct association between fighting and feasting. The chief gathered his warband around him in his hall; he feasted them and provided for them; in return they fought for him.

In generalizing about the Celts, Strabo speaks of large quantities of food, milk and all kinds of meat, especially fresh and salted pork. At formal feasts the men sat in a circle, with the chief in the centre, his attendants and warriors around

Pl 88. Rapiers, Dirks and Swords. The development of offensive bronze weapons is illustrated here. From left to right is a rapier, a dirk, and three leaf-shaped swords, two of the latter with bronze chapes. These span the period from 1400 BC until 600 BC. The central sword is from the Thames at Brentford. (The central sword is 62 cm in length)

Pl 89. Bronze Shield. This round shield with a central boss comes from Rhyd y Gorse in Dyfed, Wales. The decoration consists of concentric rows of small bosses alternating with raised ribs, beaten out from the back. The type is British and owes little to continental inspiration. (Diameter of shield is 67 cm)

and behind him, each occupying a position according to his status. When meat was served it was the custom of the chief to take the thigh piece. If someone else claimed it, a single combat might ensue. Frequently, use was made of some chance circumstance to start an argument and then a fight during a feast. The conflict might escalate through sham fights and feints to wounding and killing. There are descriptions of enormous feasts given by some chiefs. Luernius, chief of the Arverni in Gaul, put on a feast which lasted for several days, in a vast enclosure, the sides of which were 2.4 km long.

Warfare and feuding in Britain did not remain unchanged in character during the 500 years before the Roman conquest. In the earlier period leading warriors may have occupied particular hillforts. Warfare and feuding were conducted in the heroic style, with perhaps rather more feuding and raiding than warfare and pitched battles. Cattle rustling by powerful aristocratic neighbours seems to have been the initial cause of much of the hostility. In the later period, more dense occupation at larger hillforts suggests the wholesale movements of populations and food-stores into some of the forts. Large fighting forces could now be mobilized, that could control and ravage the whole countryside, and the possibility of occasional sieges at hillforts should not be discounted entirely. There was a trend to replace the expensive armament of the individual with a more general arming of the whole populace. Although society was still led by the noble warriors, developing techniques of warfare and skills of organization such as long-distance bombardment by slingmen, were breaking the heroic mould and forcing conflict and warfare upon an ever-increasing proportion of the population.

Arts and Crafts

Throughout the last one thousand years of the prehistoric period there was a trend towards more sophisticated arts, crafts and technology. In weapons and implements, but not to the same extent in decorative objects or horse fittings, bronze is gradually superseded by iron; ideas of abstract geometric and curvilinear design derived from Celtic Europe permeate through to British and Irish craftsmen and are developed to new heights of artistry; fashionable imports from the Classical powers of the Mediterranean world become more common. There is a growing emphasis on luxury items for display. In the earlier part of the first millennium BC these objects are in bronze and seem to have been frequently thrown into rivers and bogs as votive offerings. Many of these were weapons, and the arrival and subsequent popularity of the sword suggests that raiding and conflict may have been endemic even at this stage. In the latter half of the millennium much effort also went into producing exquisite weaponry for parade and use during not-so-friendly encounters. Artefacts connected with drinking and feasting became valued possessions, while horse trappings were prized throughout the period.

Yet there is much that does not survive. The archaeological record of existing artefacts is manifestly biased and owes much to the durability – or otherwise – of the materials that were used, and to the circumstances of loss and discovery. Metal, stone and pottery survive reasonably well, leather and textiles generally do not. In addition there must have been two modes of production; one that catered for the local market, or the self-sufficient needs of the immediate community; the other involving specialist craftsmen and the production of prestige items for long-distance exchange.

In the later stages of bronze working local smiths probably served several communities in a 15 to 20 km radius, manufacturing smaller objects such as tools, personal ornaments and spearheads. It is difficult to tell whether smiths moved around from settlement to settlement, or whether there was one permanent workshop. On a more regional level some smiths used a more complex casting technique to produce weapons such as rapiers, large spearheads and later, swords. The Thames valley seems to have emerged as a major production centre but there must have been others, perhaps in East Anglia and the Cornish peninsula and Ireland.

Metal ores were being worked long before 1,000 BC in the west of Britain, as the mining waste from the Great Orme in Gwynedd demonstrates. Some time after that, lead began to be added to the tin-copper mix, allowing yet more elaborate casting technology to be used in the production of leaded bronze artefacts. Indigenous smiths now drew on continental inspiration to make cauldrons, shields and buckets as prestige items. Novel artefacts were introduced such as sickles, knives, razors, horse fittings and improved weapons.

Technology changed with the advent of iron in about 650 BC. Although the techniques of roasting and smelting were more involved than with bronze, iron ores were much more widely available than copper, tin and lead. Even so, the first iron objects, which were forged rather than cast, were hardly better than their bronze counterparts, although they did possess a harder cutting edge. At Llyn Fawr, in south-east Wales, a cache of twenty-one objects was found in a votive hoard in a lake high up in the hills. The offering was an iron spearhead and sword and an iron sickle, along with a collection of bronze axes, sickles, spearheads, horse harness fittings and a sheet bronze cauldron.

The tradition of working in gold still continued and a variety of ornaments was produced (Pl 93). The widespread use of stone and flint for some tools had ceased with the growth of the metal industries, although stone remained essential for certain commonplace objects such as querns. Some specialist stone working survived, however. Kimmeridge shale on the Dorset coast was fashioned into bracelets, for instance. One of the most spectacular items produced in shale was the Caergwrle bowl found in the valley below the medieval castle of the same name in Clwyd. The bowl is considered to be a votive boat, with attached gold leaf suggesting shields, oars, waves and the framework of the boat itself.

Traces of production centres are much harder to locate than their products. At Llwyn Bryn Dinas, a hillfort in Clwyd, bowl hearths, a furnace base, iron-smithing slag and a complete handled crucible for the casting of bronze have been found immediately inside the rampart. Excavations within a small hillfort at Bryn y Castell in Gwynedd have

138

uncovered several small iron smelting furnaces, one inside a snail-shaped hut, perhaps built in that shape to assist the draught to the furnaces. Pottery kilns are extremely scarce in the excavation record and most pottery may have been fired in simple bonfires; vessels were often skillfully made but not wheel-thrown until the first century BC. Analysis of some of the mineral content of the pottery, however, has demonstrated that certain decorated forms were traded widely from about 300 BC onwards. Salt was an important commodity and troughs for evaporation have been recognized in the Cornish peninsula, in Essex and Lincolnshire. Bone weaving combs, needles, and chalk and limestone loom weights and spindle whorls attest a thriving textile industry, of which all too little survives. The craft of carpentry has similarly left few traces, though morticed joints and turned bowls survive in a small number from waterlogged sites.

Personal items of adornment became increasingly popular. A variety of pins and brooches, some influenced by continental design, became common. Much larger items were produced. Some magnificent decorated mirrors (Pl 92) and parade weaponry were manufactured, such as the shields from the river Witham in Lincolnshire or that from the Thames at Battersea (Pl 90), or the helmet from the Thames at Waterloo Bridge (Pl 87).

Between 600 and 200 BC more varied types of pottery bowls, dishes and jars replaced the earlier bucket-shaped forms. Much of this pottery can be grouped into regional styles, suggested both by the form and the type of decoration. Decorative motifs were abstract geometric and curvilinear patterns formed by stamped motifs or incised lines. Yet during this period, pottery, and most other objects, are not evenly distributed across the country. The number of artefacts decreases dramatically to the north and to the west. Many settlements in Wales and Ireland seem not to have possessed pottery at all, presumably relying on organic containers made out of basketry, leather or wood. In Scotland most of the prestigious metal items seem to date to the very end of the prehistoric period. From this category come the bronze trumpet mouth in the shape of a boar's head from Deskford, Banffshire, and the elaborate armlets from the north-east (Pl 91), like the spiral armlet with snake-head terminals from Culbin Sands, Morayshire.

In Ireland the final period of prehistoric bronze working has been named the Dowris phase, after the hoard found in boggy terrain between two midland lakes at Dowris in Co. Offaly (Pl 94). The objects in the hoard include a range of spectacular items such as gold sleeve fasteners, certain pin types, bracelets, sheet bronze cauldrons, swords, massive gold gorgets (neck ornaments), disc brooches and end-blow and side-blow horns. The gorgets are particularly out-

Pl 90. The Battersea Shield. This spectacular shield was found in the river Thames at Battersea. It is made from four bronze sheets, originally attached to a shield of wood. Inlays of red glass enhance the curvilinear design characteristic of Celtic art. (Length of shield is 77.7 cm)

Pl 91. Bronze Armlets (*above*). Some of the most distinctive products of late Celtic craftsmanship in Scotland are elaborate bronze armlets. Some have snake heads at the terminals, like that from Culbin Sands, Morayshire. The examples in this photograph have high relief curvilinear patterns, and terminals inlaid with discs of enamel. (Average diameter of armlets is 13.6 cm)

Pl 92. Desborough Mirror. One of the finest of the decorated bronze mirrors found by chance in Northamptonshire in 1908. The face of such mirrors was left plain, but the back offered a wonderful surface for curvilinear decoration. Were some of these patterns worn as tattoos? (Mirror is 35 cm long)

standing and do not occur outside Ireland. Even there they are limited in distribution, being confined to north Munster. The most numerous finds were the enigmatic crotals, which may have been used as tradesmens' weights, although their resemblance to a bull's scrotum might link them to a fertility cult. Twenty-six horns were recovered at Dowris; experiments have indicated that they are capable of a variety of sounds, not dissimilar to those emitted by the Australian aborigine instrument, the *didjeridu*.

Bronze casting, using clay moulds, seems to have occurred at several Irish centres including Whitepark Bay, Co. Antrim and Old Connaught in Co. Dublin. Later metal artefacts from Ireland are represented by the important grave goods such as the brooches from Loughey, Donaghadee, Co. Down, and the scabbards and brooches from Lambay Island, Co. Dublin; these may have been locally made or imported from Roman Britain or might have been the personal possession of refugees or traders from Britain. Personal adornment was still sought after, as the pins, finger rings and the small number of gold neckrings or torcs demonstrate. Most spectacular among the latter is the decorated gold torc, dated to the last half-century BC, and found with a hoard of gold objects at Broighter, Co. Derry. Also in gold was a remarkable model boat, complete with fifteeen oars, nine seats and a yard-arm, the first evidence for the use of the sail in Irish waters. In 56 BC Julius Caesar tells us that he defeated the sea-faring Veneti in Brittany by cutting down their sails. Was a fugitive sailor responsible for the Broighter boat?

A unique insight into prehistoric boats has come from the Hasholme logboat, found preserved in peat near what was once an estuarine tributary of the river Humber in north-east England. The boat is over 12 m long and was cut from a single tree, and finished by complex joinery at its stern and bow.

Pl 93. Golden Jewellery. These gold items of personal adornment span the period from 1,350 BC until 500 BC. Bottom left is a ribbon-torc, and above it an armlet. Bottom right is a dress-fastener and above it a bracelet. The flattish disc is an Irish find known as a gorget, and probably part of a neck ornament. Various rings and cuff-fasteners are in the centre. (Diameter of ribbon-torc is 24.7cm)

Tree-ring matching of a sample of the hull with dated tree-ring sequences, suggests that the log which was used for the boat was felled between 322 and 277 BC. The boat possessed a sloping bow and a vertical stern complete with a steering platform. The vessel probably served a number of iron smelting sites established along the banks of the inlet. The excavators concluded that the boat was probably propelled using paddles, and estimated that up to eighteen paddlers and two steersmen might have formed the crew. During her last voyage the vessel was carrying a cargo of timber and beef when she apparently foundered due to swamping.

Beliefs and Burials

The Classical authors also tell us something about religious practices in the first millennium BC in Britain and Ireland, and about the class of priests known as the Druids. The preoccupation of Celtic society with fighting and warfare, for instance, is reflected in the religious evidence. Knowledge of the Celtic war-gods is derived from the Romans, who superimposed the name of their principal war-god, Mars, on existing native deities. There can be little doubt of the widespread popularity of war-gods among the pre-Roman Celts. In lowland Britain the Romanized name of Mars is linked epigraphically to a vast number of Celtic place names. There appear to be at least three interconnected themes underlying Celtic war-gods. First, there is a close association between war and death; Ceasar recounts that the Druids encouraged the belief that the soul did not die but passed to another person at death, in order to foster bravery. Second, the protective nature of war-deities guarded the community and its territory. And finally, the war-gods' influences were thought to extend into the general area of securing prosperity, well-being and fertility.

A separate concern of society seems to have been, as we have already remarked, with head-hunting. No doubt the warriors were keen to decapitate their adversaries and bring back their heads as trophies, as a sign of personal power or virility, and as a warning to other enemies. This preoccupation with heads was extended to the domain of sculpture. Decapitated statues, for instance, have been discovered at Garton Slack in Humberside. In addition, stone heads were carved and some were placed around sacred springs and wells.

More gruesome was the apparent display of human heads noted from a number of sites. At Bredon Hill, Hereford and

Pl 94. Dowri's Hoard. Part of the cache of bronze and gold objects from the boggy terrain at Dowris, Co. Offaly. Only some of the items are displayed here, including spearheads, socketed axes, swords, horns, a bucket (an import from eastern Europe) and the round objects which are known as crotals. (Height of bucket is 40.9 cm)

Worcester, six human skulls lined the entrance to the hillfort. At Danebury in Hampshire, eight pits within the hillfort contained single human skulls. There is also a suggestion that ritual cannibalism was practised, probably as a means to ensure the complete ritual destruction of the enemy.

The veneration of places associated with water, such as rivers, springs, wells and shafts continued throughout the later prehistoric period. The wealth of prestige armour from rivers such as the Thames and the Witham has already been mentioned. Shields, swords, buckets, imported material and even broken scraps of metal all seem to have been cast into these waters during various rites. Close to Navan fort in Ireland a pool, known as the King's Stables, was constructed. Antlers of red deer, dog bones and eighteen fragments of clay moulds (for bronze sword production) were thrown or placed in the sacred waters. A votive hoard at Llyn Cerrig Bach on Anglesey had been deposited in a peat bog. It consisted of swords, shield ornaments, horse harness and vehicle fittings, a trumpet, cauldrons, gang-chains and several other items. Reverence for peat bogs is also exemplified by the

number of so-called bog burials from Britain and Ireland. The most recent and perhaps the most famous is that of Lindow Man – or Pete Marsh – from Cheshire (Pl 95). He had been struck on the head, garotted and had his throat cut before being put in the bog. Was this a punishment for some heinous crime, or a sacrifice to the deities of the bog?

There is also some evidence for more formal religious shrines or stuctures. Several Romano-Celtic temples, common in Roman Britain, have produced pre-Roman material, especially coins, as at Harlow in Essex. Here, the coins may be associated with a round-house shrine underneath the courtyard of the Roman temple. More evidence comes from the sites at Frilford in Berkshire, Lancing Down in West Sussex and Brigstock in Northamptonshire, where prehistoric structures underlie, or are adjacent to, Roman temples. Most convincing, however, is a rectangular wooden construction found beneath Heathrow Airport, which bears a striking resemblance to the standard ground plan of the square Romano-Celtic temple of the Mediterranean world, with a portico. Some hillforts seem to have possessed purpose-built

Fig 38 (*opposite*). Burials, Shrines and Ritual Sites. Our knowledge of burials in the last thousand years of the prehistoric period is extremely patchy. No definitive conclusions can be drawn from this map, other than to note the well-known concentration of square barrows in Yorkshire and Humberside, and the cluster of bog burials in the Fens.

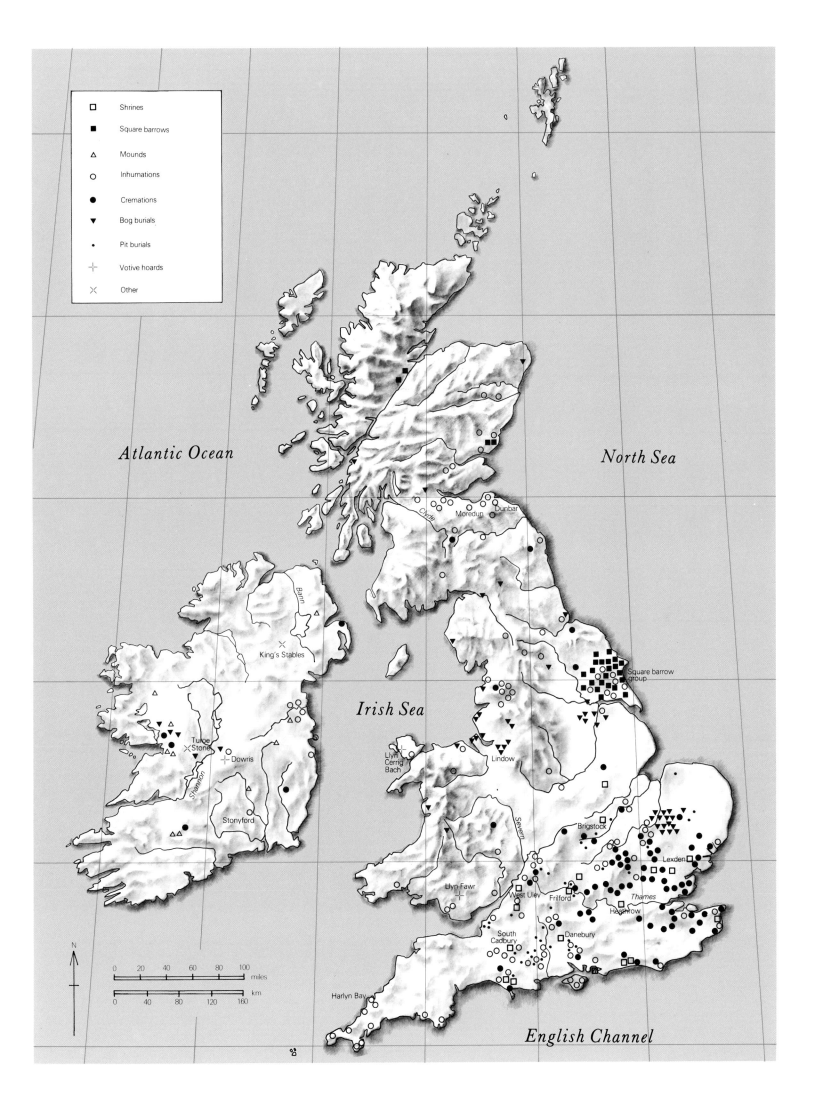

Shrines

Square barrows

Mounds

Inhumations

Cremations

Bog burials

Pit burials

Votive hoards

Other

Atlantic Ocean

North Sea

Irish Sea

Clyde

Moredun

Dunbar

Bann

△

King's Stables ✕

Tulloe
Stone ✕

✚ Dowris

Shannon

Stonyford

Square barrow
group

Llyn
Cerrig
Bach ✚

Lindow ▼

Severn

Brigstock □

Lexden □

Llyn Fawr ✚

West Uley □   Frilford □

Thames

Heathrow

South
Cadbury □

Danebury □

Harlyn Bay

N

0   20   40   60   80   100
                              miles

0   40   80   120   160
                              km

English Channel

Pl 95. Lindow Man. The body of a man found during peat
extraction at Lindow Moss, near Wilmslow in Cheshire. The
leather-like texture of the skin is the result of preservation in peat.
Lindow Man was found in 1984; other parts of different bodies
have been found in the same bog since.

shrines, such as those from Danebury in Hampshire, South
Cadbury in Somerset and Maiden Castle in Dorset. On the
Cotswolds at West Uley, in Gloucestershire, a substantial
ritual enclosure some 25 by 48 m in extent was found to
underlie an early Roman temple of Classical design. Very
nearly all the shrines were orientated so that their doors
faced east, which implies some sacred significance was attached to that direction.

The record for formal burials in Britain and Ireland during
the last millennium BC is an extremely fragmentary one (Fig
38). In some areas no burials at all have been found and it has
been assumed that if there was a uniform or popular rite it was
one which left no detectable material remains. The scattering
of cremated bone, or surface burial may have been practised,
with the corpse quickly disintegrating through decomposition. In southern England some disarticulated skeletons have
been found within hillforts like Danebury and inside defended
farms as at Gussage All Saints, Dorset where articulated
remains were put in pits, apparently with little care or ceremony. There are also a small number of warrior inhumations, complete with weapons such as swords and shields.

In the west of Britain, by contrast, inhumation graves
and cemeteries of stone-lined cists seem to have been the normal burial custom. The largest cemetery located so far is that
at Harlyn Bay, Cornwall, where some 130 burials were found
preserved beneath a sand dune. This large cemetery may
have been used from about 300 BC until the Roman conquest.
In Wales there is little evidence of burial during this period,
though the presence of a decorated bronze lid in a cist from
Cerrig y Drudion, Clwyd, may suggest the occasional rich
burial. At Stackpole Warren in Dyfed, a crouched adult was
buried in a simple grave near a standing stone that had probably been erected a thousand years earlier.

In Scotland the usual burial rite was again inhumation in
cists. At Moredun in Midlothian a small cist contained two
crouched bodies with two brooches. Multiple inhumations
also are known in Scotland. At Lochend, Dunbar, East Lothian, a long cist functioned as a burial vault in which was
found the remains of twenty adults and a child, mostly
incomplete and probably representing successive burials of
related people in the same grave. Aerial photographs have
shown several cemeteries of barrows surrounded by distinctive square ditches in Angus. Some of these may well be
late prehistoric in date and comparable to the ones from
Yorkshire described below.

In Ireland there are a number of burials that can be definitely assigned to the last millennium BC. Both cremation
and inhumation were practised, either in flat cemeteries, in

graves underneath mounds or inside ring-barrows. However, cremation seems to have been the more persistent tradition. The burial of genuine Roman type from Stonyford in Co. Kilkenny is remarkable. The human remains were cremated and contained within a glass cinerary urn. A small glass bottle and a circular bronze mirror covered the urn. It may be that this lady died in Ireland while visiting from Roman Britain during the second century AD. Given the proximity of the find to the port of Waterford a more intriguing possibility is that a small Roman trading post might have existed in the vicinity.

The best-known collection of burials dates to between 400 and 100 BC and comprises crouched inhumations beneath square barrows in North Yorkshire and Humberside. Distinctive cemeteries of square-ditched barrows are now known through aerial photography in almost every dry valley in the Wolds, and some cemeteries, like those at Burton Fleming, Garton Slack and Wetwang Slack have been extensively excavated. Most of the burials contained pottery, pig bones and small ornaments as grave goods, but there are a few in which the deceased was buried accompanied by a dismantled chariot or cart. Of three graves excavated at Wetwang, two contained males, the third a female. The sequence of burial was common to all three. First a large pit had been dug in which the wheels of the dismantled vehicle were carefully placed side by side. Then the bodies of the deceased were laid out in crouched positions between the wheels. Each interment had a range of grave goods. The woman was equipped for her journey into the next world with a side of pork, an iron mirror, a dress pin and a work box of bronze; the men lay with their swords, spears and shields. Above the bodies were placed the remaining parts of the vehicles. At nearby Garton Slack excavation showed that spears were thrown at corpses laid in the grave pits. Possibly this strange ritual was intended to kill the ghosts of the deceased so that they did not return to haunt the living. Adjacent to the Garton burials, in the parish of Kirkburn, a body was laid over the wheels of the chariot and then covered by a complete coat of chain mail.

Prehistoric Politics

During the last century and a half of the prehistoric period, communities in Britain and Ireland were increasingly influenced by the growth of Roman power in Europe, directly affected by the exploratory missions of Julius Caesar in 55 and 54 BC, and the final conquest of Britain launched under Claudius in AD 43. It is the Classical authors, supplemented by names on British coinage (which first came into use during this period) who allow us to draw a crude political map of the principal chiefdoms and their territories prior to the conquest. Sometimes more colourful details are provided. Ceasar mentions that the Britons dye their bodies with woad so as to produce a blue colour, that they wear their hair long, and shave the whole of their bodies apart from the head and the upper lip. Tacitus makes a distinction between the large-limbed red-haired people of the north, who he sur-

Pl 96. Turoe Stone, Co. Galway, Ireland. This stone, about 1m high, originally stood beside the Rath of Feerwore some kilometres away. The lower part of the stone is undecorated, the middle carries a Greek-style step-pattern, while the upper part is covered by curvilinear ornament typical of Celtic decoration.

mised to be Germanic in origin, and the more swarthy, curly-haired residents of the west.

Irish folk tales can also be used to throw some sort of reflection on the structure of Celtic society. Apparently the *tuath* signified a discrete population settled in a small territory. The social framework of the *tuath* was based on a fourfold distinction between chiefs, nobles, free commoners and slaves. The nobles were the warriors, while the freemen were mainly farmers and craftsmen. The ritual performance of the chief was as important as his secular activities. Within the *tuath* the effective social unit was the kin group, which was united around the male descendants through four generations.

Ownership of land was vested in these kin groups, and they were also responsible for obtaining redress in disputes. In addition to the ties and duties of kinship, there was also the institution of clientship. This could involve armed attendance by a commoner on a noble; in return the commoner enjoyed protection and material support without losing any independence or rights to hold property in cattle or land. A relationship of equality between individual *tuath* could change into one of overlordship, where a more powerful chief

Pl 97. Chysauster, Cornwall, England. This is a typical courtyard house, with oval and circular rooms opening off the courtyard. The entrance to the house is bottom left in the photograph. There are four pairs of courtyard houses along a street at Chysauster.

could become overlord of others less influential. Fosterage was another typical feature of Celtic society. The sons of lesser nobles were sent to, and reared in, the houses of the more powerful and were taught the rudiments of warfare. The nobles were subdivided into two groups: young warriors and older, learned men, who included Druids, seers and bards.

Throughout this century and a half there must have been widespread and continual contact between communities on either side of the Channel. The quantity of imports from Europe attests to the great volume of trade. There may also have been an influx of refugees from Gaul after the destruction of the fleet of the Veneti off the coast of Brittany, and Caesar's completion of his Gallic campaigns. If folk movements of this type happened then it must be presumed that the newcomers were quickly assimilated into the local chiefdoms since there is little in the archaeological record that would conclusively prove large-scale immigration.

New settlement forms did appear, however, especially in south-east England. Most notable are the so called oppida, the nearest equvialent to towns that late prehistoric chiefdoms created. Five such sites are known: Skeleton Green (Braughing) and Verulamium (St Albans), both in Hertfordshire, Camulodunum (Colchester) in Essex, Canterbury in Kent and Silchester in Hampshire. The principal characteristics of these oppida are their very large areas; their enclosure of discrete clusters of occupation sites, some of which can be distinguished from others on the basis of activities undertaken; and their proximity to a small hill-top enclosure. Industrial processes carried out within these sites included potting, coin production and metal-working. Rectangular houses at Silchester seem to owe much to the ideas of Classical architecture, and further evidence of Roman influences can be detected in the rectilinear street pattern that was laid out in part of the town in about 20 BC. It is noteworthy that all five oppida became Roman towns after the conquest.

Pl 98. Carn Euny, Cornwall, England. This is a village of courtyard houses. Its most striking feature is a *fogou* or souterrain, which is some 20 m long and has a unique circular side-chamber, which once had a corbelled roof. This photograph looks down into that chamber, with the souterrain passage visible in the far wall.

Away from south-eastern England the pace of change was much slower. Some new large enclosures were created, as at Bagendon in Gloucestershire, with an emphasis on trade with the south-east, but these did not approach the complexity of the oppida proper. In the very last years of the prehistoric era some sites, like Redcliff in Humberside, prospered through trade with the Roman army as the imperial frontier edged slowly towards the river Humber. Elsewhere, some hillforts were either enlarged or had their defences strengthened, as at Maiden Castle in Dorset. In eastern England, the south-west and Wales small defended farms and unenclosed settlements continued a tradition of occupation that had already endured several centuries. In Scotland brochs became larger and more architecturally sophisticated. The discoveries of iron weapons, bronze jewellery and Roman imports from brochs at Bulchlyvie and Leckie in Stirlingshire show that the inhabitants belonged to a class of warring, Celtic chiefs.

Ireland was never part of the Roman Empire and the prehistoric way-of-life continued in Ireland until the 5th century AD. Despite Agricola's boast that he could subdue the island with the assistance of only one legion, the conquest never came. Roman artefacts reached Ireland by way of trade, plunder, or with refugees, but the basic settlement form continued to be the rath. Some raths became so important that in the early medieval period these locations, like Tara in Co. Meath, emerged as the centres of royal power.

Outside south-east England gold, silver and bronze coins were produced in the immediate pre-conquest period by communities living over much of the area between Dorset and Yorkshire. Minting must have been undertaken at a variety of sites including hillforts, enclosures and open settlements. Iron currency bars (sword-shaped bars of iron) seem to have constituted another medium of exchange. The production of fine, decorated metalwork reached a peak in the last century of the prehistoric period. At Stanwick, North Yorkshire, a large fortification of high status, a well preserved iron sword complete with beautifully carved ash scabbard was located in a waterlogged section of ditch. Use of gold and silver also became more common at this time. Nowhere is this better illustrated than in the fashioning of gold torcs, particularly from East Anglia, and twisted neck-rings from other regions. Gold torcs have also been found in a hoard at Shaw Hill, Borders, and much of the fine metalwork from Scotland at this time may owe something to the influx of refugee metalworkers fleeing before the advent of the Romans.

Locally produced luxury items were also finding their way into prestige burials. At Owslebury in Hampshire a warrior was buried with his weapons and a tinned or silvered bronze belt hook dating to about 10 BC. A wealthy female was inhumed at Birdlip, near Cheltenham in Gloucestershire. She was accompanied into the after-life by a finely decorated bronze mirror, a silver brooch, a bronze expanding bangle, a bronze animal-head knife handle with an iron blade, a small bronze bowl, a drop handle, a finial loop, tweezers, bronze rings and a collection of beads; in addition a large bronze bowl had been placed carefully over the lady's face as she lay in the grave.

From Caesar to Claudius

Julius Caesar led two separate expeditions to Britain, in 55 and 54 BC. These were essentially reconnaissances since neither resulted in any territory being taken into the Roman Empire. What they did achieve, however, was political alliances with certain chiefs in the south-east of England, and also the creation of formal trading links across the Channel, thereby ensuring that a steady stream of prestigious Roman artefacts arrived in Britain. No direct archaeological evidence of Caesar's campaigns has survived. This is an interesting example of how significant historical events can leave little or no detectable trace in the archaeological record. Despite the fact that some British chiefs had submitted to Caesar before he left Gaul, others remained openly hostile and heavy casualties were inflicted on the Roman army of two legions.

After his first expedition in the summer of 55, Caesar returned with a stronger army in 54 BC, only to meet a more united opposition under a leader called Cassivellaunus, who lived north of the Thames, perhaps with his capital at Verulamium, near St Albans in Hertfordshire. After advancing beyond the Thames, and after several victorious encounters against the British, the local leaders were forced to sue for peace and to offer hostages to Caesar. The Romans accepted the surrender on condition that an annual tribute was paid to Rome. Caesar returned to mainland Europe where other matters quickly prevented him from turning his attention to Britain for a third time. Almost a century elapsed before the Romans returned, but in this time the influence of the classical world spread in Britain through trade, travel and political manoeuvring.

Contact with the civilized world obviously had a significant impact on the higher echelons of society in south-east England. Some of the leaders and nobles must have tried to imitate Roman lifestyles and an influx of exotic objects and new ideas flowed into the country, even through trading posts as far west as Hengistbury Head in Dorset. Most of the artefacts that arrived related to eating and drinking, highly valued activities in the Celtic world. Wine was imported from Italy, and fish sauce and olive oil in amphorae from Spain. Fine pottery, plates, cups and beakers were imported from production centres in France and Italy. Silver cups, bronze flagons and bronze bowls and strainers completed the table set for the well-to-do. Exported from Britain, according to Strabo, were corn, cattle, gold, silver, hides, slaves and hunting dogs. Some of these items must have been obtained in western Britain by traders from the south-east.

It was not only lifestyles that were affected by contact with Rome. New and grander burial rites date from the century before the conquest. North of the Thames is a group of particularly rich burials, known as the Welwyn type, and named after excavated examples at Welwyn Garden City and Welwyn in Hertfordshire (Pl 99). These usually comprise a deep grave pit in which the cremated remains of the deceased were heaped, together with copious supplies of food and wine and the utensils needed for their consumption. Occasionally iron fire-dogs, decorated with animal heads and originating from the hearth of the deceased, were placed in the graves. South of the Thames, cremation cemeteries at

Pl 99. Welwyn Garden Burial. From Welwyn Garden City in Hertfordshire comes one of the richest grave-pits of this type of very late prehistoric burial. The cremated remains of the deceased were accompanied into the next world by a variety of objects imported from the Roman Empire, including the five wine amphorae at the rear of the grave. (Depth of pit is 1.2 m approx.)

Aylesford and Swarling, both in Kent, suggest a different burial tradition. Here, in the richest graves, the ashes were placed in wooden buckets ornamented with decorated bronze plates, again accompanied by a variety of drinking vessels. At Lexden, near the oppidum of Camulodunum, Essex, an exceptionally large burial pit and lavishly furnished cremation burial was covered by a massive barrow over 23 m in diameter.

The final Roman invasion of Britain began in AD 43 with the landing of the fleet at Richborough in Kent. Between Caesar and Claudius the Roman world had witnessed a political transformation from Republic to Empire, and the fourth Emperor, Claudius, seems to have thought that it would add to his political standing and popularity with the army if a new province could be brought under imperial control. There were also more material concerns, such as the need for increased revenue from new mineral resources, and

the fact that since AD 40 much of south-eastern England had been ruled by two chiefs Togodumnus and Caratacus, who seemed intent on repudiating earlier alliances with Rome and stirring up anti-Roman feeling. The invasion itself was led by the commander Aulus Plautius, with four legions and about 40,000 men in total. The south-east was quickly overrun and the Emperor himself arrived in the summer of AD 43 to lead his army into Camulodunum and receive the submission of twelve British chiefs.

The conquest, however, was to prove a long drawn-out affair which was never fully completed. Many of the hillforts in southern England underwent last-minute restructuring of defences and gateways in preparation for the impending attack. The future Emperor Vespasian successfully led the second Augustan Legion against hillforts in Dorset and Somerset. The local defenders were no match for a disciplined army equipped with superior weaponry and military machines such as siege engines. The hillfort of Hod Hill, Dorset, succumbed after a barrage of ballista bolts had rained down on its interior; the Romans then built their own, smaller, fort within the prehistoric defences (Pl 100). At Maiden Castle in Dorset there is evidence that the fort was taken by force and that the defeated defenders were allowed to bury

Pl 100. Hod Hill, Dorset, England. The southern gateway of the Roman fort which occupies the north-west corner of the earlier hillfort. The Roman fort was garrisoned by 600 soldiers and 250 cavalry and was held until AD 51. The hillfort was densely packed with timber round-houses.

their fallen comrades in a war cemetery near to the east entrance. Danebury, in Hampshire, appears to have become a defended refuge point for the surrounding population during the Roman advance.

The subjugation of the other regions was much less straightforward. The suppression of communities in north Wales in AD 60 was interrupted by the revolt of Boudica, queen of the Iceni, whose headquarters may have been at Thetford in East Anglia. A large tract of Yorkshire and northern England rose in revolt when Venutius became the leader of the Brigantes, after his pro-Roman wife, Cartimandua, had divorced him. His capital was probably at Stanwick, in North Yorkshire, which was refortified with additional dyke systems in anticipation of Roman retaliation. Between AD 71–4 a series of campaigns by the Romans finally restored their military control in the north of England. It was left to the most famous of Roman governors of Britain, Agricola, to complete the conquest of the whole of Wales and to lead Roman armies northwards in AD 79, across the Clyde-Forth isthmus and into the highlands of Scotland. Suppression of the Scottish chiefdoms, however, was never sucessfully achieved and the Romans fell back on a containment policy with the construction of frontier fortifications under the Emperors Hadrian and Antoninus Pius. Agricola contemplated, but never attempted, the conquest of Ireland.

Rule from Rome ushered in the historic era of Britain and truncated the prehistoric period. In south-east England Roman customs and behaviour were imposed and imitated by a largely receptive indigenous population. In the north and west most farming communities lived on as before, conscious of the presence of the Roman military and no doubt rendering agricultural taxes to their new overlords. In Ireland only the presence of Roman imports and the occasional boatload of fugitives disturbed a pattern of life that had lasted for centuries. Christianity, not Caesar or Claudius, would bring Ireland within the ambit of written history. Traditionally, the missionary who did most to christianize Ireland, Patrick, arrived in Ireland as a slave from Britain in AD 432.

Pl 101. Ingleborough, North Yorkshire, England. On the crest of Ingleborough Hill lies one of the very few hillforts in the Pennines. This is one of the highest in Britain at 716 m above sea-level. The hillfort was defended by a huge wall of millstone grit, which enclosed an area of 6 ha.

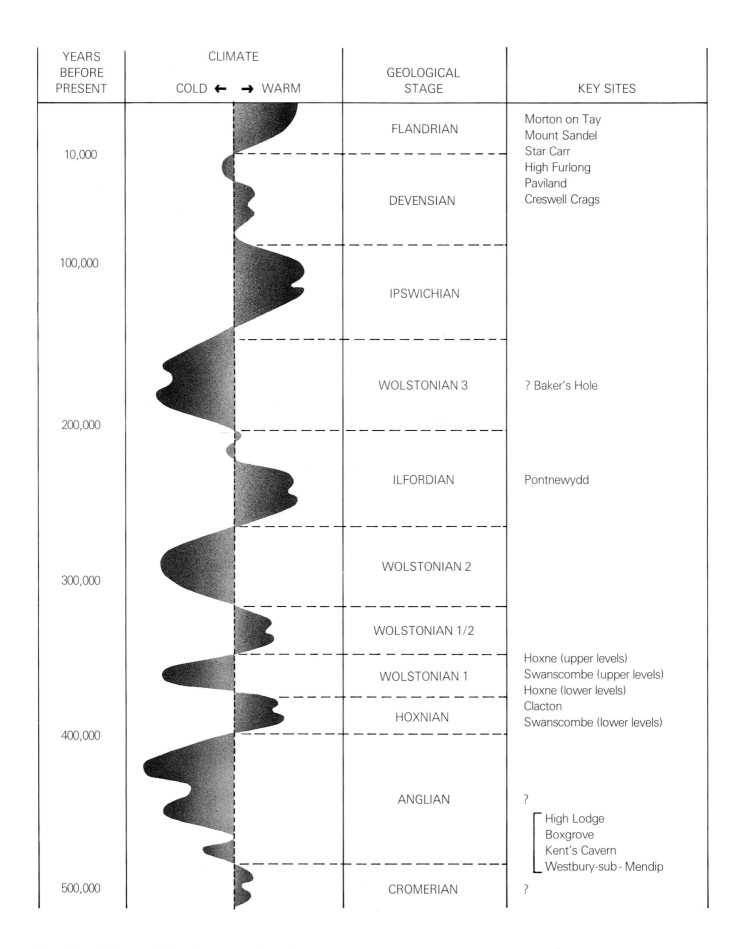

YEARS BEFORE PRESENT	CLIMATE COLD ← → WARM	GEOLOGICAL STAGE	KEY SITES
		FLANDRIAN	Morton on Tay
			Mount Sandel
10,000			Star Carr
		DEVENSIAN	High Furlong
			Paviland
			Creswell Crags
100,000		IPSWICHIAN	
		WOLSTONIAN 3	? Baker's Hole
200,000		ILFORDIAN	Pontnewydd
300,000		WOLSTONIAN 2	
		WOLSTONIAN 1/2	
		WOLSTONIAN 1	Hoxne (upper levels)
			Swanscombe (upper levels)
		HOXNIAN	Hoxne (lower levels)
			Clacton
400,000			Swanscombe (lower levels)
		ANGLIAN	?
			High Lodge
			Boxgrove
			Kent's Cavern
			Westbury-sub-Mendip
500,000		CROMERIAN	?

Date Chart I (Chapter 1). This chart covers the period conventionally known as the Palaeolithic (Old Stone Age) and Mesolithic (Middle Stone Age). Cold and warm phases in the climate of the Ice Ages are identified and tentative correlations are made with conventional geological stages and key archaeological sites. The dating of some sites is problematic, however, and may change as more research is carried out. The divide between Palaeolithic and Mesolithic occurred *c* 9,000 BC.

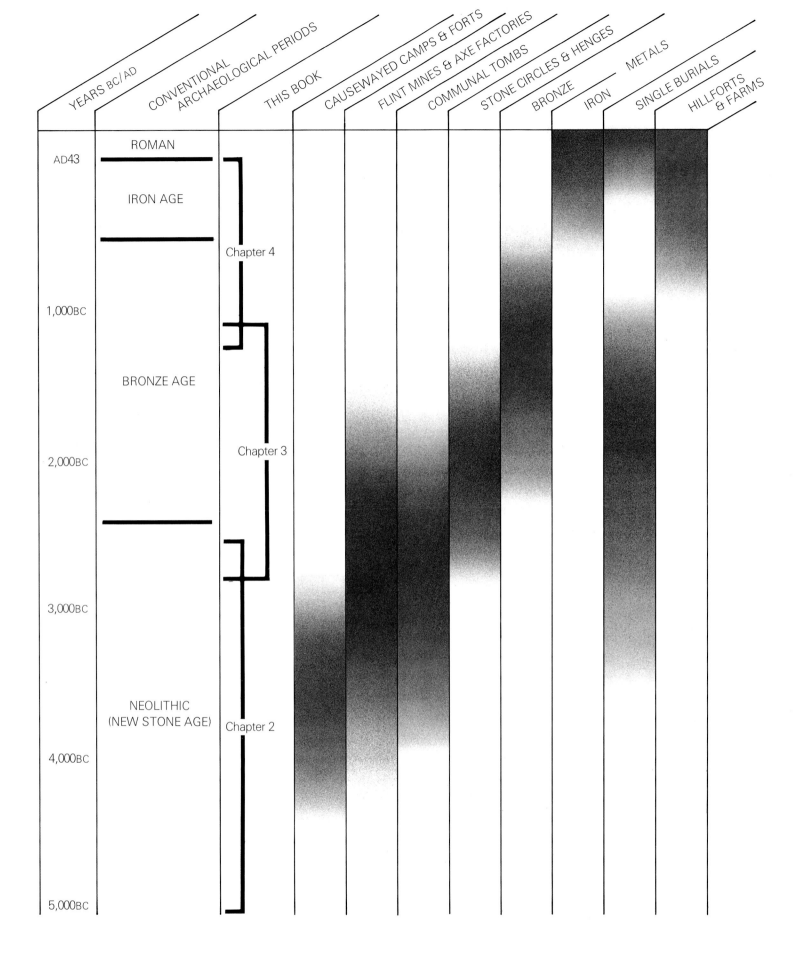

Date Chart II. (Chapters 2, 3 & 4). This chart covers the periods conventionally known as the Neolithic (New Stone Age), Bronze Age and Iron Age. The conventional archaeological periods have not been followed in this text however, as a glance at the chart will reveal. The divisions chosen for this book correlate with periods of stress and change for the prehistoric communities of these islands, rather than the centuries when new metals were introduced. There is a certain degree of overlap between the chapters, as the chart suggests. Calendar dates, not radiocarbon dates, are given on this chart and throughout the book.

Sites to Visit

There has never been a better time to visit archaeological sites and excavations. The increased profile of 'heritage attractions' in the tourism industry has led to better interpretive material at many of the major state-owned monuments. Long-running excavations are also increasingly displayed as attractions in their own right. Nevertheless, most prehistoric sites are situated in the countryside, on private land. It is, therefore, important to seek the landowner's permission before visiting such a site, and to observe the country code at all times. Certainly, permission to visit should be sought at those sites in the Sites to Visit section that are *not* prefixed by an asterisk. Good quality maps are an essential prerequisite for the serious site visitor. In Britain the ordnance survey map *Ancient Britain* is a useful start, which needs to be supplemented by OS area maps at 1:50,000 and 1:25,000 scale. In Ireland the best coverage is on OS maps at scales 1:250,000 and 1:126,720.

All national museums, and most provincial museums, will contain prehistoric finds of most periods. Useful guides to these institutions are: K Hudson & A Nicholls, *The Cambridge Guide to the Museums of Britain and Ireland*, (Cambridge University Press, 1987) and *The Museums and Galleries of Great Britain and Ireland* (British Leisure Publications, 1988). Some of the major museums containing prehistoric objects are listed below. In the Places to Visit section for Chapter 1, some museums with hunting and gathering artefacts are listed.

There are also a growing number of Interpretation and Heritage Centres dealing with the prehistoric past.

Creswell Crags and the Flag Fen Visitor Centre, the Somerset Levels Centre and the archaeological 'theme parks' in Ireland (eg Wexford) are examples. You should be able to find details of these in your local museum or tourist information centre.

Chapter 1

The best places to visit to appreciate the early prehistory of Britain and Ireland are the many splendid museums that contain artefacts relevant to the hunting and gathering bands. In contrast with the later periods there are very few actual sites that can be visited.

England

British Museum, Cromwell Road, South Kensington, London SW7 5BD. *Finds from Swanscombe and the Devonshire caves.*

British Museum, Great Russell St, London WC1B 3DG. *Axes from Hoxne and Swanscombe, and a selection of objects from Star Carr.*

Cambridge University Museum of Archaeology and Anthropology, Downing St, Cambridge CB2 3DZ. *Many finds from Star Carr.*

Cheddar Caves, Cheddar, Somerset BS27 3QF. *Artefacts from Gough's cave and guided tours of Gough's cave.*

Creswell Crags Visitor Centre, Crags Road, Creswell, Worksop, Notts. *Finds from the caves and guided tours available.*

Manchester Museum, Oxford Road, Manchester M13 9PL. *Finds from the Peak District and Creswell Crags.*

Somerset County Museum, Taunton Castle, Taunton, Somerset TA1 4AA. *Artefacts from the Mendip caves.*

Torquay Museum, 529 Babbacombe Road, Torquay, Devon TQ1 1HG. *Material from Kent's Cavern.*

Wookey Hole, Wells, Somerset BA5 1BB. *Finds from the caves and visit to Wookey Hole.*

Yorkshire Museum, Museum Gardens, York YO1 2DR. *Some material from Kirkdale Cave, North Yorks.*

Wales

National Museum of Wales, Cathays Park, Cardiff CF1 3NP. *Finds from Pontnewydd Cave and Coygan Cave, as well as the human burial from the Goat's Hole Cave.*

Swansea Museum, Victoria Road, Swansea, West Glamorgan SA1 1SN. *Some material from the Gower caves.*

Scotland

Hunterian Museum, The University, Glasgow G12 8QQ. *Finds from the islands of Jura, Risga, Isla and Oronsay.*

Royal Museum of Scotland, Queen St, Edinburgh EH2 1JD. *Extensive collection including material from excavations on Jura, from the Obanian caves and from Morton, as well as surface collections from coastal middens in various parts of Scotland.*

Ireland

National Museum of Ireland, Kildare St, Dublin. *A small amount of material including the Stackpoole collection (Co. Dublin), the Hewson collection (Co. Derry, Antrim and Down) the Dalkey hoard, which comprises some blades and large, leaf-shaped flakes. Also excavated material from Lough Boora and Lough Gara.*

The Manx Museum, Douglas, Isle of Man. *Extensive collections that reflect both Irish and mainland British traditions. Two principal stone industries represented: microlithic and heavy-bladed.*

Ulster Museum, Botanic Gardens, Belfast BT9 5AB. *Various collections made by antiquarians.*

Chapter 2

The following sites are listed alphabetically by county. The figures in brackets refer to ordnance survey maps. The asterisks mean public ownership or customary access via public footpath.

England

*Stoney Littleton, Avon (ST 735572). *Restored in 1858, this is a fine example of a megalithic tomb. There is a horned forecourt with a low entrance, and into one of the jambs the spiral cast of a fossil ammonite was built. Does this spiral pattern echo the spiral carvings which are such a feature of megalithic art?*

Maiden Bower, Bedfordshire (SP 997225). *Causewayed camp and later hillfort.*

*Lanyon Quoit, Cornwall (SW 430337). *Famous dolmen re-erected in 1824, but still hauntingly dramatic with its huge, flat capstone.*

*Trethevy Quoit, Cornwall (SX 259688). *Most impressive and accessible of the Cornish dolmens. A sloping capstone is supported by six uprights, which form the sides and ends of a burial chamber divided in two by a cross stone.*

Zennor Quoit, Cornwall (SW 469380). *This dolmen has a huge capstone some 5.4m long and weighing as much as 12t.*

Pike of Stickle, Cumbria (NY 272072). *Location of axe-quarrying and manufacture on the scree slopes below the summit. Some debris from these processes can still be found, although the visitor is urged not to remove material from the site.*

Hembury, Devon (ST 113030). *Causewayed camp and later hillfort.*

Hambledon Hill, Dorset (ST 848122). *Causewayed camp and later hillfort. Adjacent to Celtic hillfort of Hod Hill.*

Pimperne, Dorset (ST 917104). *Well-preserved long barrow, about 100m long and 2.7m in height.*

*Belas Knap, Gloucestershire (SP 022254). *There is a false entrance at the northern end of this megalithic tomb, which has projecting hornworks, creating a U-shaped forecourt and emphasizing the 'entrance'. The actual burial chambers are in the long sides of the mound.*

*Crickley Hill, Gloucestershire (SO 928161). *Causewayed camp and later hillfort. On a dramatic promontory overlooking the Severn plain.*

*Notgrove, Gloucestershire (SP 096212). *Megalithic tomb with burial chambers opening off a long gallery.*

Nympsfield, Gloucestershire (SO 794013). *Megalithic tomb which has lost its capstone and covering mound.*

*Randwick, Gloucestershire (SO 825069). *Earthen long barrow.*

*Coldrum, Kent (TQ 654607). *Four huge sarsen stones of the burial chamber remain standing.*

Jullieberrie's Grave, Kent (TR 077532). *Excellent example of an earthen long barrow.*

*Kits Coty House, Kent (TQ 745608). *One of the most famous prehistoric sites in Kent; the remains of this megalithic tomb comprise three uprights and a capstone.*

King Orry's Grave, Isle of Man (SC 438843). *Megalithic tomb.*

*Wayland's Smithy, Oxfordshire (SU 281854). *Megalithic tomb formed by a long mound with a facade of four (originally six) huge standing stones, leading to the burial passage and chamber behind. Note use of dry-stone walling between the megaliths in the facade.*

*Bant's Carn, Scilly (SV 911123). *A good example of the type of megalithic tomb to be found on Scilly. Here the grave is set within a round mound some 13m in diameter, with the burial chamber originally covered by four capstones.*

*Barkhale, West Sussex (SU 976126). *Causewayed camp.*

Cissbury, West Sussex (TQ 139080). *The major monument here is a Celtic hillfort. However, outside the southern entrance and around the west end of the fort lie over 200 depressions that mark the site of earlier flint mining.*

Trundle, West Sussex (SU 877111). *Causewayed camp and later hillfort. Commanding views of the surrounding countryside.*

*West Kennet, Wiltshire (SU 104677). *Probably the most popular of the English megalithic tombs. Close to Silbury Hill and Avebury.*

*Whitesheet Hill, Wiltshire (ST 802352). *Beautiful causewayed camp on a hill enjoying a splendid rural vista. Later hillfort shares the same hill.*

*Windmill Hill, Wiltshire (SU 087714). *The most famous of the causewayed camps, easily accessible from Avebury.*

Duggleby Howe, North Yorkshire (SE 881669). *Large chalk round barrow, originally some 9m in height and still surviving to some 6m.*

Wales

*Barclodiad y Gawres, Anglesey (SH 328708). *Megalithic tomb comprising a burial chamber set in a round mound 30m in diameter. Five of the stones used in the construction of the side walls and chambers are decorated with pecked linear designs.*

*Bryn Celli Ddu, Anglesey (SH 508702). *Passage grave consisting of a polygonal chamber formed by six uprights. A long stone found near the centre of the tomb was decorated with abstract patterns.*

*Din Lligwy, Anglesey (SH 501861). *Bizarre portal dolmen with an enormous capstone squatting on partly buried uprights.*

*Pentre Ifan, Dyfed (SN 099370). *One of the finest megalithic tombs in Wales. A capstone weighing some 17t is supported by four tapering uprights.*

*Tinkinswood, South Glamorgan (ST 092733). *Megalithic tomb with a chamber located at the eastern end of a long cairn, and set back between the horns of a facade.*

Parc Cwm, West Glamorgan (SS 537898). *Classic megalithic tomb with four side chambers.*

*Capel Garmon, Gwynedd (SH 818543). *Well-preserved megalithic tomb with a false entrance between the horns of a long cairn, and the actual entrance in the side of the tomb.*

*Dyffryn, Ardudwy, Gwynedd (SH 588228). *A portal dolmen later incorporated into a long cairn with another chamber at its eastern end. Easily accessible behind Dyffryn school. Prehistoric cultivation terraces visible on the hillside above.*

Ty-Isaf, Powys (SO 182290). *Megalithic tomb with a false entrance.*

Scotland

*Cairnholy I and II, Dumfries and Galloway (NX 518541). *Two megalithic tombs in the fine setting of Wigtown Bay. The first is the more impressive, with a horned forecourt incorporating six tall stones.*

Mid Gleniron, Dumfries and Galloway (NX 186610). *As these megalithic tombs are on private land you must ask the farmer's permission before visiting the monument.*

Balnuaran of Clava, Highland (NH 756443). *An impressive necropolis comprising three large cairns, each surrounded by a stone kerb and a stone circle. Two, those to the south-west and north-east, have passages that possibly point to the midwinter sunset.*

*Camster, Highland (ND 260442). *A long cairn over 60 m in length. A round cairn lies some 200 m to the south-east.*

Corrimony, Highland (NH 383304). *Megalithic tomb similar to Balnuaran of Clava. A low passage leads to a central, corbelled chamber, now open to the sky.*

*Knowe of Yarso, Orkney (HY 403280). *Tomb with four compartments.*

*Maes Howe, Orkney (HY 318127). *Architecturally the most sophisticated of the British passage graves.*

*Midhowe, Orkney (HY 371306). *The interior of a large burial cairn, divided into different compartments or stalls, is displayed.*

Unstan, Orkney (HY 282117). *Well-restored tomb, with compartments and a narrow entrance passage.*

*Skara Brae, Mainland Orkney (HY 231118). *One of the most famous prehistoric settlements in Europe. It comprises nine houses built of flat blocks of stone, with remarkable preservation of internal stone furniture.*

Ireland

*Lough Gur, Co. Limerick (R 640410). *Foundations of a rectangular house on Knockadoon, overlooking the lough.*

*Creevykeel, Co. Sligo (G 720540). *Spectacular court-cairn set in trapezoidal mound.*

Ballyglass, Co. Mayo (G 100380). *Court-cairn with a central court.*

Ballyrenan, Co. Tyrone (H 370830). *Portal tomb with a very complex development.*

*Poulnabrone, Co. Clare (M 240000). *Remarkable dolmen with a gracefully supported capstone. Situated on the unusual limestone formations of the Burren.*

*Newgrange, Co. Meath (O 000720). *The most impressive of the British and Irish passage graves. A visit to the neighbouring passage graves of Dowth and Knowth is also a must.*

*Carrowkeel, Co. Sligo (G 750110). *A cemetery of passage graves set on the crests of a series of hills that are aligned north-south. Most of the covering mounds are round.*

*Carrowmore, Co. Sligo (G 660330). *Largest cemetery of megalithic tombs in Ireland. Dominated by Maeve's cairn on Knocknarea.*

*Loughcrew, Co. Meath (N 580780). *Cemetery of at least thirty passage graves on two neighbouring peaks, known as Cairnbane East and West.*

Chapter 3

England

Lambourn Seven Barrows, Berkshire (SU 328828). *One of the most easily visited round barrow cemeteries in Britain. It comprises forty mounds of different types and periods arranged mostly in two rows, running north-west/south-east.*

Carn Gluze, Cornwall (SW 355313). *A complex double-walled cairn, oval in shape and measuring 11 by 9m. It incorporated a number of small stone cists as burial chambers.*

Merry Maidens, Cornwall (SW 432245). *Superb stone circle made up of nineteen regularly spaced blocks of local granite The site's Cornish name – Dans Maen (stone dance) – derives from the tale that these are nineteen maidens turned to stone for dancing on a Sunday. The chambered tomb at Tregiffian is just to the south-west.*

*Castlerigg, Cumbria (NY 292236). *A pear-shaped stone circle, some 30m in diameter, set in the beautiful Lakeland scenery.*

Long Meg and Her Daughters, Cumbria (NY 571373). *One of the largest stone circles in Britain. Of an original seventy stones, fifty-nine survive, of which twenty-seven – the daughters – are standing. Local legend says the rocks are all witches turned to stone.*

*Arbor Low, Derbyshire (SK 160636 *The most important monument of the Peak District and known as the Stonehenge of Derbyshire. A typical henge which encloses a stone circle, the fifty stones of which are all now recumbent.*

*Hob Hurst's House, Derbyshire (SK 287692 *A cairn some 10m in diameter and 1m high, with a bank and ditch around it. A stone circle formerly stood inside the bank, and a cremation burial was found in a stone cist at the cairn's centre.*

Grey Wethers, Devon (SX 638832 *Stone circles.*

*Grimspound, Devon (SX 701809 *A granite-walled enclosure on Dartmoor containing the remains of over twenty stone hut circles (in the centre and to the south), some supposed cattle-pens (to the west) and some possible storage huts (to the north).*

Reaves, Devon. *Good examples can be seen on Dartmoor looking northwards from Combestone Tor (SX 670718) across the river Dart, and from the car park at Peek Hill (SX 5577707), running northwards towards Leeden Tor.*

Five Marys, Dorset (SY 790842 *Eight round barrows of different types in a line.*

*Rudston Monolith, Humberside (TA 097677 *The tallest standing stone in Britain, some 7.8m in height, is situated in Rudston churchyard. Three cursus monuments converge on the end of the chalk ridge where the pillar stands.*

Dod Law Rock Carvings, Northumberland (NU 004317 *A major concentration of rock carvings, including cup and ring marks, in a small area of high moorland. Some of the best carvings lie between the two later forts of the same name.*

Roughting Linn Rock Carving, Northumberland (NT 984367 *Large expanse of sandstone decorated with over sixty carvings, the majority of which are cup and ring marks.*

*Rollright Stones, Oxfordshire (SP 296308 *A stone circle formed by seventy-seven stones known as the King's Men. A single stone – either part of a burial chamber or a standing stone – stands some 73m to the north-east, while some 360m south-east of the circle are the so-called Whispering Knights, five large stones that once formed a burial chamber.*

Robin Hood's Butt, Shropshire (SO 490779 *A round barrow, 27m across and 4m high. It contained the body of a teenager and a bronze knife. The body may have been burned on the site.*

Priddy Nine Barrows, Somerset (ST 538518). *Cemetery of barrows.*

Itford Hill, East Sussex (TQ 447053). *Rather overgrown but a typical downland farmstead.*

Devil's Jumps, West Sussex (SU 824173). *A fine linear cemetery of six round barrows, orientated north-west/south-east.*

*Afton Down, Isle of Wight (SZ 352857). *A group of twenty-four round barrows of different types and an earlier long barrow.*

*Avebury, Wiltshire (SU 103700). *Magnificent henge which encloses three stone circles, and the modern village.*

Normanton Barrow Cemetery, Wiltshire (SU 115413). *This cemetery is the closest to Stonehenge and stretches for over 1km in a line east-west. It contains twenty-six mounds, including an earlier long barrow. The Bush Barrow is in this cemetery, and finds from the burials can be seen in the museum at Devizes.*

*Silbury Hill, Wiltshire (SU 100685). *This is the largest man-made prehistoric mound in Europe, comprising 354,000 cubic metres of chalk, and standing to almost 40m in height.*

*Stonehenge, Wiltshire (SU 123422). *A henge, a stone circle and a stone-lined avenue make this the most visited archaeological site in Britain and Ireland.*

Devil's Arrows, North Yorkshire (SE 391666). *Three huge standing stones, lying on a north-south alignment, and naturally weathered into a fluted shape.*

Wales

Brenig, Clwyd (SH 985576). *Burial and ritual monuments are attractively laid out along an archaeological trail. There is also a Visitor Centre on the other side of the lake.*

Gop Cairn, Clwyd (SJ 086801). *The largest man-made prehistoric mound in Wales. It stands over 11m in height with a maximum diameter of 100m. Excavations in the nineteenth century failed to reveal any central features.*

Gors Fawr Circle, Dyfed (SN 134294). *Sixteen stones remain of this stone circle, which is about 22m in diameter.*

*Stackpole Warren, Dyfed (SR 985965). *Standing stone.*

Carnedd y Saeson, Gwynedd (SH 678717). *One of a group of seven cairns. This one displays a retaining circle of stones, and a side-stone and capstone of a central cist.*

Cwm Ffrydlas, Gwynedd (SH 644684). *Heaps of piled stone indicate hut sites and some clearance cairns.*

*Druids' Circle, Gwynedd (SH 722746). *Ten stones up to 2m high stand in a low bank and form an almost circular area 26m in diameter.*

Cerrig Duon Circle, Powys (SN 852206). *A fairly regular circle of twenty stones, with possibly eight missing. Outside the circle, to the north-east, are two parallel lines of stones, and, to the north, a large standing stone known as Maen Mawr.*

Scotland

*Green Knowe, Borders (NT 21244). *Unenclosed platform settlements.*

*Drumtroddan, Dumfries and Galloway (NX 362446). *Cup and ring marks and standing stones. This fine set of carvings are located on several rock faces.*

*Loanhead of Daviot, Grampian (NJ 747288). *Recumbent stone circle, with a huge horizontal stone between two uprights. The stone next to the eastern upright has five cup marks carved on it.*

*Memsie, Grampian (NJ 976620). *Impressive cairn.*

*Callanish, Lewis (NB 213330). *A stone circle 13m across and formed by thirteen tall slabs of easily split Lewis gneiss. Running north-east from the circle is a splayed avenue of two rows of tall stones, and other single rows of stones lead off from the circle in other directions.*

*Cairnpapple Hill, Lothian (NS 987717). *A huge cairn was built within the western half of a henge. A concrete cover shows the outline of the cairn, and you can descend into it by means of a ladder to view the burials found underneath it.*

*Ring of Brodgar, Mainland Orkney (HY 294133). *The finest and biggest stone circle in Scotland. There were originally sixty stones, forming a circle some 113m in diameter, and sited within a henge monument. The stones are all of local red sandstone, which splits easily and naturally.*

*Stones of Stenness, Mainland Orkney (HY 306125). *Originally a henge, a stone circle was later set up on the site, comprising twelve tall slabs of local flagstone.*

Nether Largie, Strathclyde (NR 830938). *Three cairns with cists, one decorated with axe carvings.*

Ireland

*Farranahineeny, Co. Cork (W 220610). *An alignment of four standing stones and one fallen on the slopes of the Shehy mountains.*

*Kealkil, Co. Cork (W 054556). *Five stones form a miniature stone circle; there are also two standing stones and the remains of another circle with small stones nearby.*

*Knocknakilla, Co. Cork (W 290840). *Stone circle with five stones standing. Nearby is a standing stone.*

Ballynoe, Co. Down (J 481404). *Stone circles and a cairn.*

*Punchestown Stone, Co. Kildare (N 920160). *Tall granite stone tapering to a height of over 7m. When it fell and was re-erected in 1930, a burial was found at its base.*

The Lios, Co. Limerick (R 640410). *Stone circle.*

*Lough Gur, Co. Limerick (R 640410). *Several stone circles, the most impressive of which has a bank outside the stones. A variety of other prehistoric monuments can be visited around the Lough, including burial mounds and standing stones.*

Beaghmore, Co. Tyrone (H 685842). *Stone circles and cairns.*

*Castleruddery, Co. Wicklow (S 920940). *Stone circle, some 35m in diameter, with an interior and exterior facing of stones with a bank in between.*

Chapter 4

England

*Flag Fen, Cambridgeshire (TL 280960). *A remarkably well-preserved late prehistoric crannog. Visitor centre open from Easter to Autumn.*

Eddisbury Hillfort, Cheshire (ST 553695). *A hillfort of 4.5ha with a double rampart and ditch.*

*Carn Euny, Cornwall (SW 403288). *Remarkable restored late prehistoric village, with courtyard houses and a 20m long souterrain.*

Chun Castle, Cornwall (SV 405339). *Small round fort with a diameter of 85m, and defended by a double dry-stone rampart of granite.*

*Chysauster, Cornwall (SV 472350). *Late prehistoric village with courtyard and houses and a souterrain.*

*Treryn Dinas, Cornwall (SW 397222). *Promontory fort.*

*Mam Tor, Derbyshire (SK 128837). *The largest hillfort in Derbyshire lies at an altitude of 500m and dominates the modern town of Castleton.*

*Badbury Rings, Dorset (ST 964030). *Oval hillfort of 7.3ha, with massive defences and a complex western gateway.*

Chalbury Hillfort, Dorset (SY 695838). *A pear-shaped fort on a very steep hill dominating Weymouth Bay. Two earlier round barrows are situated at the centre, while numerous hut-platforms can be seen inside the fort.*

*Eggardon Hillfort, Dorset (SY 541948). *Impressive hillfort with defences formed by three banks and two ditches. Storage pits and hut-platforms inside.*

Hod Hill, Dorset (ST 857106). *Rectangular hillfort which was attacked and taken by the Romans, who built a fort in its north-west corner.*

*Maiden Castle, Dorset (SY 668885). *One of the biggest and most spectacular prehistoric sites in Britain. The defences have a circumference of 2.5km and enclose an area of 18ha.*

*Butser Hill, Hampshire (SU 712201). *Late prehistoric farm reconstruction, complete with round-houses and ancillary farm buildings. Sited in the Queen Elizabeth Country Park.*

*Danebury Hillfort, Hampshire (SU 323377). *Oval hillfort of 5.3ha.*

Close ny Chollagh, Isle of Man (SC 246671). *Promontory fort.*

Cronk ny Merriu, Isle of Man (SC 319703). *Promontory fort.*

Humbleton Hill, Northumberland (NT 967283). *Hillfort, protected by steep slopes on all sides, with a walled enclosure at its centre and visible hut-circles.*

Caer Caradoc, Shropshire (SO 477953). *Another hillfort of the same name is at SO 310758.*

*Old Oswestry, Shropshire (SJ 296310). *Massive hillfort with complex defences.*

*Ingleborough, North Yorkshire (SD 740750). *One of the highest hillforts in Britain.*

Wales

*Moel Arthur, Clwyd (SJ 145660). *Small hillfort on prominent hill in the Clwydians. Adjacent to other hillforts – Penycloddiau to the north, and Moel-y-Gaer, Llanbedr to the south. Information on these hillforts available from Loggerheads Countryside Centre, between Mold and Ruthin.*

*Moel-y-Gaer, Rhosesmor, Clwyd (SJ 210680). *Easily accessible hillfort overlooking Dee estuary.*

Carn Goch Hillfort, Dyfed (SO 691243). *10.5ha hillfort with massive dry-stone walls enclosing a rectangular area.*

*Castell Henllys, Dyfed (SN 050390). *A small defended farmstead which has been excavated and reconstructed. The site lies just to the north of the A407 Fishguard to Cardigan road and is well signposted. Open Easter to autumn.*

The Bulwark Hillfort, West Glamorgan (SS 443927). *An oval hillfort formed by multiple enclosures.*

High Pennard, West Glamorgan (SS 567864). *Promontory fort.*

*Tre'r Ceiri, Gwynedd (SH 373446). *Superb hillfort on the Rivals. Stone defences and internal huts, but an arduous climb to the top.*

Ffridd Faldwyn, Powys (SO 216970). *Multiphase hillfort which in its final form enclosed 4ha.*

Scotland

Eildon Hill, Borders (NT 555328). *Massive hillfort comparable to Traprain Law in size. The Romans placed a small wooden signal station at its western end.*

Hownam Rings, Borders (NT 790194). *A hillfort at the north end of a long hilltop. The multivallate defences were probably constructed to meet the Roman advance.*

Burnswark Hillfort, Dumfries and Galloway (NY 185785). *A 7ha hillfort in a commanding position, and later used for training exercises in sieges by the Romans.*

*Dun Carloway Broch, Lewis (NB 190412). *Well-preserved broch still standing up to 9m high.*

Traprain Law, Lothian (NT 581746). *The largest hillfort in Scotland, in its final form enclosing an area of 16ha. It was the capital of the Votadini.*

*Gurness Broch, Mainland Orkney (HY 383268). *Formidable broch protected by strong and complex outer defences, including three rock-cut ditches.*

*Clickhimin Broch, Mainland Shetland (HV 465408). *Complex broch with fortifications from several periods.*

*Mousa Broch, Mainland Shetland (HV 457237). *By far the best in preservation of the 500 brochs known.*

Finavon, Tayside (NO 506556). *Hillfort with stone vitrified defences still standing over 2m high.*

Ireland

*The King's Stables, Co. Armagh (H 838455). *Ritual pool set within a bank and measuring 30m across.*

Caherconell, Co. Clare (R 240000). *Impressive stone fort.*

*Craggaunowen, Co. Clare (R 450700). *Reconstructed crannog with internal round-houses.*

*Aran Islands, Co. Galway (L 76-99. 00-13). *The islands are dotted with spectacular archaeological sites, including stone forts at Dun Aengus (L 820100), Dun Oghil (L 860100) and Dun Doocaher (L 870090) on Inishmore. On Inishmaan is the great fort of Dun Conor.*

*Turoe Stone, Co. Galway (M 630220). *Round-headed boulder with intricate Celtic carving.*

*Staigue, Co. Kerry (V 610630). *One of the finest stone forts in Ireland. The circular wall is up to 6m high and 4m wide, surrounding an area 30m in diameter.*

*Dun Aillinne, Co. Kildare (N 820080). *Hillfort of some 8ha enclosed by a circular rampart 450m in diameter, with an internal ditch.*

*Tara, Co. Meath (N 920600). *Hillfort defended by a single bank and external ditch. The hillfort is sited on Tara Hill and contains two raths or ring-forts, and the earlier passsage grave known as Mound of the Hostages. Other raths lie north and south of the hillfort.*

*Baltinglass Hill, Co. Wicklow (S 880890). *Concentric rings of stone form the defences of this hillfort.*

*Rathgall, Co. Wicklow (S 900730). *Stone hillfort built on a small hillock, and formed by three concentric stone ramparts with external ditches.*

Select Bibliography

Listed below are a few of the principal text books and guide books on prehistory in Britain and Ireland. Most will be equipped with bibliographies that will allow you to look up additional sources and reports on specific sites.

C Burgess, *The Age of Stonehenge*, J M Dent & Sons, London, 1980

A Burl, *The Stone Circles of the British Isles*, Yale University Press, 1976

D V Clarke, T G Cowie & A Foxon, *Symbols of Power at the Time of Stonehenge*, National Museum of Antiquities of Scotland, HMSO, Edinburgh, 1985

P Clayton, *Guide to the Archaeological Sites of Britain*, Batsford, London, 1985

B Cunliffe, *Iron Age Communities in Britain*, Routledge & Kegan Paul, London, 1978

T Darvill, *Prehistoric Britain*, Batsford, London, 1987

T Darvill, *Ancient Britain*, A A Glovebox Guide, Basingstoke, 1988

P J Fowler, *The Farming of Prehistoric Britain*, Cambridge University Press, 1983

A Hamlin, C Lynn, ed., *Pieces of the Past*, Belfast, HMSO, 1988

P Harbison, *Pre-Christian Ireland*, Thames and Hudson, London, 1988

P Harbison, *Guide to the National Monuments in the Republic of Ireland*, Gill & Macmillan, Dublin, 1975

J Hawkes, *The Shell Guide to British Archaeology*, Michael Joseph, London, 1986

M Herity & G Eogan, *Ireland in Prehistory*, Routledge & Kegan Paul, London, 1977

C Houlder, *Wales: An Archaeological Guide*, Faber & Faber, London, 1975

I Longworth & J Cherry, *Archaeology in Britain since 1945*, British Museum Publications, 1986

E W Mackie, *Scotland: An Archaeological Guide*, Faber & Faber, Lodon, 1975

J V S Megaw & D D A Simpson, *An Introduction to British Prehistory*, Leicester University Press, 1979

A Morrison, *Early Man in Britain and Ireland*, Croom Helm, London, 1980

R Muir & H Welfare, *The National Trust Guide to Prehistoric and Roman Britain*, George Philip, London, 1983

C Renfrew, (ed), *The Prehistory of Orkney*, Edinburgh University Press, 1985

G & A Ritchie, *Scotland: Archaeology and Early History*, Thames & Hudson, London, 1981

A Ritchie, *Scotland BC*, HMSO, Edinburgh, 1988

D A Roe, *The Lower and Middle Palaeolithic Periods in Britain*, Routledge & Kegan Paul, London, 1981

If you do have difficulty in finding a particular publication, or if you want to study a certain period or area in greater detail, then an excellent bibliographic service is organized by the Council for British Archaeology. The CBA can be contacted at 112 Kennington Road, London SE11 6RE. In addition, the CBA will help you out if you wish to become more involved in archaeology, perhaps by taking a series of evening classes, or joining in an excavation.

Two excellent illustrated magazines, often containing the latest results of excavations before they are more comprehensively published, are *Current Archaeology* and *Archaeology Ireland*. *Current Archaeology* can be obtained on subscription by writing to 9 Nassington Road, London NW3 2TX, while *Archaeology Ireland* is similarly available on subscription from Irish Academic Publications, 9 Herbert Street, Dublin 2.

Index

All numbers refer to pages
Plate references are in **bold**
Figure references are in *italics*